Special Education Law:
Issues & Implications for the '90s

Stephen B. Thomas
&
Charles J. Russo

NATIONAL ORGANIZATION ON LEGAL PROBLEMS OF EDUCATION

DISCLAIMER

The National Organization on Legal Problems of Education (NOLPE) is a private, nonadvocacy, and nonprofit association of educators and attorneys. The opinions expressed in this publication are those of the author and do not represent official views of the Organization.

Copyright © 1995

Stephen B. Thomas & Charles J. Russo

ISBN 1-56534-088-4

Published by

NATIONAL ORGANIZATION ON LEGAL PROBLEMS OF EDUCATION

3601 S.W. 29th Street, Suite 223

Topeka, Kansas 66614

(913) 273-3550 • FAX (913) 273-2001

About the Authors

Stephen B. Thomas is a Professor of Educational Administration, College of Education, Kent State University. He has been a consultant to several state departments of education, national organizations, and school districts. Dr. Thomas has presented papers at more than 150 national and regional conferences, has over 150 publications (including eighteen books), and has conducted a number of funded research studies. Among his publications are *Legal Issues in Special Education* and *Health Related Issues in Education,* both published by NOLPE. Additionally, he coauthored a publication entitled *Special Education Law: Case Summaries and Federal Regulations*—the companion book to this one. Over the years, Dr. Thomas has served NOLPE as a Board Member, President, and Interim Executive Director. He also has served as a member of the Authors Committee for West's *Education Law Reporter* since its beginning in 1981.

Charles J. Russo is Associate Professor with a joint appointment in the Departments of Administration and Supervision and Special Education and Rehabilitation Counseling in the College of Education at the University of Kentucky. He has contributed to NOLPE in a number of ways. In addition to being a member of NOLPE's Board of Directors, Program Chair of the 40th Annual NOLPE Convention in 1994, he has written the Chapter on Bargaining for *The Yearbook* of *Education Law,* has edited three citations volumes, is a regional reporter for the *School Law Reporter,* and is author of the *Law Review Digest* in *NOLPE Notes.* Most recently he was appointed Editor of *The Yearbook of Education Law,* succeeding his co-author, Dr. Stephen B. Thomas. A member of the Author's Committee of West's *Education Law Reporter* since 1987, Dr. Russo has authored more than 100 articles and has presented many papers at national and regional conferences.

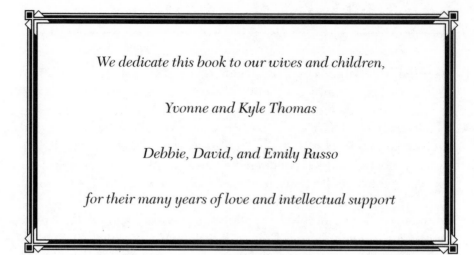

We dedicate this book to our wives and children,

Yvonne and Kyle Thomas

Debbie, David, and Emily Russo

for their many years of love and intellectual support

TABLE OF CONTENTS

Chapter 1
Introduction and History

Chapter 2
Free Appropriate Public Education

Chapter 3
Related Services

Chapter 4
Disease

Chapter 5
Student Records

Chapter 6
Discipline

Chapter 7
Minimum Competency Testing

Chapter 8
Sport Participation

Chapter 9
Child Abuse

Chapter 1
Introduction and History

Introduction

The *Declaration of Independence,* written more than two hundred years ago, guarantees Americans the right to life, liberty, and the pursuit of happiness. Yet, these rights have not been available uniformly to all citizens, for as the adage purports, although all are created equal, some are created more equal than others. Individuals with disabilities, for example, have received unequal treatment and have been victims of both intentional and unintentional discrimination.

Historically, it was more convenient, both legislatively and socially, to remove the disabled from the social mainstream than it was to integrate them in public schools or to provide them with jobs or training.

An attitude of not always such benign neglect toward the disabled permeated federal, state, and local governments, which systematically segregated or excluded persons with disabilities through a variety of means. Laws were enacted that restricted the rights of individuals with disabilities to immigrate, to vote, to obtain a driver's license, to purchase a hunting or fishing license, to hold office, and, in the case of newborn infants, to live.[1] Moreover, numerous states selectively restricted or denied persons with disabilities the right to enter into contracts based on an irrebuttable presumption of incapacity. One of the earliest reported cases of this type occurred in 1821 in Connecticut where the court decided a controversy concerning a person who was deaf, dumb, and blind. The court reasoned that such a person was "considered in law as incapable of any understanding, being deficient in those inlets which furnish the human mind with ideas."[2]

During the late 1950s, twenty-eight states required persons with feeblemindedness, epilepsy, idiocy, imbecility, or insanity to be sterilized. Numerous other states proscribed marriages between persons who were handicapped or where one of the parties was mentally ill, mentally retarded, or epileptic. As recently as 1952, a Kentucky decision[3] quoted with approval the language of an 1834 ruling which observed that "[a] person 'of unsound mind' . . . is, as to all intellectual purposes, dead; and such a thing, destitute of intellectual light and life, is as incapable as a dead body of being a husband or a wife in a legal, rational, or moral sense."[4]

Also of note were state and local laws that deprived the disabled of opportunities to participate fully in the mainstream, discriminated against them, or treated them in demeaning ways. For example, a former Wisconsin law gave the superintendent of each home for the

---

[1] *See* Marcia Pearce Burgdorf & Robert Burgdorf, Jr., *A History of Unequal Treatment: The Qualifications of Handicapped Persons as a "Suspect Class" under the Equal Protection Clause*, 15 SANTA CLARA LAWYER 855 *passim* (1975), for a related discussion.

[2] Brown v. Brown, 3 Conn. 299 (1821).

[3] Beddow v. Beddow, 257 S.W.2d 45, 48 (Ky. 1952).

[4] Jenkins v. Jenkins' Heirs, 32 Ky. 102, 104 (1834).

mentally retarded the authority to order exploratory brain surgery following the death of a resident, if such an examination were considered beneficial to scientific research.[5]   In addition, in 1958 the Supreme Court of Illinois held that existing compulsory attendance legislation did not require the state to provide a free public education program for "feeble minded" or "mentally deficient" children who, because of limited intelligence, were unable to receive a good common school education.[6]   Similarly, a Chicago Municipal Code, repealed in 1974, made it unlawful for a person who was "diseased, maimed, mutilated or in any way deformed so as to be an unsightly or disgusting object or improper person to be allowed in or on the public ways or other public places."[7]

In education, as in society, the disabled were segregated, excluded, or treated poorly. Although Horace Mann believed that every person has a natural law right to an education,[8] history has shown that few children with disabilities were provided with such an opportunity prior to the 1970s.

Formal public education in the United States began in Massachusetts in 1647 with the adoption of a series of local laws. These laws required the creation of public schools to teach reading and writing as the means to defeat "ye old deluder Satan" in the battle to save souls.[9]   Over the next three centuries, as public schools focused their attention on providing education for waves of immigrants, many schools diversified and specialized.[10]   Yet, educators were seldom willing to adapt their programs to accommodate the "special" needs of children with disabilities.   In fact, many school

---

[5] WIS. STAT. ANN., § 52.04 (1930), as amended (1945) (repealed 1947).

[6] Department of Pub. Welfare v. Haas, 154 N.E.2d 265 (Ill. 1958).

[7] CHICAGO, ILL., MUN. CODE § 36-34 (1966) (repealed 1974).

[8] Horace Mann, Tenth Annual Report to Massachusetts State Bd. of Educ., OLD S. LEAFLETS V. No. 109, 177-80 (1846).   The cited literature was discussed in Burgdorf & Burgdorf, *supra* note 1, at 868.

[9] The "Ye Old Deluder Satan" Act can be found in DOCUMENTS OF AMERICAN HISTORY (Henry Steele Commager, 7th Ed. 1963), citing *Records of the Governor and Company of the Massachusetts Bay in New England, Vol. II*, p. 203.   *See also* L. DEAN WEBB, MARTHA M. MCCARTHY, & STEPHEN B. THOMAS, FINANCING ELEMENTARY AND SECONDARY EDUCATION, at 2 (1988) for a related discussion.

[10] *See* DAVID B. TAYAK, THE ONE BEST SYSTEM: A HISTORY OF AMERICAN URBAN EDUCATION (1974) for a discussion of the development of public education.

officials actually moved to restrict the admission of such students or to have them expelled.

Behavior that today would be determined to be a manifestation of a child's disability, historically was viewed as misbehavior requiring an appropriate punishment. For example, in 1893 a child in Massachusetts was suspended from school because he was "so weak in mind as not to derive any marked benefit from instruction," and because he was "troublesome to other children, making unusual noises, pinching others, etc." He also was found to be "unable to take ordinary, decent, physical care of himself."[11] The court compared his behavior, which it ruled was caused by "incapacity and mental weakness," to that of a normal child who had "willfully and carelessly" violated school regulations. It opined, however, that although the situations differed regarding student ability and motive, the result was the same–other scholars were being disturbed. As a result, the court upheld his suspension and labeled the local school committee's decision as a "good faith" action aimed at eliminating disruptive students from the school environment. A similar situation existed in 1919 when the Wisconsin Supreme Court permitted the expulsion of a child with cerebral palsy who had the academic ability to benefit from being in school. Yet, the court upheld his exclusion for three related reasons: first, he drooled uncontrollably and had facial contortions and a speech impairment; second, he had a "depressing and nauseating" effect on the teachers and students; and third, his physical disabilities required an undue portion of the teacher's time.[12]

Treatment of the disabled began to change at the dawn of the twentieth century when "special" classes, intended to assist students who were experiencing learning difficulties, were made available. However, most students in these classes did not have difficulty because of mental, emotional, or physical limitations; rather, they suffered from language deficiencies. Accordingly, instruction was more often similar to that afforded in either English as a second-language or bilingual education classes than to that provided within today's individualized education programs. Nevertheless, due to these and other special programs, children with disabilities began

---

11 Watson v. City of Cambridge, 32 N.E. 864, 864 (Mass. 1893).
12 State *ex rel.* Beattie v. Board of Educ. of Antigo, 172 N.W. 153, 154 (Wis. 1919).

attending school in greater numbers. The presence of these students presented educators with both the incentive and the opportunity to develop methods and materials for communicating with and educating this newly accepted population of children.[13]

New Jersey, in 1911, became the first state to enact a statute authorizing the establishment of classes for the mildly mentally retarded, although several cities, such as Providence, Boston, and Chicago, had already initiated offerings for this and other special populations. New York State passed related statutes in 1917 and Pennsylvania followed suit in 1920.[14] However, most early programs for the retarded accepted only students classified as "educable." With few exceptions, "trainable" students who required more individual attention were not served until the late 1920s and 1930s, while "subtrainable" students continued to be excluded from almost all schools. Moreover, with the onset of the Great Depression in 1929, money to fund programs for individuals with disabilities all but disappeared.

Over the next forty years, many school districts slowly but deliberately expanded their offerings in special education and admitted a growing number of children. Statistics from the Department of Education indicate that the number of programs grew slowly, but surely, through the 1960s as the percentage of all children with disabilities who were served increased from 12% in 1948 to 21% in 1963 and to 38% in 1968.[15] Additionally, a Report by the Committee on Education and Labor of the House of Representatives, prior to the enactment of the Education for All Handicapped Children Act (EAHCA), showed that growth in the number of programs continued during the early 1970s. As significant as was the growth in the number of students, the results were, at best, mixed.

Effective July 1, 1974, the Bureau for the Education of the Handicapped estimated that 78.5% of the 8,150,000 eligible children received some form of public education. However, only 47.8% of these students received special education and related services, 30.7% did not receive related services, and the remaining 21.5% received

---

[13] Burgdorf & Burgdorf, *supra* note 1, at 873.

[14] H.R. REP. NO. 332, 94th Cong., 1st Sess. at 20 (1975).

[15] Weintraub & Ballard, *Introduction: Bridging the Decades,* SPECIAL EDUCATION IN AMERICA: ITS LEGAL AND GOVERNMENTAL FOUNDATIONS (1982), at 2.

no educational services at all.[16] Accordingly, despite the improvement, schools were far from "zero reject,"[17] and were even further from providing appropriate programs. As a result, it is not surprising that the initial reliance of persons with disabilities on the "good intentions" of educators and legislators was eventually supplanted by their dependence on the courts.

Case law relevant to equal educational opportunities for all children dates back to 1954 and *Brown v. Board of Education of Topeka,* the most significant ruling on education in the history of the United States.[18] In *Brown,* a decision involving the segregation of racial minority students, the Supreme Court concluded that "[i]n these days, it is doubtful that any child may reasonably be expected to succeed in life if he is denied the opportunity of an education. Such an opportunity, where the state has undertaken to provide it, is a right which must be made available to all on equal terms."[19]

The principles of equal educational opportunity enunciated in *Brown* have ensured its place in history as the cornerstone upon which all subsequent legal developments protecting the rights of the disenfranchised, including individuals with disabilities, are grounded. Consequently, *Brown* has been applied in a number of cases involving the disabled, beginning in 1969 with *Wolf v. Legislature of Utah.*[20]

In *Wolf,* the judge not only identified education as the most important function of state and local governments, but also declared it to be a fundamental right under both the state and federal constitutions. Although in *San Antonio Independent School District v. Rodriguez*[21] the Supreme Court later disagreed with the conclusion that education was fundamental under the United States Constitution, this decision served as a presage for the more than forty special education-related cases to follow. Of these cases, two federal district court suits, *Pennsylvania Association for Retarded Children*

---

16 H.R. REP. No. 332, 94th Cong., 1st Sess. at 11 (1975).
17 The concept of "zero reject" requires states to provide education to all children, regardless of the nature or severity of their respective disabilities.
18 Brown v. Board of Educ. of Topeka, 347 U.S. 483 (1954).
19 *Id.* at 493.
20 Wolf v. Legislature of Utah, Civil No. 182646 (Utah 3d Jud. Dist. Ct., Jan. 8, 1969).
21 San Antonio Indep. Sch. Dist. v. Rodriguez, 411 U.S. 1, 44 (1973).

(PARC) v. Pennsylvania and *Mills v. Board of Education of the District of Columbia*, were of particular significance.

Pennsylvania Association for Retarded Children v. Pennsylvania involved a consent decree pursuant to 42 U.S.C. section 1981 (Equal Rights Under the Law)[22] and 42 U.S.C. section 1983 (Civil Action for the Deprivation of Rights)[23] on behalf of all retarded persons between the ages of six and twenty-one who were excluded from public schools in Pennsylvania. The original complaint challenged state statutory provisions that relieved the State Board of Education of the responsibility to educate students who were classified as uneducable or untrainable by a public school psychologist; permitted an indefinite postponement of admission to public schools of children who had not attained the mental age of five years; and excused children from compulsory attendance if a psychologist found them unable to profit from schooling, even though attendance was required of all children ages eight to seventeen.

The original decree, entered into in 1971,[24] and as amended in 1972,[25] greatly enhanced the educational rights of students with disabilities while setting the stage for subsequent developments in federal statutory law. Under the settlement in *PARC*, the parties recognized that a child could neither be denied admission to a public school nor be subjected to a change in educational status unless formal due process was provided. The parties also acknowledged that persons who were mentally retarded were capable of benefiting from an education, and that the state must provide them with a free public

---

[22] 42 U.S.C. § 1981 states that "[a]ll persons within the jurisdiction of the United States shall have the same right in every [s]tate and [t]erritory to make and enforce contracts, to sue, be parties, give evidence, and to the full and equal benefit of all laws and proceedings for the security of persons and property as is enjoyed by white citizens, and shall be subject to like punishment, pains, penalties, taxes, licenses, exactions of every kind, and to no other."

[23] 42 U.S.C. § 1983 states that "[e]very person, who under color of any statute, ordinance, regulation, custom, or usage, of any [s]tate or [t]erritory, subjects, or causes to be subjected, any citizen of the United States or other persons within the jurisdiction thereof to the deprivation of any rights, privileges, or immunities secured by the Constitution and laws, shall be liable to the party injured in an action at law, suit in equity, or other proper proceedings for redress."

[24] Pennsylvania Ass'n for Retarded Children v. Pennsylvania, 334 F. Supp. 1257 (E.D. Pa. 1971).

[25] Pennsylvania Ass'n for Retarded Children v. Pennsylvania, 343 F. Supp. 279 (E.D. Pa. 1972).

program appropriate to their capacity. Furthermore, the litigants agreed that placement in a regular classroom was preferable to any of the more restrictive and segregative options.

Mills v. Board of Education of the District of Columbia[26] was decided in 1972. The suit was brought on behalf of seven exceptional children who were certified as a class representing 18,000 similarly situated students whose educational needs were not being served by the public schools of the District of Columbia. Their suit, based on the Fourteenth Amendment charged that they were improperly excluded from school without due process of law. *Mills* was similar to *PARC* in that it greatly increased the educational rights of children with disabilities. However, *Mills* differed from *PARC* in that it dealt with a wider class of students labeled as having behavioral problems, mental retardation, emotional disturbances, and hyperactivity (*PARC* was limited to students who were mentally retarded), and in that it was a judgment on the merits, not a consent decree.

The *Mills* court held that the "insufficiencies" of the school system not be permitted to bear more heavily on exceptional children than on "normal" children, that no child could be totally excluded from publicly supported education, and that children with disabilities must be provided with due process prior to education being denied. Also, since *Mills* originated in the nation's capitol, it is likely that it was among the more significant influences that moved federal law makers to act to ensure adequate statutory protection for children (and adults) with disabilities.

Given the success of the plaintiffs in *PARC* and *Mills,* it was not surprising to see the filing of a myriad of related complaints. In fact, by June 1975 no less than forty-six law suits in twenty-eight states were brought seeking clarification of the educational rights of students with disabilities.[27] The plaintiffs in these cases generally were successful and, as a result, were provided additional services. Many even received programs that were specially designed to meet their unique needs. However, in states where litigation was neither present nor threatened, incidents of segregation or exclusion continued.

---

[26] Mills v. Board of Educ. of D.C., 348 F. Supp. 866 (D.D.C. 1972).
[27] H.R. REP. NO. 332, 94th Cong., 1st Sess. at 3 (1975).

School districts that did not comply with the law by providing educational services for students with disabilities presented a variety of arguments. Among the most common justifications offered were that funds were not available (or that they were unsure which governmental unit was to provide funds), that programs had not been developed, that existing faculty had not completed training, that current facilities were inadequate, or that instructional materials and equipment either were not available or had not been received or purchased. Other districts, where state legislation was not sufficiently specific, restricted admission to only selected populations, required partial funding from parents, or maintained no specific timetable for testing, classifying, or placing. Students often complained of the dearth of offerings in residential institutions, misclassifications, unjust residency requirements, tuition reimbursement ceilings, and a lack of due process.[28]

Four years before the adoption of the EAHCA in 1975, only seven states had mandatory legislation in all categories of exceptionality while twenty-six others had some form of mandatory provisions. These figures improved dramatically in the interim so that by 1975 only a handful of states had failed to pass related statutes.[29] However, the laws varied substantially among the states as no "great design" existed for all to follow. Most states had developed neither sufficient guidelines for compliance nor administrative machinery capable of handling complaints.

The success enjoyed by litigants in special education cases mirrored developments in federal law that reflected evolving public sentiment favoring support for the disabled (i.e., The Elementary and Secondary Education Act, P.L. 89-10 and The National Technical Institute for the Deaf Act, P.L. 89-36). Today, the most important laws affecting children with disabilities are the Fourteenth Amendment to the Federal Constitution, 42 U.S.C. section 1983, section 504 of The Rehabilitation Act of 1973, The Individuals with Disabilities Education Act (IDEA) (formerly the Education of the Handicapped Act (EHA)), and The Americans with Disabilities Act (ADA) of 1990.[30] A brief discussion of each of these laws is provided below.

---

[28] Burgdorf & Burgdorf, *supra* note 1, at 879-83.
[29] H.R. REP. NO. 332, 94th Cong., 1st Sess. at 10 (1975).
[30] 42 U.S.C. § 12101 *et seq.*

Fourteenth Amendment

The Fourteenth Amendment to the United States Constitution prohibits states and their local subdivisions from denying to any person within their respective jurisdictions the equal protection of the law, or from taking life, liberty, or property without due process of the law. Consequently, because public schools are local subdivisions of the state, school personnel are required to treat similarly all classes of persons and to provide proper due process where liberty and property interests may be denied.[31]

Equal Protection

Over the years, three judicially created standards of review have evolved (i.e., the strict scrutiny test, the rational relationship test, and the intermediate test) for facially discriminatory practices,[32] while the standard of intent exists for those practices that are facially neutral.[33] Each of these standards is discussed below.

Strict Scrutiny. Under strict scrutiny, if a governmental policy or a law facially discriminates on the basis of a "suspect" classification (i.e., alienage, race, or national origin[34]), or if it infringes upon a fundamental right (i.e., explicit or implicit constitutional rights such as those to assemble, to vote, or to procreate[35]), the provision will be strictly scrutinized. Consequently, any such policy or law will be justified only if a compelling state interest can be proven. This level of

---

[31] Furthermore, the Fifth Amendment provides protection similar to that established by the Fourteenth Amendment, but has been interpreted by the courts to prohibit federal, rather than state, acts that deny due process. Although the Fifth Amendment does not contain a comparable Equal Protection Clause, the Supreme Court has ruled that the two (due process and equal protection) are not mutually exclusive. Bolling v. Sharpe, 347 U.S. 497, 499 (1954).

[32] An example of facial discrimination is when a person with a disability is not admitted to a public school or is denied employment admittedly due to disability.

[33] Examples of a practice that is facially neutral, yet results in disparate impact, are the use of tests or physical requirements that eliminate students with disabilities in disproportionate numbers.

[34] *E.g.,* Graham v. Richardson, 403 U.S. 365 (1971) (alienage); Hunter v. Erickson, 393 U.S. 385 (1969) (race); Korematsu v. United States, 323 U.S. 214 (1944) (nationality).

[35] *E.g.,* Police Dep't of Chicago v. Mosley, 408 U.S. 92 (1972) (right to assemble); Reynolds v. Sims, 377 U.S. 533 (1964) (right to vote); Skinner v. Oklahoma, 316 U.S. 535 (1942) (right to procreate).

scrutiny is based on the principle that certain actions must be subjected to strict scrutiny in order to preserve equality and liberty. Although the compelling interest standard has, at times, been met,[36] most laws, policies, regulations, and practices have not withstood this level of scrutiny.

Rational Relationship. If neither a suspect class nor a fundamental right is involved, a challenged law or policy must bear only a rational relationship to a legitimate governmental objective. Under this standard, the governmental action is presumably constitutional and will be struck down only if it is "clearly wrong, a display of arbitrary power, not an exercise of judgment."[37] Given the comparative ease of meeting this standard, it is not surprising that most challenged practices have been found constitutional under this level of review.[38]

Intermediate Level. In addition to these two extreme standards, the Supreme Court has established an intermediate level of scrutiny that requires the classification to serve important governmental objectives while the discriminatory act must be substantially related to the achievement of those objectives. This standard is applied where a court is convinced that mere rationality is too lenient and strict scrutiny is too demanding. Intermediate scrutiny is employed when a significant, though not necessarily fundamental, interest allegedly is infringed, or a sensitive, though not necessarily suspect, class is affected. In so far as the Burger and Rehnquist Courts have been reluctant to increase the number of rights that have been classified as fundamental, or to identify additional classes that are suspect, the intermediate standard has been of particular importance to persons who have sought protection from discriminatory practices. To date, however, only a few claims have succeeded at the Supreme Court under this standard.[39]

It often has been argued that persons with disabilities should be identified as a suspect (or at least as a quasi-suspect) class and that

---

[36] *E.g.,* Hirabayashi v. United States, 320 U.S. 81 (1943).

[37] Mathews v. De Castro, 429 U.S. 181, 185 (1976).

[38] *But see* James v. Strange, 407 U.S. 128, 140 (1972); Eisenstadt v. Baird, 405 U.S. 438, 447 (1972); Reed v. Reed 404 U.S. 71, 76 (1971); Rinaldi v. Yeager, 384 U.S. 305, 309 (1966).

[39] Plyer v. Doe, 457 U. S. 202 (1982)(illegal elementary children cannot be denied a public education); Mississippi Univ. for Women v. Hogan, 485 U. S. (1982) (gender discrimination); Clark v. Jeter, 486 (1988) (illegitimacy).

the rational relationship standard is too lenient for evaluating laws or policies affecting them.[40] Historically, federal courts have not agreed as to the "traditional indicia of suspectness," and numerous criteria have been proposed, both by the courts and by commentators. Many, if not all, individuals with disabilities meet most, if not all, of these standards: they represent a discrete and insular minority;[41] they evoke stereotypes that carry the stigma of inferiority and a badge of opprobrium;[42] they often have conditions that are immutable;[43] they have been subjected to a history of purposefully unequal treatment;[44] they are in a position of political power-less-ness;[45] and they are often "saddled" with physical, mental, and emotional disabilities depending upon the nature and severity of their respective disabilities.[46]

This discussion notwithstanding, persons with disabilities have been identified as a suspect class, or a quasi-suspect class, only by select state and federal courts.[47] In fact, most courts, including the Supreme Court, refuse to place persons with disabilities in a suspect class, and require the use of only the rational relationship test as a means of supporting allegedly discriminatory acts.[48]

Intent. Along with the difficulty of obtaining relief under the Constitution when confronted by a facially discriminatory policy or law, victims with disabilities also encounter a formidable task when the challenged act is facially neutral, but is applied or enforced in a

---

[40] *E.g.*, Burgdorf & Burgdorf, *supra* note 1; Thomas E. McClure, Comment, *The Equal Protection and Due Process Clauses: Two Means of Implementing "Integrationism" for Handicapped Applicants for Public Employment*, 27 DEPAUL L. REV. 1169 (1978).

[41] United States v. Carolene Prod. Co., 304 U.S. 144, 152-53 n.4 (1938)

[42] *See, e.g.*, Charles L. Black, *The Lawfulness of the Segregation Decisions*, 69 YALE L.J. 421, 424 (1960).

[43] *See, e.g.*, Weber v. Aetna Casualty and Sur. Co., 406 U.S. 164 (1972).

[44] San Antonio Indep. Sch. Dist. v. Rodriguez, 411 U.S. 1, 28 (1973).

[45] *Id.*

[46] *Id.*

[47] *See, e.g.*, Frederick L. v. Thomas, 408 F. Supp. 832, 836 (E.D. Pa. 1976), *aff'd*, 557 F.2d 373 (3d Cir. 1977); Fialkowski v. Shapp, 405 F. Supp. 946, 958-59 (E.D. Pa. 1975); *In re* G.H., 218 N.W.2d 441, 446-47 (N.D. 1974).

[48] *See* City of Cleburne v. Cleburne Living Center, 473 U.S. 432 (1985). *See also* Schweiker v. Wilson, 450 U.S. 221 (1981); Gurmankin v. Costanzo, 411 F. Supp. 982, 992 n.8 (E.D. Pa. 1976); New York State Ass'n for Retarded Children v. Rockefeller, 357 F. Supp. 752, 762 (E.D.N.Y. 1973); *In re* Levy, 345 N.E.2d 556 (N.Y. 1976).

discriminatory manner. In such a situation, the plaintiff must prove that the discriminatory act was both purposeful and performed with an intent to discriminate. While it is not impossible to establish intent, it may prove exceedingly difficult in the majority of cases, even if actual discrimination exists.

Due Process

The Fourteenth Amendment also requires that neither life, liberty, nor property may be withdrawn or withheld from an individual unless there is an adequate determination that the deprivation is justified.[49] When a due process violation is claimed, a court must make a tripartite determination: first, whether the plaintiff had a life, liberty, or property interest at stake; second, whether government action infringed that interest; and, third, whether adequate due process procedures were followed.[50] The Due Process Clause has a direct application in public education, for although education is not a fundamental right, it can be a property right.[51] Consequently, if a student is denied an education without due process, a Fourteenth Amendment violation may exist. Furthermore, if a student's reputation or otherwise good name is injured by a state actor a liberty infringement also may be present.

42 U.S.C. Section 1983

Section 1983 was originally section 1 of the Ku Klux Klan Act of 1871, but is now codified in volume 42, section 1983 of the United States Code. That section stipulates that "[e]very person who, under color of any statute, ordinance, regulation, custom, or usage, of any [s]tate or [t]erritory, subjects, or causes to be subjected, any citizen of the United States or other person within the jurisdiction thereof to the deprivation of any rights, privileges, or immunities secured by the Constitution or laws, shall be liable to the party injured in an action at law, suit in equity, or other proper proceeding for redress."

---

[49] *See* Wolff v. McDonnell, 418 U.S. 539, 557-58 (1974).
[50] *See* Board of Curators Univ. of Mo. v. Horowitz, 435 U.S. 78 (1978); Bishop v. Wood, 426 U.S. 341 (1976); Goss v. Lopez, 419 U.S. 565 (1975); Perry v. Sindermann, 408 U.S. 593 (1972); Goldberg v. Kelly, 397 U.S. 254 (1970). *See also* Kathleen De Santis, *The Disabled Student Athlete: Gaining a Place on the Playing Field*, 5 COMM/ENT L.J. 517, 535-37 (1983) for a related discussion.
[51] Goss v. Lopez, 419 U.S. 565, 574 (1975).

Although this law appears fairly direct, its application has been complex. Six of the more obvious questions regarding section 1983 are addressed at this time, while several related issues are discussed in the body of this book.

Who qualifies as a "person"?

The term "person" is not defined in the Act. The Supreme Court has concluded, however, that local governments in the form of school boards, cities, or counties that are acting under color of state law are persons and therefore can be sued under section 1983.[52]

Who, if anyone, is responsible for punitive damages?

Individuals acting in bad faith may be responsible for punitive damages, compensation in excess of actual damages which are awarded in rare instances of malicious or willful misconduct, but school districts may not.[53]

Who, if anyone, can claim good faith immunity?

Individuals acting in good faith may claim immunity from suit, but school districts that qualify as persons and which act under color of state law are not eligible for good faith immunity. Accordingly, as long as individuals are performing their responsibilities in good faith, even if later proven to be in error, they may not be personally sued under this law.

What substantive rights are provided?

None. A section 1983 suit has to identify another federal constitutional or statutory right that is allegedly being infringed. It must "attach" to another federal law and may not stand alone.

---

[52] For a full discussion of § 1983 *see* RONALD D. ROTUNDA & JOHN E. NOWAK, 3 TREATISE ON CONSTITUTIONAL LAW: SUBSTANCE AND PROCEDURES 568 *et seq.* (2d ed. 1992).

[53] City of Newport v. Fact Concerts, 453 U.S. 247 (1981).

Is it necessary to exhaust remedies?

Generally, there is no requirement that administrative remedies be exhausted prior to a section 1983 suit.[54] However, if section 1983 is being attached to an IDEA suit, exhaustion is required, not due to provisions of section 1983, but because of mandates in the IDEA. Section 1983 cannot typically be used to circumvent administrative review when it otherwise is required.

Does this law apply to private schools?

Private schools are "persons" as that term is usually applied in the law; however, such institutions are not generally subject to liability under section 1983 because they do not typically act under color of state law.[55]

42 U.S.C. Section 1988

This section allows the prevailing party to recover reasonable attorney fees. However, the statute has been interpreted to establish a higher standard for the award of fees to the defendant than to the plaintiff. For a defendant to receive fees, most courts will require that the complaint be ruled as "frivolous, unreasonable, or without foundation."

Rehabilitation Act of 1973—Section 504

On September 23, 1973, The Rehabilitation Act, P.L. 93-112, was enacted by Congress. Included among its many provisions was section 504,[56] which represents the first federal civil rights law protecting the rights of the disabled. The language of the Act is almost identical to the wording in title VI of the Civil Rights Act of 1964[57] and to the wording in title IX of the Education Amendments of 1972:[58] "No otherwise qualified individual with a disability in the United States...

---

[54] Patsy v. Board of Regents of Fla., 457 U.S. 496 (1982).

[55] Rendell-Baker v. Kohn, 457 U.S. 830 (1981); Lugar v. Edmonson Oil Co., 457 U.S. 922 (1981).

[56] 29 U.S.C. § 794. The most significant regulations enacted pursuant to § 504, those dealing with the Department of Education, may be found at 34 C.F.R. § 101.4-104.51; those for the Department of Health and Human Services are at 45 C.F.R. § 84.1-84.61; and those for the Office of Elementary and Secondary Education are at 34 C.F.R. § 222.70-222.79.

[57] 42 U.S.C. § 2000d.

[58] 20 U.S.C. § 1681 *et seq.*

shall, solely by reason of her or his disability, be excluded from the participation in, be denied the benefits of, or be subjected to discrimination under any program or activity receiving [f]ederal financial assistance . . . ."[59]

History

The regulations implementing section 504 took over three years to evolve due to numerous administrative concerns that needed to be addressed and several political roadblocks that had to be removed. Following the passage of section 504, five months elapsed before the enforcement responsibility of the Act was assigned to the Office of Civil Rights (OCR) in the Department of Education (formerly the Department of Health, Education, and Welfare). Thus, it was May 1976 before draft regulations were issued and before twenty-two public hearings were conducted.

Although the regulations were finalized soon thereafter, they were not made public for nearly a year. Secretary Mathews was reluctant to have them issued for a number of reasons, primary of which was his concern over the inclusion of alcoholics and drug addicts within the definition of "handicapped." Due to this delay, lobbying groups took a number of steps to force the issuance of the regulations, including the filing of a law suit, *Cherry v. Mathews*.[60] Even so, Secretary Mathews left office on January 20, 1977 without taking action. Secretary Califano, Mathews' successor, shared some of his predecessor's concerns about the political repercussions of the Act, but continued the delay only three and one-half additional months. On May 4, 1977, the regulations were issued; the total process had lasted nearly three years and eight months.

In spite of the fact that department rules were finally formalized and promulgated, relief was not quickly forthcoming, because the OCR already had a substantial backlog of complaints dealing with race and gender. As a general rule, cases were investigated on a first-come, first-served basis. Therefore, the claims of disability discrimination received little initial attention. In fact, organizations concerned with race and gender discrimination were able to acquire a

---

[59] 29 U.S.C. § 794(a).
[60] Cherry v. Mathews, 419 F. Supp. 922 (D.D.C. 1976).

court order in *Adams v. Califano*,[61] which required the processing of existing cases prior to the investigation of new complaints, including all of those related to disability. After substantial political pressure, however, the order was modified to permit the OCR to expand its investigations.

Section 504 requires recipients of federal financial assistance to file an assurance of compliance; to take remedial action where violations are proven; to take voluntary action, in addition to that required by the Act, to overcome the effects of conditions that resulted historically in limiting participation of persons with disabilities in the recipient's program; to conduct a self evaluation; to designate a particular employee to coordinate compliance; to adopt grievance procedures; and to give notice to participants that the recipient's program does not discriminate against persons with disabilities.[62]

Individual with a Disability Defined

Section 504 offers broad-based protection for a wide array of persons. It defines an individual with a disability as one "who (i) has a physical or mental impairment which substantially limits one or more of such person's major life activities, (ii) has a record of such an impairment, or (iii) is regarded as having such an impairment."[63] The regulations enacted pursuant to section 504 define physical or mental impairments as including:

> (A) any physiological disorder or condition, cosmetic disfigurement, or anatomical loss affecting one or more of the following body systems: neurological; musculoskeletal; special sense organs; respiratory, including speech organs; cardiovascular; reproductive, digestive, genito-urinary; hemic and lymphatic; skin; and endocrine; or (B) any mental or psychological disorder, such as mental retardation, organic brain syndrome, emotional or mental illness, and specific learning disorders.[64]

---

[61] Adams v. Califano, 430 F. Supp. 176 (D.D.C. 1977).
[62] 45 C.F.R. § 84.5-84.8.
[63] 29 U.S.C. § 706(7)(B).
[64] 45 C.F.R. § 84.3(j)(2)(i), 34 C.F.R. § 104(j)(2)(i).

A note accompanying this list indicates that it is not intended to be exhaustive.[65] Additionally, prior to an individual's being classified as having a disability, it must also be shown that a major life activity (i.e., caring for one's self, performing manual tasks, walking, seeing, hearing, speaking, breathing, learning, and working[66]) is limited due to the nature and severity of the disability.

In order to have a record of impairment, an individual must have a history of, or have been misclassified as having, a mental or physical impairment that substantially limits one or more of life's major activities.[67] For example, a person with a history of hospitalization due to tuberculosis who currently tests negative could qualify as a person with a record of impairment.[68]

> An individual who is regarded as having an impairment is one who: (A) has a physical or mental impairment that does not substantially limit major life activities but that is treated by a recipient as constituting such a limitation; (B) has a physical or mental impairment that substantially limits major life activities only as a result of the attitudes of others toward such impairment; or (C) has none of the impairments . . . but is treated by a recipient as having such an impairment.[69]

An illustration of "being regarded as having an impairment" can be seen when dealing with a person who is HIV positive, but who is fully qualified to perform the job without any form of accommodation. If the employer terminates or makes a change in the individual's job status solely as a result of her or his testing positive for HIV, a section 504 suit may be forthcoming.[70] The person would not technically qualify as being an "otherwise qualified person with a disability" under definition (i) above in part because no major life activity has yet been affected (i.e., the person is only HIV positive and does not

---

[65] 45 C.F.R. Part 84 App. A, § 3 pp. 376-377.

[66] 45 C.F.R. § 84.3(j)(2)(ii), 34 C.F.R. § 104.3(j)(2)(ii).

[67] 45 C.F.R. § 84.3(j)(2)(iii), 34 C.F.R. § 104.3(j)(2)(iii).

[68] Arline v. School Bd. of Nassau County, Fla., 480 U.S. 273 (1987).

[69] 45 C.F.R. § 84.3(j)(2)(iv), 34 C.F.R. § 104.3(j)(2)(iv).

[70] *See* Chalk v. United States Dist. Ct., Cent. Dist. of Cal., 840 F.2d 701 (9th Cir. 1988) (where a teacher who was diagnosed as having HIV was an "otherwise qualified person" under section 504 and, as such, was ordered reinstated to his teaching position from the administrative post to which he had been assigned).

have active AIDS, related diseases, or a weakened condition). Furthermore, definition (ii) also would not be met, since there is no record of impairment. However, if the employer were to regard or treat the individual as having an impairment, definition (iii) would be met and a section 504 violation would exist.

Once a person is determined to have a disability, the next step is to ascertain whether the individual is qualified. To be qualified, as the term is applied to preschool, elementary, and secondary school students, one must be "(i) of an age during which nonhandicapped persons are provided such services, (ii) of any age during which it is mandatory under state law to provide such services to handicapped persons, or (iii) [a person] to whom a state is required to provide a free appropriate public education [under the IDEA]."[71]

Even when an individual appears to be "otherwise qualified" within the meaning of section 504, institutions often assert defenses to avoid being charged with noncompliance. A discussion of at least one of the defenses was part of the Supreme Court's ruling in *Southeastern Community College v. Davis*.[72] The Court held that an institution is not required to make accommodations that would result either in "a fundamental alteration in the nature of [a] program"[73] or impose an "undue financial burden"[74] upon it. The language of the Court has since been addressed in regulations pertaining to schools[75] and employers.[76] A second defense is that an otherwise qualified person with a disability can be excluded from a program or position if his or her presence creates a substantial risk of injury to him or herself or to others.[77] These forms of defense, and others, are discussed further in the remaining portions of this book.

Prohibits Discrimination

Along with the guidelines related to the education of children with disabilities, section 504 also prohibits discrimination. It requires

---

[71] 45 C.F.R. § 84.3(k)(2).

[72] Southeastern Community College v. Davis, 442 U.S. 397 (1979).

[73] *Id.* at 410.

[74] *Id.* at 412.

[75] 45 C.F.R. §§ 84.31-39, 41-47 (1993).

[76] 45 C.F.R. § 84.12 *et seq.* (1993).

[77] The concern over safety seems to have originated in Southeastern Community College v. Davis, 442 U.S. 397, 403 (1979). *See also* 29 C.F.R. § 32.14 (1994).

institutions to make individualized modifications for otherwise qualified students with disabilities[78] by providing aid, benefits, or services
that are comparable to those provided students who are not disabled.
Accordingly, students with disabilities must receive comparable
materials, teacher quality, length of school term, and daily hours of
instruction. Moreover, programs for these students should not be
separate from those available to the nondisabled, unless such segregation is necessary for the program to be effective. Where programs
are permissibly separate, facilities must be comparable.[79]

In demonstrating compliance with section 504, an institution is
required to identify every qualified individual with a disability residing within its jurisdiction who is not receiving a public education, and
it must inform each of them of their rights under the Act. Once
identified, an appropriate public education must be made available
to each qualified person with a disability, regardless of the nature or
severity of the disability. In order to guarantee that an appropriate
education is made available, section 504 regulations include due
process requirements for evaluation and placement.[80] These criteria
are similar to ones mandated under the IDEA and are discussed in
Chapter 2.

Civil Rights Restoration Act

The requirements for programs and activities receiving federal
financial assistance under section 504 were broadened significantly
with the passage of the Civil Rights Restoration Act (CRRA) in
1987.[81] The CRRA impacted upon four of the primary recipient
statutes (i.e., title VI, title IX, the Age Discrimination Act, and section 504), by expanding the scope of each to make them "institution
wide," rather than "program specific." Accordingly, if any program
or activity within a university or school district qualifies as a recipient, the entire institution/district must demonstrate compliance with
each of these laws.

---

78 *See* Southeastern Community College v. Davis, 442 U.S. 397, 406 (1979) (where
   the Court held that "[a]n otherwise qualified person is one who is able to meet all
   of a program's requirements in spite of his handicap").

79 34 C.F.R. § 104.34(c).

80 34 C.F.R. §§ 104.35, 104.36.

81 20 U.S.C. § 1687.

The CRRA was a legislative response to the Supreme Court's decision in *Grove City College v. Bell.*[82] In this case, the Court held that while the college qualified as a recipient of federal financial assistance because its students received federal grants and loans, only the student financial aid department had to demonstrate compliance, given that it alone qualified as a recipient. The position taken by the Court was politically unpopular and, as a result, Congress enacted the CRRA to "correct" the "error" made by the Court and to "restore" civil rights which allegedly had been withdrawn.[83]

Individuals with
Disabilities Education Act (IDEA)[84]

The content of the original Education of the Handicapped Act (EHA), as amended by P.L. 94-142, and now the IDEA, reflects a long history of state and federal legislation and case law. As noted earlier, by 1975 most states had passed laws requiring local school districts to admit and provide some degree of education for all resident children regardless of the nature or severity of their respective disabilities. In addition, the courts were instrumental in mandating appropriate programs, individualized testing, equal access to nonacademic and extracurricular programs, and the like. Federal legislation addressed several related problems in an effort to provide minimum guarantees for all children regardless of where they lived or whether legal action had been filed on their behalf. Yet, despite these efforts, legislation failed to establish a comprehensive vehicle for enforcing the rights of children with disabilities by either maintaining appropriate programs or providing necessary funding. Accordingly, the time was ripe for the passage of additional, more comprehensive, legislation.

---

[82] Grove City College v. Bell, 465 U.S. 555 (1984).

[83] It should be noted, however, that the history of each of these laws, as well as their express terms, refute the claim that the Court was in error. The decision may have been unpopular, but arguably was not "incorrect."

[84] Except for the history section of this Chapter, "IDEA" will be used instead of EHA, EAHCA, or P.L. 94-142. The use of multiple terms is confusing to the reader and has been omitted for that reason.

The evolution of laws that significantly affected the education of children with disabilities began with the passage of The Elementary and Secondary Education Act (ESEA) of 1965, P.L. 89-10, which aided educationally-deprived children who resided in school districts with high concentrations of low-income families. Although this law was not designed specifically to assist children with disabilities, such youngsters were among those who were served. Additionally, over the next several years the ESEA was amended in a number of ways that benefited special needs students.

Among the more important revisions were The Elementary and Secondary Education Act Amendments of 1966 (P.L. 89-750), which included a new title VI called the Education of Handicapped Children, and The Education of the Handicapped Act of 1970 (P.L. 91-230). Public law 89-750 created both the Bureau of Education for the Handicapped and the National Advisory Council on Handicapped Children (eliminated under The Education of the Handicapped Amendments of 1977, P.L. 95-49). It provided federal assistance for states to initiate, expand, and improve programs for children with disabilities. Title VI of this law was expanded in 1967 (P.L. 90-247, The Education of the Handicapped Act) to authorize federal funds to improve the education of children with disabilities through the use of regional resource centers. Three years later, P.L. 91-230 further amended title VI of the ESEA, increased assistance for programs, and consolidated previous provisions. Part B of the Act became the most important over time because it dealt with federal funding. The EHA was re-authorized and expanded by The Education Amendments of 1974 (P.L. 93-380). Along with substantially increasing federal funding, these Amendments required states to give assurances that all children with disabilities would be provided with special education services, that they would work toward affording full educational opportunities for resident children with disabilities, that records would be kept confidential, and that procedural safeguards consistent with the statute would be established.[85]

On November 29, 1975, the role of the federal government increased dramatically when President Ford signed The Education

---

[85] *See* James A. Shrybman, DUE PROCESS IN SPECIAL EDUCATION (1982), at 9-28 for a related discussion.

for All Handicapped Children Act, also known as P.L. 94-142, into law. This enactment was a complete revision of Part B of the EHA. Although sections other than Part B remained basically unchanged, the impact of these modifications was so significant that P.L. 94-142 became known as the "Bill of Rights" for the education of children with disabilities. In fact, Senator Harrison Williams, one of the principal architects of the EAHCA, went so far as to say that it "fulfills the promise of the Constitution that there shall be equality of education for all people, and that handicapped children will no longer be left out."[86]

The federal government's maximum contribution under the EHA/IDEA is determined by multiplying 40% of the national average per pupil expenditure by the number of children with disabilities (ages three through twenty-one) being served.[87] The number of children with disabilities to be used in the formula is equal to the number of children receiving special education and related services on December 1 of the preceding fiscal year.[88] However, that number may not be greater than 12% of the total number of children ages three to seventeen within the state.[89] Funds received under the Act must supplement, not supplant, state and local dollars, while 75% of the federal contribution is intended for local school districts and merely "flows through" the state, which is to have no direct control over its use.[90] This apparently high level of theoretical support notwithstanding, the federal government has never come close to its

---

[86] 121 CONG. REC. 37413, Part 129 (Nov. 19, 1975).

[87] 20 U.S.C. § 1411(a)(1). The multiplier increased to its present authorized level from 5% for the year ending September 30, 1978, to 10% for 1979, to 20% for 1980, to 30% for 1981.

[88] 20 U.S.C. § 1411(a)(3).

[89] 20 U.S.C. § 1411(a)(5)(A)(i). However, if the state does not serve children aged three to five, the 12% calculation involves children aged five to seventeen only. 20 U.S.C. § 1411(a)(5)(A)(ii).

[90] 20 U.S.C. § 1411(c); 34 C.F.R. §§ 300.705-706.

goal of reimbursing states for 40% of the national average expenditure associated with educating children with disabilities.[91]

The IDEA is designed to ensure that a free appropriate public education (FAPE), emphasizing special education[92] and related services,[93] is made available in the *least restrictive environment* (LRE) to each child with a disability between the ages of three and twenty-one, except where state law or practice or a court order restricts the participation of children aged three, four, five, eighteen, nineteen, twenty, or twenty-one.[94] Concomitantly, it is intended "to assure that the rights of children with disabilities and their parents or guardians are protected, to assist [s]tates and localities to provide for the education of all children with disabilities, and to assess and assure the effectiveness of efforts to educate children with disabilities."[95] Pursuant to its provisions, children with disabilities who are not receiving an education are the first priority while those with severe

---

[91] *See, e.g.*, Leslie A. Collins & Perry A. Zirkel, *To What Extent, If Any, May Cost be a Factor in Special Education Cases*, 71 EDUC. L. REP. 11 (1992) (reporting that federal funding in 1990 was at the level of 9%). Moreover, for the 1993 fiscal year, the federal government appropriated $411 per child under the Part B State Grant Program to each state to pay for the cost of educating children with disabilities; for the 1977 fiscal year, the first year for which funds were available, $77.00 was allocated per child. UNITED STATES DEP'T OF EDUC., TO ASSURE THE FREE APPROPRIATE PUBLIC EDUCATION OF ALL CHILDREN WITH DISABILITIES: SIXTEENTH ANNUAL REPORT TO CONGRESS ON THE IMPLEMENTATION OF THE INDIVIDUALS WITH DISABILITIES EDUCATION Act 3, Table 1.1, Part B State Grant Program: Funds Appropriated, 1977-93 (1994).

[92] 20 U.S.C. § 1401(a)(16). Special education is defined as "specially designed instruction, at no cost to parents or guardians, to meet the unique needs of a child with a disability, including (A) instruction conducted in the classroom, in the home, in hospitals and institutions, and in other settings; and (B) instruction in physical education." Related regulations may be found at 34 C.F.R. § 300.17(a)(1).

[93] 20 U.S.C. § 1401(a)(17). Related services are defined as "transportation, and such developmental, corrective, and other supportive services (including speech pathology and audiology, psychological services, physical and occupational therapy, recreation, including therapeutic recreation, social work services, counseling services, including rehabilitation counseling, and medical services, except that such medical services shall be for diagnostic and evaluative purposes only) as may be required to assist a child with a disability to benefit from a special education, and includes early identification and assessment of disabling conditions in children." Related regulations may be found at 34 C.F.R. § 300.16.

[94] 20 U.S.C. § 1412(2)(B).

[95] 20 U.S.C. § 1400(c).

disabilities who are receiving an inadequate education are accorded second priority.[96]

In order to qualify for coverage under the IDEA, a child must meet two eligibility requirements. First, a child must be evaluated as having "mental retardation, hearing impairments including deafness, speech or language impairments, visual impairments including blindness, serious emotional disturbance, orthopedic impairments, autism, traumatic brain injury, other health impairments, or specific learning disabilities."[97] Second, a child must be in need of special education and related services.[98] Thus, a child with a disability who is not in need of special education and related services may not qualify for assistance under the IDEA. For example, a child who has lost sight in one eye and is not otherwise qualified for special education, but can be served by being moved to the front of a classroom, is not entitled to protection under the IDEA. However, the student may, under certain circumstances, be covered under section 504 if discriminated against due to the disability by a recipient of federal financial assistance.

The IDEA is designed to provide full educational opportunities to all children with disabilities.[99] More specifically, it requires all educational agencies, including states and local school districts, receiving assistance under the Act to identify, locate, and evaluate all resident children with disabilities.[100] Subsequently, each child must be provided with a FAPE[101] in the LRE[102] based on an individualized edu-

---

[96] 20 U.S.C. § 1414(a)(1)(C)(ii). Related regulations may be found at 34 C.F.R. § 300.320 *et seq.*

[97] 20 U.S.C. § 1401(a)(1)(A)(i). Related regulations may be found at 34 C.F.R. § 300.7.

[98] 20 U.S.C. § 1401(a)(1)(A)(ii). Related regulations may be found at 34 C.F.R. § 300.7.

[99] 20 U.S.C. § 1412(2)(A)(i).

[100] 20 U.S.C. § 1412(2)(C).

[101] 20 U.S.C. § 1401(a)(18). Related regulations may be found at 34 C.F.R. § 300.300 *et seq.* As defined by the IDEA, a FAPE requires that special education and related services be provided at public expense, under public supervision and direction, and without charge; meet the standards of the state education agency; include an appropriate preschool, elementary, or secondary school education; and be provided in conformity with the child's IEP.

[102] 20 U.S.C. §§ 1412(5)(B), 1414(a)(1)(C)(iv). Related regulations may be found at 34 C.F.R. § 300.550.

cation program (IEP).[103] In addition, these agencies must not only establish procedural safeguards to protect the rights of students and their parents or guardians,[104] but must also preserve the confidentiality of all information and data used in the evaluation, placement, and education of students.[105]

In 1986, the EHA was amended to include P.L. 99-457, which offers funding for preschool and early childhood programs, and establishes two age categories of children: three to five and birth to two. The amended law requires states applying for funds to establish programs for youngsters aged three to five and to assure that they are providing a FAPE to all eligible children.[106] A state's failure to offer such services to all children may result in a loss of funding as well as the loss of grants and contracts related to preschool special education authorized under IDEA discretionary programs. Furthermore, if a state seeks federal financial assistance to provide preschool services for children with disabilities, these students must receive the full benefits of the substantive and procedural due process safeguards of the IDEA.

The early intervention provisions of P.L. 99-457 are intended to establish state level programs for infants and toddlers (birth to age two) with disabilities. Children may receive services if they are expe-

---

[103] 20 U.S.C. § 1401(a)(20). An IEP is defined as a "written statement for each child with a disability developed in any meeting by a representative of the local educational agency or an intermediate educational unit who shall be qualified to provide, or supervise the provision of, specially designed instruction to meet the unique needs of children with disabilities, the teacher, the parents or guardian of such child, and, whenever appropriate, such child, which statement shall include (A) a statement of the present levels of educational performance of such child, (B) a statement of annual goals, including short term instructional objectives, (C) a statement of the specific educational services to be provided to such child, and the extent to which such child will be able to participate in regular educational programs, (D) a statement of the needed transition services for students beginning no later than age 16 . . . , (E) the projected date for initiation and anticipated duration of such services, and (F) appropriate objective criteria and evaluation procedures and schedules for determining, at least on an annual basis, whether instructional objectives are being achieved." Related regulations may be found at 34 C.F.R. § 300.340 *et seq.*

[104] 20 U.S.C. § 1415. Related regulations may be found at 34 C.F.R. § 300.500 *et seq.*

[105] 20 U.S.C. § 1417(c). Related regulations may be found at 34 C.F.R. § 300.560 *et seq.*

[106] 20 U.S.C. § 1419.

riencing developmental delays or have a diagnosed physical or mental condition that has a high probability of resulting in developmental delay. Additionally, at a state's discretion, children who are "at risk" of having substantial developmental delays may also be served.[107] States wishing to provide such programs are subject to requirements that differ slightly from those applicable to the rest of the IDEA.[108] For example, programs were phased in over five years,[109] parents may be charged fees on a sliding scale,[110] and due process rights need not be as extensive.[111] Moreover, the criteria for eligibility to participate in early intervention programs are not as stringent.

Similar to the IEP component of the IDEA, early intervention services must include a multidisciplinary assessment and a written individualized family service plan (IFSP). The IFSP must include a statement of the child's current level of development (including physical, cognitive, speech/language, psychosocial, motor, and self help); identification of the strengths and needs of the family related to enhancing the child's development; identification of major outcomes expected to be achieved; the criteria, procedures, and time lines for determining progress; a list of specific early intervention services (including the method, frequency, and intensity of the service); a statement of natural environments in which to serve the child; the date for initiation of services and expected duration; procedures for transition from early intervention into the preschool program; and the name of the case manager.[112] In addition, the IFSP should be evaluated annually and reviewed at six-month intervals, or more often if needed.[113]

---

[107] 20 U.S.C. § 1472(1).
[108] 20 U.S.C. §§ 1471-1485. Related regulations may be found at 34 C.F.R. § 303 *et seq.*
[109] 34 C.F.R. § 303.140 *et seq.*
[110] 20 U.S.C. § 1472(2)(B). *See* 303 C.F.R. § 521 for applicable regulations.
[111] 20 U.S.C. § 1480. *See* 300 C.F.R. § 304.400 *et seq.* for applicable regulations.
[112] 20 U.S.C. § 1477(d). Related regulations may be found at 34 C.F.R. § 303.340.
[113] 20 U.S.C. § 1477(b).

Comparing the IDEA with Section 504

In light of the complexities and overlapping nature of the IDEA and section 504, an edited version[114] of a table originally published by the Council of Administrators of Special Educationi is included. (See Table 1-1.) The table helps summarize much of the aforediscussed material and should help clarify the similarities and differences between the two laws.

Table 1-1

IDEA & Section 504: A Comparison

Component	IDEA	Section 504
General Purpose	A federal funding statute whose purpose is to provide financial aid to states in their efforts to ensure adequate and appropriate services for children with disabilities.	A broad civil rights law which protects the rights of individuals with disabilities in programs and activities that receive federal financial assistance from the U.S. Department of Education.
Who is Protected	Identifies all school-aged children who fall within one or more specific categories of qualifying conditions.	Identifies all schoolaged children as disabled who meet the definition of a person with a disability: (1) has or (2) has had a physical or mental impairment which substantially limits a major life activity, or (3) is regarded as disabled by others. Major life activities include walking, seeing, hearing, speaking, breathing, learning, working, caring for oneself, and performing manual tasks. The handcapping condition need only substantially limit one major life activity in order for the student to be eligible.

---

[114] The table was edited slightly from the original: the form was changed to be consistent with the rest of this publication; the term "disability" and its variations were substituted for the term "handicapped" and its variations.

Component	IDEA	Section 504
Responsibility to Provide a Free & Appropriate Public Education (FAPE)	See comment under section 504.	Both laws require the provision of a Free Appropriate Public Education (FAPE) to eligible students covered under them including individually designed instruction. The Individualized Education Program (IEP) of the IDEA will suffice for a section 504 written plan.
	Requires a written IEP docu- ment with specific content and a required number of specific participants at the IEP meeting.	Does not require a written IEP document, but does require a plan. It is recommended that the district document that a group of persons knowledgeable about the student convened and specified the agreed upon services.
	"Appropriate education" means a program designed to provide "educational benefit." Related services are provided if required for the student to benefit from specially designed instruction.	"Appropriate" means an education comparable to the education provided to students without disabilities, requiring that [individualized modifications] be made. Related services, independent of any special education services as defined under the IDEA, may be the reasonable accommodation.
Special Education v. Regular Education	A student is only eligible to receive IDEA services if the multi-disciplinary team determines that the student is disabled under one or more of the specific qualifying conditions and requires specially designed instruction to benefit from education.	A student is eligible so long as she or he meets the definition of person with a disability (see above). It is not required that the disability adversely affect educational performance, or that the student need special education in order to be protected.

Component	IDEA	Section 504
Funding	Provides additional funding for eligible students.	Does not provide additional funds. IDEA funds may not be used to serve children found eligible only under section 504.
Accessibility	Requires that modifications must be made if necessary to provide access to a FAPE.	Has regulations regarding building and program accessibility, requiring that reasonable accommodations be made.
Procedural Safeguards	See comment under section 504.	Both laws require notice to the parent or guardian with respect to identification, evaluation, and/or placement. IDEA procedures will suffice for section 504 implementation.
	Requires written notice.	Does not require written notice, but a district would be wise to do so.
	Delineates required components of written notice.	Written notice is not required, but indicated by good professional practice.
	Requires written notice prior to any change in placement.	Requires notice only before a "significant change" in placement.
Evaluations	A full comprehensive evaluation is required, assessing all areas related to the suspected disability. The child is evaluated by a multi-disciplinary team or group.	Evaluation draws on information from a variety of sources in the area of concern; [placement] decisions are made by a group knowledgeable about the student, evaluation data, and placement options.
	Requires informed consent before an initial evaluation is conducted.	Does not require consent, only notice . . . .

Component	IDEA	Section 504
Evaluations (continued)	Requires reevaluation to be conducted at least every three years.	Requires periodic reevaluations. The IDEA schedule for reevaluation will suffice.
	A reevaluation is not required before a significant change in placement. However, a review of current evaluation data, including progress monitoring, is strongly recommended.	Reevaluation is required before a significant change in placement.
	Provides for independent educational evaluation at district expense if the parent disagrees with the evaluation obtained by the school and [on appeal] the hearing officer concurs.	No provision for independent evaluations at district expense. The district should consider any such evaluations presented.
Placement Procedures	See comment under section 504.	When interpreting evaluation data and making placement decisions, both laws require districts to: (a) draw upon information from a variety of sources; (b) assure that all information is documented and considered; (c) ensure that the eligibility decision is made by a group of persons, including those who are knowledgeable about the child, the meaning of the evaluation data, and placement options; and (4) ensure that the student is educated with her or his nondisabled peers to the maximum extent appropriate (least restrictive environment).
	An IEP review meeting is required before any change in placement.	A meeting is not required for any change in placement.

Component	IDEA	Section 504
Grievance Procedure	Does not require a grievance procedure, or a compliance officer.	Requires districts with more than 15 employees to (a) designate an employee to be responsible for assuring district compliance with section 504 and (b) provide a grievance procedure for parents, students, and employees.
Due Process [Hearing]	See comment under section 504.	Both statutes require districts to provide impartial hearings for parents or guardians who disagree with the identification, evaluation, or placement of a student.
	Delineates specific requirement.	Requires that the parent have an opportunity to participate and be represented by counsel. Other details are left to the discretion of the local school district. Policy statements should clarify specific details.
Exhaustion	Requires the parent or guardian to pursue an administrative hearing before seeking redress in the courts.	An administrative hearing is not required prior to OCR involvement or to court action; compensatory damages are possible.
Enforcement	Enforced by the U.S. Office of Special Education Programs (OSEP). Compliance is monitored by the State Department of Education and OSEP.	Enforced by the U.S. Office for Civil Rights (OCR).
	The State Department of Education resolves complaints.	State Departments of Education have no monitoring, complaint resolution, or funding involvement.

Source: CASE, Student Access, A Resource Guide for Educators; Section 504 of the Rehabilitation Act of 1973, at 4-7. This table was reprinted in edited form with the permission of the Council of Administration of Special Educators, Inc.

Americans with Disabilities Act (ADA)

The Americans with Disabilities Act (ADA)[115] is not specifically aimed at education. Yet, the ADA is notable because it provides broad-based protection for a variety of persons with disabilities by imposing far-reaching obligations on employers, public services and accommodations, transportation, and telecommunications to make reasonable accommodations for otherwise qualified individuals.[116]

Title I of the law affects employment discrimination in businesses or institutions that employ fifteen or more employees for at least twenty weeks per year. Such employers may not discriminate in hiring, promotion, termination, compensation, training, application, or other terms or conditions of employment. Furthermore, they must make reasonable accommodations for individuals who can perform the essential functions of the job.

Title II regulates public services such as mass and public transportation vehicles and facilities. It also requires that new purchases and newly constructed buildings be accessible to the disabled.

Title III deals with privately operated public accommodations (e.g., private schools, athletic associations) and services including inns, restaurants, museums, and retail establishments. Such facilities must take readily achievable action to remove barriers to persons with disabilities.

And finally, title IV affects telecommunications relay services which must now provide lines allowing equal access by graphic non-voice communications devices such as TDDs used by the deaf.

The ADA's broad definition of a disability is comparable to the one in section 504, but the ADA may prove to have an even greater impact because its coverage is not limited to recipients of federal financial assistance. Accordingly, it reaches a part of the population heretofore unregulated by federal disability law—the private nonrecipient sector. The ADA greatly strengthens existing laws against

---

[115] 42 U.S.C. § 12101 *et seq.* (1994).

[116] For a more detailed discussion of the ADA's impact on education, *see* Albert S. Miles, Charles J. Russo, & William M. Gordon, *The Reasonable Accommodations Provisions of the Americans with Disabilities Act*, 69 EDUC. L. REP. 1 (1991); Ronald D. Wenkart, *The Americans with Disabilities Act and its Impact on Public Education,* 82 EDUC. L. REP. 291 (1993).

discrimination on the basis of disability while not limiting any federal or state law that provides greater or equal protection.

The ADA's impact on education may be most dramatic in the area of reasonable accommodations for employees and students, especially in the nonpublic, nonrecipient sector. While it may take some time for litigation or increased regulation to provide a more definitive answer, it appears that if a school is faithful in its implementation of section 504, it is not likely to have difficulties with the ADA.

Civil Rights Act of 1991

The Civil Rights Act of 1991[117] amended three primary laws: title VII of the Civil Rights Act of 1964 (a law prohibiting employment discrimination based on race, color, or national origin), section 1981 (a law requiring that all citizens have the same right as white citizens to enter into contracts), and the ADA. The Act allows plaintiffs alleging intentional discrimination (i.e., disparate treatment) to recover compensatory damages (e.g., future pecuniary losses, emotional pain, suffering, inconvenience, mental anguish, loss of enjoyment in life, and other nonpecuniary losses) and punitive damages. Punitive damages may be acquired, however, only if the defendant acted with malice or reckless indifference. Furthermore, the law established a series of caps for combined compensatory and punitive damages depending upon the size of the business or institution: 15-100 employees ($50,000); 101-200 employees ($100,000); 201-500 employees ($200,000); and 500+ employees ($300,000). Also advantageous from the plaintiff's perspective is the fact that jury trials can be requested where damages are sought.

Rights to compensatory and punitive damages and to a jury trial are not limited to instances where plaintiffs allege intentional discrimination, however; they also may be requested under the ADA where an employer failed to provide reasonable accommodation. This, of course, assumes the absence of good faith and undue hardship.

---

[117] Pub. L. No. 102-166; 105 Stat. 1071 (1991)

Conclusion

As this discussion indicates, section 504 and the IDEA (and to a lesser extent the ADA) offer broad-based protection for students with disabilities. However, these laws and their accompanying regulations have been interpreted by both educators and the courts in a variety of ways, thereby giving rise to the many lawsuits[118] that have taken place since the late 1970s. Furthermore, with the addition of the ADA, the revision of the IDEA, the expansionist interpretations of the courts (see Appendix 1) regarding section 504, the proactive stance recently taken by both OSERS and OCR, and a quickly changing Supreme Court (see Appendix 2), the future is anything but clear.

These rapid changes notwithstanding, this book ideally will help practitioners better understand the law and more confidently address related problems. Several of the more commonly addressed issues are reviewed in this publication, including the nature of FAPE, related services, disease as a disability, access to school records, discipline, minimum competency testing, sport participation, and child abuse.

---

[118] For a summary of the majority of these cases, as well as a copy of the Federal Regulations for the IDEA, *see* STEPHEN B. THOMAS & CAROL A. DENZINGER, SPECIAL EDUCATION LAW: CASE SUMMARIES AND FEDERAL REGULATIONS (1993).

Chapter 2

Free Appropriate
Public Education

Introduction

In providing a free appropriate public education (FAPE) in the least restrictive environment (LRE) for all eligible children with disabilities, educational agencies need to be aware of several related concerns. Among these are preliminary matters on residency and pre-identification procedures; notice, consent, and evaluation issues; aspects of preparing an individualized education program (IEP);

concerns over appropriate placement, whether in private schools, segregated settings, or the mainstream; and procedural safeguards and relief.

Preliminary Matters

Residency Requirements

Eligibility for special education provided by a particular educational agency or school district often hinges on whether the children are considered "residents," as defined under state statute and/or regulations. Determining residency, however, may not be as simple as might be imagined. As a rule, children are considered to be residents of the same district as their parents as long as they are physically present with the intent of remaining.[1] Additional questions may be raised about where children reside who are from separated families (i.e., with the mother, father, relative); who have no identifiable parents; and who are wards of the court, or are incarcerated.[2] Furthermore, there is no clear-cut solution concerning the residency of children who live with a noncustodial adult or in a "family home at board," homeless, or are emancipated minors. These questions are not answered in federal statute or regulation and, although the courts have ruled with relative consistency on some of these matters, there have been a number of unique and seemingly contradictory decisions, generally based on state law.

Children whose parents are divorced and who are living with the custodial parent are typically residents of the district within which the custodial parent resides.[3] Issues related to joint custody are more complex, and must be resolved under family, divorce, custody, and residency laws of the respective states. Where parents retain custody and control of children who have been placed in a residential facility in another district, the district where the parents reside generally is

---

[1] Martinez v. Bynum, 461 U.S. 321 (1983). The Department of Education adopted this position in Mills, 13 EHLR 213:139 (OSEP 1988). *But see In re* Gary B., 466 A.2d 929 (N.H. 1983) (where the law does not consider intent in determining residency with regard to special education). *See also* Connelly v. Gibbs, 445 N.E.2d 477 (Ill. 1983) (where the parents failed to establish residency when the father and son lived in a condominium within the school district in which the student attended school, but over the weekend the family lived in a house it owned in another district).

[2] Green v. Johnson, 513 F. Supp. 965 (D. Mass. 1981).

[3] Mathias v. Richland Sch. Dist., 592 A.2d 811 (Pa. Commw. Ct. 1991).

responsible for related costs;[4] however, if the parents cannot be located, state laws vary regarding financial responsibility for the child's education. The state, the district where the residential facility is located, or the district of last known residence of the parents may be responsible for related costs, depending upon state statutes and regulations. Additionally, children who are wards of the court and are living with foster parents,[5] are under the supervision of a legal guardian,[6] or minors living apart from their parents for reasons other than to obtain an education in a different district[7] are likely to be entitled to attend classes and receive services within the districts in which they are living. Children who do not meet residency requirements may, at a district's discretion, still be permitted to enroll.[8] Enrollment could be free of charge, or be on a tuition basis, dependent on state law and local district policy. Moreover, where an admissions officer unknowingly admitted a student who was not a resident, one court has ruled that the school may not recover tuition, assuming that the student's basis for application was in good faith and was not fraudulent.[9]

Pre-identification Procedures

States typically delegate at least a portion of their responsibility to develop policies and procedures to identify, locate, and evaluate children with disabilities to local educational agencies or school districts.[10] Consequently, practices vary not only between states, but between districts. Among the many different practices are those related to referral and identification.

---

[4] *See* William C. v. Board of Educ. of Chicago, 390 N.E.2d 479 (Ill. 1979); School Dist. No. 153 v. School Dist. No. 154 1/2, 370 N.E.2d 22 (Ill. App. Ct. 1977). *But see In re* Children Residing at St. Aloysius Home, 556 A.2d 552 (R.I. 1989) (where children in need of special services were deemed residents of the town in which the facility was located; however, the town was able to seek reimbursement from surrounding locations).

[5] Rabinowitz v. New Jersey State Bd. of Educ., 550 F. Supp. 481 (D.N.J. 1982).

[6] Sonya C. v. Arizona Sch. for the Deaf and Blind, 743 F. Supp. 700 (D. Ariz. 1990).

[7] Major v. Nederland Indep. Sch. Dist., 772 F. Supp. 944 (E.D. Tex. 1991).

[8] *In re* Curry, 318 N.W.2d 567 (Mich. Ct. App. 1982).

[9] Teel v. Hamilton-Wenham Regional Sch. Dist., 433 N.E.2d 907 (Mass. Ct. App. 1982).

[10] 34 C.F.R. § 300.128(a)(1).

Districts in all states are required to do more than simply wait for parents to refer their own children.[11] It can be convincingly argued that if parents were solely responsible for preliminary referrals leading to identification, it is unlikely that all (or even most) eligible children would be served. Before parents are likely to make a referral, they would need to be able to recognize that their child is not functioning at age or grade level; understand that special education could help ameliorate the problem; be knowledgeable of the procedures to acquire the necessary services; and properly comply with those procedures. Since most parents lack sufficient training, experience, or knowledge regarding disabilities, child development, and educational practice, many children would not be identified or provided with services if their parents were singularly responsible for referrals. As a result, parental referrals represent only one of many methods used by districts in their efforts to identify all eligible children residing within their respective service areas. Additional methods of identifying children may vary by location, but typically include census taking, community surveys, public awareness activities (information dissemination regarding procedural rights and special education programs), screening of kindergarten children, and referrals by teachers and medical doctors.

Referrals generally are made to the chairperson of the committee responsible for the evaluation of children with disabilities or to the administrator of the school the child attends or is likely to attend. These "child-find" provisions of IDEA require states to identify, locate, and evaluate all children with disabilities from birth to age twenty-one.[12] Once "found" and evaluated, appropriate programs can be developed for pupils with disabilities.

Evaluation Procedures

When a child has been referred with a recommendation that assessment is needed to determine whether a disability is present, it is the responsibility of the educational agency to provide an appropriate evaluation. "Evaluation," as that term is defined within the

---

[11] 20 U.S.C. § 1412.
[12] 34 C.F.R. § 300.128 (note 1), 300.300 (note 3).

IDEA, means procedures (not just tests) used to determine (1) whether a child has a disability, and (2) the nature and extent of the special education and related services that the child needs.[13] "Procedures" used to evaluate include only those that are used selectively with an individual child and do not include those administered to all children in a school, grade, or class (e.g., a standardized ability test or a competency test).[14] Prior to the administration of a test that is used selectively with an individual child, the parents must be notified, and informed consent must be acquired.

Notice

As a rule, notice is provided for all tests administered to the entire population of in-coming and current students. Both notice and consent are required where the types of assessment are for particular children, using specific (rather than general) tests. Notice for "general" testing can be in local newspapers, fliers, letters taken home by students, or other methods designed to communicate to parents. Notice for "specific" testing must be in writing with an explanation of the proposed action.[15] The notice must also inform the parents of each evaluation procedure, test, record, or report the district has or will rely on and a description of other factors that influenced its decision to proceed.[16]

As a rule, parental notice must be written in a language understandable to the general population. When necessary, it must be provided in the native language of the parent, or in other modes of communication as needed, unless it is not feasible to do so.[17] Although compliance with notice requirements clearly is important, where parents have received actual if not procedurally correct notice, federal courts have sustained placement decisions based on IEPs that were found to be appropriate.[18]

---

[13] 34 C.F.R. § 300.500(b).

[14] *Id.*

[15] *See* Hall v. Vance County Bd. of Educ., 774 F.2d 629 (4th Cir. 1985) (where failure to notify parents of their rights resulted in a district's failure to provide a FAPE).

[16] 34 C.F.R. § 300.505.

[17] 34 C.F.R. § 300.505(b)(c).

[18] *See* Thomas v. Cincinnati Bd. of Educ., 918 F.2d 618 (6th Cir. 1990) (where a board's failure to provide written notice was not a prejudicial error because the child's mother had actual notice and participated in the IEP conference). Scituate Sch. Comm. v. Robert B., 620 F. Supp. 1224 (D.R.I. 1985), *aff'd without opinion,* 795 F.2d 77 (1st Cir. 1986) (where inadequate notice to parents was not a fatal

Consent

Along with appropriate notice, an educational agency cannot conduct an individual assessment until it has received consent indicating that the parent "understands and agrees in writing to the carrying out of the activity for which . . . consent is sought [and that] the granting of consent is voluntary on the part of the parent and may be revoked at any time."[19]

If parents refuse to consent or withdraw their approval, and if school officials choose to challenge the parents' refusal to permit the testing of their child, they first must consult state law. If state law requires consent, state procedures will govern any attempt to override the refusal.[20] In the event that there are no specific practices mandated by the state, or state law does not require consent, IDEA appeals procedures may be followed by filing a request for an impartial hearing. If the state is a "one-tier" state, such as Arkansas, the hearing will be held at the state level, with an appeal available in state or federal court; if the state is a "two-tier" state, such as Kentucky,[21] the initial hearing will be held at the school district level, with an appeal available at the state level. If the hearing officer determines that the child should be evaluated, the parents may then allow the evaluation, appeal the hearing officer's decision to the appropriate appeal body,[22] or withdraw their child from public schools. However, consistent with state compulsory attendance laws, parents who withdraw their children from public schools generally must enroll them in private schools or acquire approval for home-instruction programs.

If a school does not challenge a parent's refusal to permit evaluation and places the child in a regular classroom without an IEP or

---

defect because the mother had attended a previous IEP meeting and was aware of its purpose). Where defects were major, the courts have invalidated placements—*see* Board of Educ. of County of Cabell v. Dienelt, 843 F.2d 813 (4th Cir. 1988) (where a board's failure to involve a child's parents in the IEP process resulted in its failure to provide a FAPE); Spielberg v. Henrico County Pub. Sch., 853 F.2d 256 (4th Cir. 1988), *cert. denied*, 489 U.S. 1016 (1989) (where failure to comply with procedural requirements of the law invalidated a change in a student's placement).

19 34 C.F.R. § 300.500(a)(2)(3).
20 34 C.F.R. § 300.504(b)(2).
21 707 KY. ADMIN. REGS. 1:170 § 12.
22 34 C.F.R. § 300.510 and § 300.511.

supplemental aids and services, such a placement could prove disadvantageous both for the inappropriately served child and the other pupils assigned to the class. Moreover, where a child has not been classified as having an IDEA disability, the IDEA's procedural safeguards generally[23] do not apply to a proposed change in the youngster's education (e.g., access to a tutor or to intervention assistance) or when the child is subject to discipline. However, there are exceptions to this position. For example, in a Ninth Circuit case, administrators expelled a student from school who had not at that time qualified as a person with a disability under the IDEA without following section 1415 procedures. The parents filed suit.[24] The court ruled that the student's rights had been violated because the school failed to properly classify him as disabled and since there was no effort to determine whether his behavior was disability-related or whether he was receiving an appropriate education at the time of his expulsion. To rule otherwise, the court held, would allow districts simply to fail to identify qualified students so that appropriate programs and due process would not have to be provided. (See Chapter 6 for a more thorough discussion of this topic.)

Assessment

Once consent is acquired, either voluntarily or following administrative hearings and/or civil action, personalized assessment of a child may begin. The initial assessment must be conducted "in all areas related to the suspected disability, including, if appropriate, health, vision, hearing, social and emotional status, general intelligence, academic performance, communicative status, and motor abilities."[25] These measures typically include data on the family, related social and economic circumstances, health and psychological assessments, educational background (including academic and social perfor-

---

[23] This area of the law may be changing, however, because more courts are holding that a child need not be identified as disabled to seek protection under § 1415 of the IDEA. *See* Hacienda La Puente Sch. Dist. of Los Angeles v. Honig, 976 F.2d 487 (9th Cir. 1992); M.P. *ex rel.* D.P. v. Governing Bd. of the Grossmont Union High Sch. Dist., 858 F. Supp. 1044 (S.D. Cal. 1994).

[24] Hacienda La Puente Unified Sch. Dist. of Los Angeles v. Honig, 976 F.2d 487 (9th Cir. 1992).

[25] 34 C.F.R. § 300.532(f).

mance), test scores, parent and teacher interviews, observations of the child within school and home environments, and the like.

All tests and other evaluation materials must be selected and administered in a fashion that is neither racially nor culturally discriminatory.[26] In addition, no one measure can be the single criterion for determining a child's educational program, while all tests must be administered in the child's native language (or other mode of communication) when feasible; validated for the specific purpose for which they are used; administered by trained personnel in such a way that they accurately reflect a child's aptitude or achievement level rather than the disability; and tailored to assess specific areas of educational need. Finally, the evaluation must be made by a multidisciplinary team.[27]

Independent Educational Evaluation

If parents disagree with the evaluation of their child, they have the right to obtain an independent educational evaluation at public expense.[28] This right is not without restriction, however, because if the educational agency requests a hearing which substantiates that its initial assessment was appropriate, the parents still retain the right to an independent evaluation, but must pay for it themselves.[29] When parents pay for an independent evaluation, the committee making decisions about FAPE must "consider" its findings,[30] but it is not required to follow or to base its IEP on the independent evaluation. After careful consideration of all information available to the team, it is possible that the initial evaluation by the district may still be viewed as appropriate. If the parents disagree with this decision, they have the right to request an impartial due process hearing.[31]

In addition to the original and independent evaluations, there may be atypical circumstances where additional information is needed

---

[26] 34 C.F.R. § 300.530(b).

[27] 34 C.F.R. § 300.532(a)(b)(c)(d).

[28] 34 C.F.R. § 300.503(e). Whenever an independent evaluation is at public expense, the criteria under which the evaluation is obtained, including the location of the evaluation and the qualifications of the examiner, must be the same as the criteria which the public agency uses when it initiates an evaluation.

[29] 34 C.F.R. § 300.503(b).

[30] 34 C.F.R. § 300.503(c).

[31] 20 U.S.C. § 1415(b).

during the hearing process. At such times, it is within the authority of the hearing officer to request that a third evaluation be performed. When this occurs, the cost of the evaluation will be the responsibility of the district and the findings must once again be "considered" by the IEP team.[32] Furthermore, the child must be reevaluated at least every three years, or more frequently if conditions warrant or if requested by the parent or teacher.[33]

Individualized Education Program Preparation

IEP Team

The development, review, and revision of IEPs is the responsibility of an interdisciplinary team.[34] The IEP team should include a representative of the educational unit (other than the child's teacher) who is qualified to provide (or at least to supervise) the instruction and services; the child's teacher; one or both of the child's parents;[35] the child, where appropriate; and other persons at the discretion of the educational agency or parent.[36] Moreover, at the initial meeting, the local education agency is required to have present a member of the evaluation team or someone else who is knowledgeable about the results and their interpretation.[37]

As with many other aspects of special education, before an IEP meeting can take place, parents must be notified and provided sufficient planning time to allow them to attend the meeting at a mutually agreed upon time and place.[38] In addition, the agency is required to take whatever steps (e.g., translators) are necessary to ensure that the parents can participate fully.[39] If the parents are unable to attend, the agency must use other methods (e.g., conference calls) to ensure their involvement. Where neither parent is available or willing to participate, the agency must maintain records of its attempts to arrange a meeting.

---

[32] 34 C.F.R. § 300.503(d).

[33] 34 C.F.R. § 300.534(b).

[34] 34 C.F.R. § 300.343(a).

[35] For a discussion of parental rights, *see* Carol A. Denzinger & Stephen B. Thomas, *Rights, Entitlements, and Responsibilities of Parents of Disabled Children*, in THE PRINCIPAL'S LEGAL HANDBOOK (William E. Camp, et al. eds.) 61, 61-74 (1993).

[36] 34 C.F.R. § 300.344(a).

[37] 34 C.F.R. § 300.344(b).

[38] 34 C.F.R. § 300.345(a).

[39] 34 C.F.R. § 300.345(e).

In situations where the parents are divorced, the noncustodial parent also has a right to attend IEP sessions and other meetings about the child's education, absent a court order to the contrary.[40] If there is significant disagreement between the parents as to the content of their child's IEP and consensus is not possible, it appears prudent for the educators on the team, along with the custodial parent, to design what is in their collective professional judgment an appropriate program. Ideally, the custodial parent will then approve the IEP and implementation can proceed. Had the educators acted independently of the custodial parent,[41] or had they developed an IEP agreed to only by the noncustodial parent, a request for an impartial hearing (and its related cost and inconvenience) no doubt would be forthcoming. Clearly, the custodial parent has the right to request such a hearing, while the rights of the noncustodial parent are less clear.[42]

When no parent can be identified, when no parent can be located after reasonable efforts, or when a child is a ward of the state, a surrogate parent must be appointed.[43] A surrogate has all of the rights and responsibilities of an actual parent regarding the identification, evaluation, educational placement, and provision of a FAPE to the child. Accordingly, the surrogate may view educational records, receive notice, grant consent, appeal decisions, and request due process hearings. The person serving as a surrogate may not have interests that conflict with those of the child, must have knowledge and skills to ensure adequate representation, and may not be an employee of the public agency involved in the care or education of the child.[44]

IEP Development

Within thirty days of a decision that a child is in need of special education and related services, a meeting must be held to formulate an IEP.[45] The IEP serves two primary purposes: it is a formal writ-

---

[40] Doe v. Anrig, 651 F. Supp. 424 (D. Mass. 1987).

[41] *See* Henderson v. Morristown Memorial Hosp., 487 A.2d 742 (N.J. Super. Ct. App. Div. 1985) (where the rights of the custodial parent were upheld).

[42] Accordingly, legal counsel should be consulted before preparing or administering related policy limiting the rights of noncustodial parents.

[43] 34 C.F.R. § 300.514(a)(b).

[44] 34 C.F.R. § 300.514(c)(d)(e).

[45] 34 C.F.R. § 300.343(c).

ten plan to direct the education of an individual child; and it is a management tool for assessing the child's progress. It must include a statement of the child's present level of educational performance; annual goals, including short-term instructional objectives; specific educational services to be provided; the extent to which the child will be able to participate in the mainstream; needed transitional services for students no later than age sixteen (and, as appropriate, as early as age fourteen), including a statement of interagency responsibilities or linkages; the projected date for initiation and projected duration of services; and appropriate objective criteria, evaluation procedures, and schedules for determining, at least annually, whether the identified objectives are being met.[46] When educators find it necessary to make minor modifications in an IEP that do not significantly alter a child's placement (e.g., hiring an aide to observe the student's behavior[47]), they may do so without notifying the parents. Any change that would substantially alter the IEP, however, requires that the parents be given notice.[48]

Placement

Once an IEP has been developed and agreed upon, its implementation and the child's placement in the LRE must follow as soon as possible.[49] The placement committee is not limited by the availability of existing programs; in fact, by law, the team is required to shape the placement to fit the child, not simply to place the child into an available public program. Moreover, a student with a disability may be placed in a private facility at public expense as long as the child's education is under public supervision and direction.[50] Since significant legal controversies have arisen over the interpretation of the IDEA concerning the meaning of both an appropriate education and the LRE, as well as over the rights of parents and students relating to private placements, a discussion of each of these ensues.

Appropriate Education. The IDEA unequivocally requires "a free appropriate public education . . . to assure that the rights of [all]

---

[46] 34 C.F.R. § 300.346.
[47] Clyde K. v. Puyallup Sch. Dist., No. 3, 35 F.2d 1396 (9th Cir. 1994).
[48] 34 C.F.R. § 300.504(a).
[49] 34 C.F.R. § 300.342(b)(2).
[50] 20 U.S.C. § 1401(a)(18)(A); 34 C.F.R. § 300.8(a); 34 C.F.R. § 300.302.

children with disabilities and their parents or guardians are protected."[51] Yet, neither the IDEA nor its accompanying regulations offer more than a few limited definitions to help the practitioner understand this mandate. Accordingly, it was perhaps inevitable that litigation would be necessary to clarify the law.

The first case reviewed by the Supreme Court regarding FAPE requirements was *Board of Education of the Hendrick Hudson Central School District v. Rowley.*[52] The plaintiff, Amy Rowley, was a deaf first-grade student who had excellent lip-reading skills. In an effort to communicate with her and her deaf parents, local school administrators took a course in sign-language interpretation, installed a teletype machine, and provided Amy with an FM hearing aid. Amy's IEP stipulated that she be assigned to a regular first-grade class along with tutorial instruction for one hour per day and receive assistance from a speech therapist for three hours per week. The Rowleys were willing to accept each of these provisions, but requested that Amy also have a sign-language interpreter assigned to her when she attended academic classes. The district previously had provided Amy with an interpreter for a two-week period while in kindergarten, but this practice was discontinued based on information provided by the former interpreter and by the placement committee. It was their collective opinion that Amy did not need such assistance, and, at times, actually was distracted by the interpreter's presence.

Following the administrative decision not to provide an interpreter, the Rowleys were granted an impartial hearing. The officer ruled in favor of the district, observing that Amy was achieving educationally, academically, and socially without such aid. On further appeal, the New York State Commissioner of Education affirmed the examiner's decision.

Having exhausted administrative remedies, the Rowleys filed suit in federal district court. The trial court observed that Amy was remarkably well-adjusted, that she interacted and communicated well with her peers, and that she maintained extraordinary rapport

---

[51] 20 U.S.C. § 1400 (c).

[52] Board of Educ. of the Hendrick Hudson Cent. Sch. Dist. v. Rowley, 483 F. Supp. 528 (S.D.N.Y. 1980), *aff'd*, 632 F.2d 945 (2d Cir. 1980), *rev'd*, 458 U.S. 176 (1982).

with her teachers. Yet, it found that while Amy's performance in school was above average, she would have learned even more had she not had a disability. This disparity between Amy's achievement and theoretical potential led the court to conclude that a free appropriate education had not been provided and that a sign-language interpreter was necessary. The Second Circuit affirmed and the Supreme Court granted certiorari.

In a six-to-three decision, the Supreme Court reversed the lower courts. It reasoned that "if personalized instruction is being provided with sufficient supportive services to permit the child to benefit from the instruction, . . . the child is receiving a 'free appropriate public education'. . . ."[53] Furthermore, in determining whether an education is "appropriate," the Court stated the position that due weight should be given to administrative proceedings, and that courts should not substitute their own notions of sound educational policy for those of school authorities.[54] To rule otherwise, the Court maintained, would frustrate the preparation of IEPs, particularly if a court were "to set state decisions at nought."[55]

In supporting its interpretation of a FAPE, the Court rejected a holding that equal educational opportunity required services sufficient to maximize a child's potential commensurate with the opportunities provided other children.[56] Moreover, it stated that Congress did not intend to achieve strict equality of services and opined that:

> [f]urnishing handicapped children with only such services as are available to nonhandicapped children would in all probability fall short of the statutory requirement of 'free appropriate public education;' to require, on the other hand, the furnishing of every special service necessary to maximize each handicapped child's potential is, we think, further than Congress intended to go. Thus to speak in terms of 'equal' services in one instance gives less than what is required by the Act and in another instance more. The theme of the Act

---

[53] Board of Educ. of the Hendrick Hudson Cent. Sch. Dist. v. Rowley, 458 U.S. 176, 189 (1982).

[54] *Id.* at 206

[55] *Id.*

[56] *Id.* at 186, referencing a position taken by the district court, 483 F. Supp. 528, 534 (S.D.N.Y. 1980).

is 'free appropriate public education,' a phrase which is too complex to be captured by the word 'equal' whether one is speaking of opportunities or services.[57]

In conclusion, the Court noted that because Amy was receiving personalized instruction and related services to meet her needs, and was earning passing grades in her regular classroom and advancing from grade to grade, she was the recipient of an appropriate education. Thus, the state complied with the IDEA, given that Amy's IEP was reasonably calculated to enable her to receive some educational benefit. The Act, according to the Court, does not require that the "best" program be selected or provided; it requires only that the selected program be appropriate.[58]

Despite being criticized by some commentators[59] for allegedly reducing the IDEA to a floor of educational opportunity rather than an open-ended ceiling under which students with disabilities can reach their maximum potential, it is improbable that the Court will revise its position. Also, since none of the Court's subsequent rulings on special education has altered this interpretation of an appropriate education,[60] it appears that the *Rowley* standard is unlikely to change.

Least Restrictive Environment. The concept of "least restrictive alternative" developed over the years and requires government to narrowly tailor its requirements to avoid stifling fundamental personal liberties when the desired end can be more narrowly achieved.[61] Today, this least restrictive approach to government reg-

---

[57] *Id.* at 198-199.

[58] *Id.* at 198.

[59] *See, e.g.,* Bonnie Tucker, *Board of Education of the Hendrick Hudson Central School District v. Rowley: Utter Chaos,* 12 J. LAW & EDUC. 235 (1983); John Myers & William R. Jensen, *The Meaning of "Appropriate" Educational Programming Under the Education for All Handicapped Children Act,* 1984 S. ILL. U. L.J. 401 (1984).

[60] In addition to its ruling in *Rowley,* the Supreme Court has addressed special education in Irving Indep. Sch. Dist. v. Tatro, 468 U.S. 883 (1984); Smith v. Robinson, 468 U.S. 992 (1984); Burlington Sch. Comm. v. Department of Educ., 471 U.S. 359 (1985); Honig v. Doe, 484 U.S. 305 (1988); Dellmuth v. Muth, 491 U.S. 223 (1989); Zobrest v. Catalina Foothills Sch. Dist., 113 S. Ct. 2462 (1993); Florence County Sch. Dist. Four v. Carter, 114 S. Ct. 361 (1993). *See also* Board of Educ. of Kiryas Joel Village Sch. Dist. v. Grumet, 114 S. Ct. 2481 (1994).

[61] Shelton v. Tucker, 346 U.S. 479 (1960). *See also* Pennsylvania Ass'n for Retarded Children v. Pennsylvania, 343 F. Supp. 279 (E.D. Pa. 1972); Mills v. Board of Educ. of D.C., 348 F. Supp. 866 (D.D.C. 1972).

ulation is no better exemplified than in the IDEA mandate for least restrictive environment.

The IDEA requires that a FAPE must be provided, to the maximum extent appropriate, in settings[62] with children who are not disabled. Moreover, it mandates separate programs only when the nature or severity of the disability is such that education in regular classes, with the use of supplemental aids and services, cannot be achieved satisfactorily.[63] Striking the balance between FAPE and the preference for education in regular education settings requires placement in the LRE. In other words, LRE represents the setting closest to the mainstream in which a FAPE can be delivered. Accordingly, a placement team must provide a least restrictive appropriate program selected among alternatives included within the following continuum: regular classes alone or in conjunction with itinerant teachers or resource rooms; special classes; special schools; home bound instruction; and instruction in hospitals and residential institutions.[64] Although the regular classroom theoretically represents the least restrictive placement, it is not appropriate for all students. Indeed, residential care may be the LRE for some children with disabilities.[65] Furthermore, IDEA regulations stipulate that children are to be placed as close to their homes as possible.[66]

As the courts have struggled with a means of determining whether a child has been provided a FAPE in the LRE, a trio of related judicial standards has emerged.[67] The earliest of the three tests origi-

---

[62] 34 C.F.R. § 300.550(b)(1).

[63] 34 C.F.R. § 300.550(b)(2). *See* Department of Educ., Haw. v. Katherine D., 727 F.2d 809 (9th Cir. 1983), *cert. denied*, 471 U.S. 1117 (1985) (where a home treatment program did not qualify as an LRE).

[64] 34 C.F.R. § 300.551.

[65] *See, e.g.*, Abrahamson v. Hershman, 701 F.2d 223 (1st Cir. 1983) (where the child's needs demanded that he receive "round-the-clock" training and reinforcement in order to make any educational progress).

[66] 34 C.F.R. § 300.552(a)(3).

[67] A fourth measure, not drawn from an LRE placement case, also raised similar issues. In Lachman v. Illinois State Bd. of Educ., 852 F.2d 290 (7th Cir. 1988), *cert. denied*, 488 U.S. 925 (1988) the court ruled that the school district's proposal that all or half of the child's day be spent in a self-contained classroom with other pupils who were hearing-impaired was appropriate. The Seventh Circuit held that where the dispute revolved around whether the child's education would be better facilitated by a cued speech technique, preferred by the parents, or total communication concept, as contained in the proposed IEP, the parents had no right to compel the school to provide a specific program or to employ a particular methodology in providing the child with a FAPE.

nated in a Sixth Circuit decision, *Roncker v. Walter*,[68] and has been adopted by the Eighth[69] and Fourth Circuits.[70] Under *Roncker*, a court is required to apply a three-part test determining whether it is feasible to move services to a mainstream setting from a more restrictive setting that is considered superior. The court must first compare the educational benefits that a child would receive in a segregated setting with those that could be expected in a regular education setting; second, it must consider the extent to which the child's being placed in a regular setting would be disruptive; and third, it must keep in mind the cost of the placement in a regular education setting.[71]

In explicitly declining an opportunity to adopt the *Roncker* test, the Fifth Circuit, in *Daniel R.R. v. State Board of Education*[72] relied heavily on language from the Supreme Court's ruling in *Rowley* to offer a two-part test that has been adapted and/or enhanced by both the Eleventh[73] and Third Circuits.[74] First, a court must determine whether a student with a disability can be educated satisfactorily in a regular classroom with the use of supplemental aids. Second, if it is not possible to educate the child in such a fashion, the court must decide whether the pupil has been mainstreamed to the maximum extent appropriate.

The first prong of *Daniel R.R.* requires three further determinations: (1) in light of the nature and severity of a child's disability, along with the curriculum and goals of a regular classroom, determine whether the child will receive an educational benefit, including both academic and nonacademic aspects, in a regular classroom;

---

[68] Roncker v. Walter, 700 F.2d 1058 (6th Cir. 1983), *cert. denied*, 464 U.S. 864 (1983).

[69] A.W. v. Northwest R-1 Sch. Dist., 813 F.2d 158 (8th Cir. 1987).

[70] Devries v. Fairfax County Sch. Bd., 882 F.2d 876 (4th Cir. 1989).

[71] Roncker v. Walter, 700 F.2d 1058, 1063 (6th Cir. 1983).

[72] Daniel R.R. v. State Bd. of Educ., 874 F.2d 1036, 1046 (5th Cir. 1989).

[73] Greer *ex rel.* Greer v. Rome City Sch. Dist., 950 F.2d 688, 696-697 (11th Cir. 1991). The court subsequently withdrew its ruling on jurisdictional grounds, 956 F.2d 1025 (11th Cir. 1992), but later reinstated it with a new effective date, 967 F.2d 470 (11th Cir. 1992). For a full discussion of this and other relevant cases, see Larry D. Bartlett, *Mainstreaming: On the Road to Clarification*, 76 EDUC. L. REP. 17 (1992); Allan G. Osborne, *The IDEA's Least Restrictive Environment Mandate: A New Era*, 88 EDUC. L. REP. 541 (1994).

[74] Oberti v. Board of Educ. of Borough of Clementon Sch. Dist., 995 F.2d 1204 (3d Cir. 1993).

(2) evaluate the child's total educational experience in a main-streamed environment, balancing the benefits of regular and special education; and (3) measure the effect, in terms of disruptiveness, that the child with a disability will have on other students in the class.[75] The Eleventh Circuit also asked whether the costs involved in educating a child in a regular setting outweighed the potential benefits.[76] The Third Circuit questioned whether the school had taken steps to accommodate the child in the mainstream, and, if so, whether it had attempted to mitigate initial behavior problems in that setting. If it had not provided such accommodations, the Third Circuit found it unnecessary to consider the second prong of the *Daniel R.R.* test.[77]

The second prong of the *Daniel R.R.* test (i.e., has the child been mainstreamed to the maximum extent appropriate) applies when a child cannot be educated satisfactorily in the mainstream. When a placement other than the mainstream is necessary to provide a FAPE, the child must still be integrated with peers who are not disabled to the maximum extent appropriate and possible. Note, however, that "least restrictive environment" and "mainstreaming" are different goals and that the effort to place children in less and less restrictive settings without regard to the appropriateness of their placements will ultimately result in the provision of inappropriate placements. The primary objective remains the provision of a FAPE in the LRE, not "full inclusion" or "mainstreaming" without regard to whether appropriate programs can, in fact, be effectively delivered in those settings.

The third and most recent standard was enunciated by the Ninth Circuit in *Sacramento City Unified School District, Board of Education v. Rachel H.* The court approved and adopted a hybrid test employed by the trial court that included factors in both *Daniel R.R.* and *Roncker,* but did not specifically adopt *Daniel R.R.* over

---

[75] Daniel R.R. v. State Bd. of Educ., 874 F.2d 1036, 1049 (5th Cir. 1989).

[76] *See* Greer *ex rel.* Greer v. Rome City Sch. Dist., 950 F.2d 688 (11th Cir. 1991).

[77] *See* Oberti v. Board of Educ. of Borough of Clementon Sch. Dist., 995 F.2d 1204, 1218-1224 (3d Cir. 1993).

Roncker.[78] This test requires that four factors be considered in developing an appropriate placement:

(1) the educational benefits available to the child in a regular classroom, supplemented with appropriate aids and services, as compared with the educational benefits of a special education classroom;[79]

(2) the nonacademic benefits of interaction with children who are not disabled;

(3) the effect of the child's presence on the teacher and other children in the classroom; and

(4) the cost of mainstreaming the child in a regular classroom.[80]

Based on these similar, yet distinct, tests, it is clear that the standards used to determine whether a child is receiving a FAPE in the LRE are still evolving. If there is to be a single standard, the Supreme Court will have to intervene and render an authoritative ruling.

Placement in Private Facilities. In providing a FAPE, the committee may consider both public and private facilities that are capable of providing the necessary special education and related services. If an appropriate public placement is available, most states require/prefer that it be selected; however, if no public facility is capable of providing a FAPE, or if one is not available, the committee may than choose among private programs.

---

[78] Sacramento City Unified Sch. Dist., Bd. of Educ. v. Rachel H., 14 F.3d 1398, 1404 (9th Cir. 1994), *cert. denied,* 114 S. Ct. 2679 (1994). For a full discussion of this case and related developments, *see* Ralph E. Julnes, *The New Holland and Other Tests for Resolving LRE Disputes,* 91 EDUC. L. REP. 789 (1994).

[79] Although the circuit court adopted the same general standards as proposed by the district court, its list was slightly different—*see* Sacramento City Unified Sch. Dist., Bd. of Educ. v. Rachel H., 14 F.3d 1398, 1400-1404 (9th Cir. 1994). The court did not explicitly require the comparison of educational benefits of the regular classroom with those of a special education classroom; this omission could have been deliberate, although it is more likely an editorial omission or error, given the general wording of the decision.

[80] Sacramento City Unified Sch. Dist., Bd. of Educ. v. Rachel H., 14 F.3d 1398, 1400-01 (9th Cir. 1994).

When a private program, whether in a residential setting[81] or in a day school,[82] is selected by the committee (or required through court order) as an appropriate placement, educational costs are paid by the public school system for as long as the child receives services or until the student turns twenty-two, graduates, or the IEP is altered following a change of placement hearing. Additionally, the local educational agency remains responsible for assuring that the student continues to receive a FAPE, for monitoring the child's program, and for ensuring that all procedural safeguards are met.

If, on the other hand, the placement committee has identified an appropriate public placement, the parents may, of course, enroll their child in a private program, but they will be responsible for related costs.[83] Such costs may be as low as a few thousand dollars or as great as $50,000 to $100,000 and more for residential placement. In contrast, had residential placement been required for special education purposes, and had the district not offered a FAPE, the district would bear the nonmedical costs for the program, including room and board.[84] However, in this instance assume that the placement was made unilaterally by the parents due to the significant health care needs of their child and that the facility was medical rather than educational in nature. In such a case, since the placement was for other than special education purposes (e.g., health, family problems, convenience, or preference), resulting costs (except for actual special education costs) are unlikely to be the responsibility of the district.[85]

The aforementioned notwithstanding, where the institution is both medical and educational, separating costs can be quite

---

[81] *See, e.g.,* Kerr Center Parents Ass'n v. Charles, 897 F.2d 1463 (9th Cir. 1990); Drew P. v. Clarke County Sch. Dist., 877 F.2d 927 (11th Cir. 1989), *cert. denied,* 494 U.S. 1046 (1990); Abrahamson v. Hershman, 701 F.2d 223 (1st Cir. 1983); Doe v. Anrig, 692 F.2d 800 (1st Cir. 1982).

[82] *See, e.g.,* Board of Educ. of Community Consol. Sch. Dist. No. 21, Cook County, Ill. v. Illinois State Bd. of Educ., 938 F.2d 712 (7th Cir. 1991), *cert. denied,* 112 S. Ct. 957 (1992); Block v. District of Columbia, 748 F. Supp. 891 (D.D.C. 1990).

[83] *See, e.g.,* Mountain View—Los Altos Union High Sch. Dist. v. Sharron B.H., 709 F.2d 28 (9th Cir. 1983) (where a child was withdrawn from a public placement and enrolled in a private program due to long administrative delays, the court reasoned that circumstances may dictate that the public educational unit is responsible for the costs); Walker v. Cronin, 438 N.E.2d 582 (Ill. App. Ct. 1982).

[84] Papacoda v. Connecticut, 528 F. Supp. 68 (D. Conn. 1981).

[85] Clovis Unified Sch. Dist. v. California Office of Admin. Hearings, 903 F.2d 635 (9th Cir. 1990).

complex.[86] In assessing financial responsibility, the district needs to consider the availability of appropriate public placements, the appropriateness of the parentally selected placement, the accreditation of the facility (i.e., medical or educational), the student's current medical condition, the nature of the actual services to be delivered, and the degree of oversight provided by medical and nursing staff.[87]

Where a child with a disability is enrolled in a "regular education" private school at parental expense, the parents may discover that the procedural safeguards and guarantee of appropriate education available to them in the public schools are not necessarily available. For example, if the private school is not a recipient of IDEA funds, it does not have to demonstrate compliance with the IDEA. Similarly, if the school receives no federal financial assistance, it does not have to demonstrate compliance with section 504. The limited protection that would be afforded such children would then be restricted to the ADA, as well as to state statutes and regulations governing the operations of private schools, and the contract signed by the parents when the child enrolled in the school. However, many children with disabilities would simply be denied admission to such schools (with the school claiming either that the child was not otherwise qualified or would require excessive accommodations). At that point, the parents could still refer the name of their child to the appropriate local education agency for a multifactored evaluation and an agreed-upon public school placement—often the mainstream.

Extended School Year

When examining case law regarding extended school years (ESYs), two types of cases can be identified that, taken together, present a reasonably clear picture of the rights of students relative to extended year placements. The earlier cases established the right of qualified students with disabilities to an ESY, while later cases set forth the criteria for determining whether a particular child was entitled to such a placement.

---

[86] Taylor v. Honig, 910 F.2d 627 (9th Cir. 1990).

[87] For a related article, *see* Dixie Snow Huefner, *Special Education Residential Placements for Students with Severe Emotional Disturbances: The Implications of Recent Ninth Circuit Cases,* 67 EDUC. L. REP. 397 (1991).

Battle v. Pennsylvania,[88] the earliest federal case[89] on point, set the standard with regard to the rights of students to receive ESY placements. In *Battle,* the plaintiff class constituted students who were severely and profoundly impaired (SPI) and those who were severely emotionally disturbed (SED). By the nature of their respective disabilities, many of these children often were unable to generalize skills they had learned in one setting to another, to accept changes in routine or environment, or to effectively deal with frustration. Moreover, significant numbers of SPI and SED students regress more dramatically than other children during summer months when instruction is not available.

Summer programs were not available in Pennsylvania, for any students, regardless of whether they had disabilities, based on an administrative policy promulgated by the State Department of Education. In fact, the needs of individual students never were considered, nor was the probability of individual regression studied. When the dispute reached the Third Circuit, the court ruled in favor of the students. It held that Pennsylvania's 180-day instructional limit violated the IDEA since, under FAPE requirements, a particular child could conceivably require instruction beyond the 180-day limit. Accordingly, in light of *Battle* and its progeny, there is little doubt that qualified students are entitled to an ESY placement.[90]

The second line of cases provides some guidance as to the circumstances under which ESY placements may be available. In *Alamo Heights Independent School District v. State Board of Education,*[91] the Fifth Circuit ruled that the determining factor is whether a student would suffer a severe or substantial regression without an ESY

---

[88] Battle v. Pennsylvania, 629 F.2d 269 (3d Cir. 1980), *cert. denied,* 452 U.S. 968 (1981).

[89] An earlier state case, Mahoney v. Administrative Sch. Dist. No. 1, 601 P.2d 826 (Or. App. Ct. 1979), required an ESY for a child who was mentally retarded.

[90] For cases that have followed *Battle, see, e.g.,* Yaris v. Special Sch. Dist. of St. Louis County, 728 F.2d 1055 (8th Cir. 1984); Georgia Ass'n of Retarded Citizens v. McDaniel, 716 F.2d 1565 (11th Cir. 1983), *vacated and remanded on other grounds,* 468 U.S. 1213 (1984), *modified,* 740 F.2d 902 (11th Cir. 1984), *cert. denied,* 469 U.S. 1228 (1985); Crawford v. Pittman, 708 F.2d 1028 (5th Cir. 1983); Phipps v. New Hanover County Bd. of Educ., 551 F. Supp. 732 (D.N.C. 1982); Birmingham & Lamphere Sch. Dist. v. Superintendent of Pub. Instruction for Mich., 328 N.W.2d 59 (Mich. Ct. App. 1982).

[91] Alamo Heights Indep. Sch. Dist. v. State Bd. of Educ., 790 F.2d 1153 (5th Cir. 1986).

placement (i.e., whether the benefits accrued would be significantly jeopardized by a lack of ESY).[92] Four years later, the Tenth Circuit, in *Johnson ex rel. Johnson v. Independent School District No. 4 of Bixby, Oklahoma,* augmented this standard.[93] The Tenth Circuit ruled that in determining whether a child was entitled to an ESY retrospective and predictive factors should be taken into account such as: the degree of a child's impairment, regression and recovery; the child's rate of progress; the child's behavioral and physical problems; the ability of the child to interact with peers who are not disabled; the parent's ability to provide education structure at home; and the availability of alternative resources.[94] Based on these cases, it appears that where a student's progress in special education would be hindered to the point of not incurring educational benefit without an extended year placement, such a placement should be made available.

Although the above may appear direct, in practice determining whether a child is eligible for an ESY is a complex process and often results in a parental appeal. Figure 2-1 provides a flow chart of a "typical" process. Observe that the IEP team, not the administration, is responsible for determining eligibility.

To assist practitioners in identifying eligible students and determining the nature, extent, and duration of services, Rapport and Thomas have identified a series of questions to be answered:

(1) Is the child's current educational program based on individual needs?

---

[92] For earlier cases that have applied a regression standard similar to *Alamo Heights, see* Cordrey v. Euckert, 917 F.2d 1460 (6th Cir. 1990), *cert. denied,* 499 U.S. 938 (1991); Holmes *ex rel.* Holmes v. Sobol, 690 F. Supp. 154 (W.D.N.Y. 1988); Bucks County Pub. Sch., Intermediate Unit No. 22 v. Commonwealth Dep't of Educ., 529 A.2d 1201 (Pa. Commw. Ct. 1987). For earlier cases where students who demonstrated regression were entitled to extended year placements, *see* Garrity v. Gallen, 522 F. Supp. 171 (D.N.H. 1981), *aff'd,* 697 F.2d 452 (1st Cir. 1983); Stacey G. *ex rel.* William G. v. Pasadena Indep. Sch. Dist., 547 F. Supp. 61 (S.D. Tex. 1982).

[93] Johnson *ex rel.* Johnson v. Independent Sch. Dist. No. 4 of Bixby, Okla., 921 F.2d 1022 (10th Cir. 1990), *cert. denied,* 500 U.S. 905 (1991).

[94] Extended year placements have been denied on the ground that students would benefit from special education without such a modification. *See, e.g.,* Rettig v. Kent City Sch. Dist., 539 F. Supp. 768 (N.D. Ohio 1981), *aff'd in part, vacated and remanded in part,* 720 F.2d 463 (6th Cir. 1983), *cert. denied,* 467 U.S. 1201 (1984); Bales v. Clarke, 523 F. Supp. 1366 (E.D. Va. 1981).

Figure 2-1
Extended School Year Flow Chart

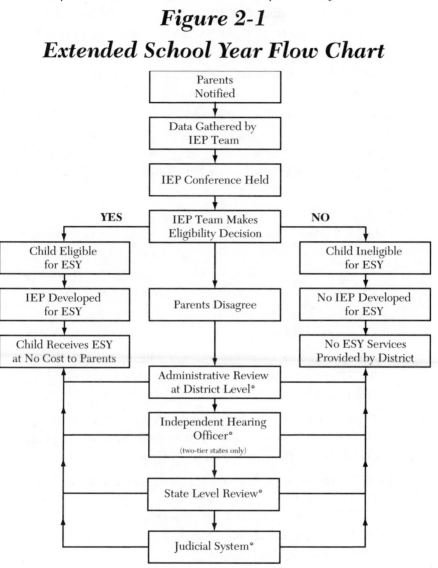

°Process continues until agreement is reached

Source: Mary Jane K. Rapport & Stephen B. Thomas, *Extended School Year: Legal Issues and Implications,* 18 JASH 16, 19 (1993).

(2) Have the nature and severity of the child's disability been considered among other factors in determining eligibility for an ESY?

(3) Is the child receiving "some educational benefit" from the current program?

(4) Has the child experienced regression, or is the child likely to experience regression, during an interruption in programming? If so, was or is the regression likely to be sufficiently significant as to support the inclusion of an ESY in the IEP?

(5) Was the regression sporadic or did it occur only during an extended interruption in programming? If regression was sporadic, is an ESY needed to ensure that the child receives "some education benefit"? (Sporadic regression, in and of itself, is not a sufficient qualifier for an ESY.)

(6) Is the child likely to recoup any losses within an acceptable period of time?

(7) Were goals of self-sufficiency and independence being met? If not, would providing an ESY enable the child to develop these attributes?

(8) Is the child failing, or is the child likely to fail, to meet short-term objectives? If so, would an extended program assist in meeting the goals and objectives?

(9) Was the decision to offer an ESY program during the current year influenced by the child's eligibility in prior years? If so, the decision to provide an ESY this year should be reexamined. Need, rather than prior eligibility, should be used as the criterion.[95]

Finally, it should be noted that an ESY is not synonymous with an extended IEP. An ESY may require the district to provide something as simple as parental assistance, or something as extensive as a full IEP. The IEP team is responsible for determining the combination of instruction and services that need to be provided to enable the child to incur educational benefit.

---

[95] Mary Jane K. Rapport & Stephen B. Thomas, *Extended School Year: Legal Issues and Implications*, 18 JASH 16, 25-26 (1993).

Procedural Safeguards & Relief

A student's substantive right to special education under the IDEA is accompanied by the safeguard of procedural due process.[96] Parents may request a due process hearing to resolve disputes related to identification, evaluation, placement, and the provision of FAPE. Similarly, the educational agency may seek a due process hearing for any of the same reasons, as well as if the parents refuse to provide consent to the initial evaluation or initial provision of special education.[97] In addition, if parents challenge the appropriateness of an evaluation, the agency may initiate a hearing to establish that its assessment was correct.[98]

Administrative Hearings

Prior to initiating a due process hearing, aggrieved parents have the right to voice their complaint before local school officials. If an agreement is not reached, some local educational agencies request the parents to join them in mediation. Although mediators have no authority to make binding decisions, they often are able to identify common ground and to propose a plan that both parties are willing to accept. Mediation is less expensive than an impartial hearing, generally takes less time, and should be less adversarial. Furthermore, when information and data are shared, the parties ideally will better understand each other's position and become more cooperative. Even when this does not occur, however, the required disclosure of all evidence helps ensure that both parties are fully informed and have an adequate opportunity to prepare related statements or rebuttals.

If mediation is rejected, unsuccessful, or unavailable, either party has the right to request an impartial due process hearing. During the pendency of any administrative or judicial review, the child must remain in the current educational placement, unless an alternative arrangement is agreed to by the parties or by court order.[99] In effect, the stay-put provision of the IDEA operates as an automatic preliminary injunction,[100] prohibiting the transfer of a student until appeals

---

[96] 20 U.S.C. § 1415(a); 34 C.F.R. § 300.500 *et seq.*
[97] 34 C.F.R. § 300.504(b)(2), (3).
[98] 34 C.F.R. § 300.503(b).
[99] 34 C.F.R. § 300.513(a); Honig v. Doe, 484 U.S. 305 (1988).
[100] Zvi D. v. Ambach, 694 F.2d 904, 906 (2d Cir. 1982).

are completed. Where possible, this requirement should be strictly adhered to. Note, however, that a student who is currently enrolled in a parentally selected private school may remain there during the appeal of the initial evaluation,[101] but the local educational agency is not responsible for the costs since public educators did not place the child in the facility. In addition, if the parents withdraw their child from a public setting during an appeal and place the child in a private program, the educational unit will not be responsible for the costs of the new, unapproved placement, unless the parents ultimately prevail.[102] (See a related discussion later in this Chapter.)

In order to ensure impartiality, the IDEA prohibits hearing officers from being either an employee of the agency involved or affected by the controversy.[103] At the hearing, the parties may be accompanied and advised by counsel and by persons with special knowledge or training with respect to the child's disability; may present evidence and confront, cross-examine, and compel the attendance of witnesses; may prohibit the introduction of any evidence that was not disclosed at least five days prior to the hearing; may receive a written or electronic verbatim record of the hearing; and may acquire written findings of facts and decisions.[104] However, the school district is not responsible under the IDEA or the Fourteenth Amendment to provide an attorney for the plaintiffs.[105]

A local educational agency has forty-five days from the receipt of a request for a hearing to render a decision.[106] Should either party be dissatisfied with the results of the hearing, it may appeal to the state education agency, assuming that the first hearing was provided by a local or intermediate educational unit and not by the state.[107] The state reviewing official then examines the record of the hearing officer and has the discretion to seek additional evidence. This review

---

[101] *See* Stacey G. *ex rel.* William G. v. Pasadena Indep. Sch. Dist., 695 F.2d 949 (5th Cir. 1983).

[102] *See* Rowe v. Henry County Sch. Bd., 718 F.2d 115 (4th Cir. 1983); Stemple v. Prince George's County Bd. of Educ., 623 F.2d 893 (4th Cir. 1980), *cert. denied,* 450 U.S. 911 (1981); Lillian S. v. Ambach, 461 N.Y.S.2d 501 (App. Div. 1983).

[103] 34 C.F.R. § 300.507(a).

[104] 34 C.F.R. § 508(a).

[105] Daniel B. v. Wisconsin Dep't of Pub. Instruction, 581 F. Supp. 585 (E.D. Wis. 1984).

[106] 34 C.F.R. § 300.512(a).

[107] 20 U.S.C. § 1415(c).

also determines whether adequate due process procedures were followed during the lower administrative hearing. Federal regulations dictate that the state must render its decision within thirty days following the request for review.[108]

Civil Action

Remedies available through due process hearings are designed to be quicker and less adversarial, maximize reliance on administrative processes designed specifically for special education, and minimize the drain on the limited resources of the courts.[109] All too often, however, one or both parties are dissatisfied with the administrative hearing officer's decision, and suit is filed. Assuming that administrative remedies have been exhausted, either party may commence a civil action in federal district court, or the appropriate state forum, without regard to the amount in controversy.[110] Note, however, that a significant number of appeals have been dismissed for failure to exhaust administrative remedies.[111]

There are two important exceptions to the exhaustion rule. As noted in *Honig v. Doe*,[112] in exceptional circumstances where administrative review would be either futile or inadequate, a party may bypass the requirement to exhaust remedies.[113] However, the burden of proof to demonstrate the futility or inadequacy of administrative review rests with the party making the claim. Exhaustion may also be

---

[108] 34 C.F.R. § 300.512(b).

[109] *See, e.g.,* Gardner v. School Bd. of Caddo Parish, 958 F.2d 108 (5th Cir. 1992); Frutinger v. Hamilton Cent. Sch. Dist., 928 F.2d 68 (2d Cir. 1991); Kerr Center Parents Ass'n v. Charles, 897 F.2d 1463 (9th Cir. 1990); Doe *ex rel.* Doe v. Smith, 879 F.2d 1340 (6th Cir. 1990); Cox v. Jenkins, 878 F.2d 414 (D.C. Cir. 1989); Christopher W. v. Portsmouth Sch. Comm., 877 F.2d 1089 (1st Cir. 1989).

[110] 112.20 U.S.C. § 1415(e); 34 C.F.R. § 300.511.

[111] *See, e.g.,* Garro v. Connecticut., 23 F.3d 734 (2d Cir. 1994); Jacky W. v. New York City Bd. of Educ., 848 F. Supp. 358 (E.D.N.Y. 1994); Norris *ex rel.* Norris v. Board of Educ. of Greenwood Community Sch. Corp., 797 F. Supp. (S.D. Ind. 1992); Moss *ex rel.* Mutakabbir v. Smith, 794 F. Supp. 11 (D.D.C. 1992).

[112] Honig v. Doe, 484 U.S. 312, 327 (1988). *See also* Smith v. Robinson, 468 U.S. 992, 1014 n.17 (1984); Marcus X *ex rel.* Jessica X v. Adams, 856 F. Supp. 395, 397 (E.D. Tenn. 1994); Bray *ex rel.* Bray v. Hobart City Sch. Corp., 818 F. Supp. 1226, 1233 (N.D. Ind. 1993); Heldman v. Sobol, 962 F.2d 148, 158 (2d Cir. 1992); Kerr Center Parents Ass'n v. Charles, 987 F.2d 1463, 1469 (9th Cir. 1990).

[113] *See also* Diamond v. McKenzie, 602 F. Supp. 632 (D.D.C. 1985) (where the school system had not communicated with the parents, failed to justify its decision, and had not complied with the directives of the hearing officer).

excused in emergency situations where it would cause severe or irreparable harm to a party.[114]

When judicial action is initiated, the court receives the records of the administrative hearings, hears arguments, and may view additional evidence at the request of either party. It is important to note that in reviewing the decision of an administrative hearing, a court, although providing de novo review, generally will defer to the administrative proceedings with respect to the facts, unless factual determinations are proven arbitrary or clearly erroneous. Predictably, however, the courts are split with regard to who bears the burden of proof in court when an IEP is challenged. Some courts have placed the burden on the local school district to establish the adequacy of a child's IEP,[115] while the majority expect the party (e.g., parent, district) attacking the results of administrative hearings to bear the burden of proof.[116] In rendering its decision, the court must base its decision on the preponderance of the evidence, and may grant such relief as it considers appropriate,[117] within statutory parameters.

Relief & Fees

Under the IDEA, courts have been authorized to provide such relief as they determine appropriate.[118] Most courts agree that money damage awards are not available under the IDEA for FAPE

---

[114] *See, e.g.,* Marcus X *ex rel.* Jessica X v. Adams, 856 F. Supp. 395, 397 (E.D. Tenn. 1994); Komninos v. Upper Saddle River Bd. of Educ., 13 F.3d 775, 778-779 (3d Cir. 1994); Christopher W. v. Portsmouth Sch. Comm., 877 F.2d 1089, 1097 (1st Cir. 1989) (where the court noted the existence of an exception but denied its application).

[115] *See* Lascari v. Board of Educ. of Ramapo Indian Hills Regional High Sch. Dist., 560 A.2d 1180, 1188 (N.J. 1989) ("[w]e believe the obligation of parents at the due process hearing should be merely to place in issue the appropriateness of the IEP. The school board should then bear the burden of proving that the IEP was appropriate"). *See also* Grymes v. Madden, 672 F.2d 321 (3d Cir. 1982); S-1 *ex rel.* P-1 v. Turlington, 635 F.2d 342 (5th Cir. 1981), *cert. denied,* 454 U.S. 1030 (1981).

[116] *See* Johnson *ex rel.* Johnson v. Independent Sch. Dist. No. 4 of Bixby, Okla., 921 F.2d 1022, 1026 (10th Cir. 1990) (where it was held that the burden of proof rests with the party attacking the child's IEP). *See also* Doe v. Defendant I, 898 F.2d 1186 (6th Cir. 1990); Spielberg v. Henrico County Pub. Sch., 853 F.2d 256 (4th Cir. 1988), *cert. denied,* 489 U.S. 1016 (1989); Alamo Heights Indep. Sch. Dist. v. State Bd. of Educ., 790 F.2d 1153, 1158 (5th Cir. 1986).

[117] 20 U.S.C. § 1415(e)(2)

[118] 20 U.S.C. § 1415(e)(1).

related disputes.[119]   As a result, plaintiffs tend to seek injunctive relief[120] (e.g., to prohibit the district from expelling a child with a disability or to order ESY services), declaratory relief (e.g., to declare that a violation of the IDEA occurred when a student was not provided with an ESY), compensatory awards (e.g., where the plaintiff received one additional year of schooling beyond the age of twenty-one when he received two years of inappropriate services and had not received a high school diploma), reimbursement (e.g., where the parents were reimbursed for the costs of a private placement when their child was removed from a public inappropriate placement and enrolled in a private appropriate placement), and attorney fees. Of the above, compensatory education, reimbursement, and attorney fees require additional discussion.

Compensatory Education

Prior to about 1984, most courts were of the opinion that compensatory education beyond age twenty-one was not available under the IDEA.[121]   Then, in 1984, district and circuit court decisions virtually reversed their early perspectives of the IDEA, despite the fact that there had been no identifiable change in the law.[122] Subsequently, there was a policy letter in 1990 from OSEP supporting the awarding of compensatory education by hearing officers where a FAPE has been denied.[123]   The position that compensatory education is avail-

---

[119] Some courts, however, have been willing to grant monetary damages where there is bad faith, the child was placed in danger, or the child's general welfare was at stake. *But see* Bonadonna v. Cooperman, 619 F. Supp. 401 (D.N.J. 1985) (where damages could not be recovered because none of the aforementioned exceptional circumstances existed).

[120] An injunction is a prohibitive writ issued by a court of equity and requires the person to whom it is directed to do or to refrain from doing a particular thing. Injunctive relief is available under the IDEA, § 504, and the Fourteenth Amendment.

[121] *See, e.g.,* Powell v. Defore, 699 F.2d 1078 (11th Cir. 1983); Adams Cent. Sch. Dist. v. Deist, 334 N.W.2d 775 (Neb. 1983), *modified,* 338 N.W.2d 591 (Neb. 1983), *cert. denied,* 464 U.S. 893 (1983); and Carter v. Independent Sch. Dist. No. 6, Sequoyah County Okla., 550 F. Supp. 172 (W.D. Okla. 1982). *But see* Timms v. Metropolitan Sch. Dist. of Wabash County, Ind., 654 F.2d 726 (7th Cir. 1981), *on appeal from remand,* 718 F.2d 212 (7th Cir. 1983); Campbell v. Talladega County Bd. of Educ., 518 F. Supp. 47 (N.D. Ala. 1981).

[122] *See, e.g.,* Helms v. Independent Sch. Dist., 750 F.2d 820 (10th Cir. 1984), *cert. denied,* 471 U.S. 1018 (1985); Max M. v. Thompson, 592 F. Supp. 1450 (N.D. Ill. 1984); Stock v. Massachusetts Hosp. Sch., 467 N.E.2d 448 (Mass. 1984).

[123] *Inquiry of Margaret Kohn,* 17 EHLR 522 (OSEP 1990).

able under the IDEA has persisted to the present day.[124]   Accordingly, where a child is denied a FAPE, offered a diploma to prematurely terminate services,[125] excluded inappropriately,[126] or denied services altogether, he or she may be found eligible for compensatory education. A recent case is illustrative. In *Murphy v. Timberlane Regional School District*,[127] the First Circuit affirmed the lower court decision providing two years of compensatory education to a student who was then twenty-five. The school district had failed to provide him with special education for two years prior to his turning twenty-one. Rather than provide the services, the district appealed the lower court decision and used, among others, a laches defense (i.e., the failure to raise an issue at the proper time). The court did not accept this, for it found that the claim was neither unreasonable nor would it result in prejudice to the opposing party in since a sufficient number of relevant witnesses were available to allow the district to structure its defense.

Reimbursement

Although there have been literally dozens of cases dealing with reimbursement, two are Supreme Court cases: *Burlington School Committee v. Department of Education*[128] and *Florence County School District Four v. Carter.*[129]

---

[124] *See* Valerie J. v. Derry Coop. Sch. Dist., 771 F. Supp. 483 (D.N.H. 1991); Board of Educ., Strongsville City Sch. Dist. v. Theado, 566 N.E.2d 667 (Ohio 1991); Lester H. v. Gilhool, 916 F.2d 865 (3d Cir. 1990), *cert. denied sub nom.*, Chester Upland Sch. Dist. v. Lester H., 499 U.S. 923 (1991); Lester H. *ex rel.* Octavia P. v. Gilhool, 916 F.2d 865 (3d Cir. 1990); Burr v. Ambach, 863 F.2d 1071 (2d Cir. 1988), *vacated sub nom.* Sobol v. Burr, 492 U.S. 902, *on remand*, 888 F.2d 258 (2d Cir. 1989), *cert. denied*, 494 U.S. 1005 (1990); Puffer v. Raynolds, 761 F. Supp. 838 (D. Mass. 1990); Burr v. Ambach, 863 F.2d 1071 (2d Cir. 1988); Jefferson County Bd. of Educ. v. Breen, 853 F.2d 853 (11th Cir. 1988); White v. State, 240 Cal. Rptr. 732, 743 (Cal. Ct. App. 1987); Miener v. Missouri, 800 F.2d 749 (8th Cir. 1986) (where the court found compensatory education to be indistinguishable from reimbursement allowed in *Burlington*); Martin v. School Bd. of Prince George County, 348 S.E.2d 857, 865 (Va. Ct. App. 1986). *But see* Natrona County Sch. Dist. v. McKnight, 764 P.2d 1039 (Wyo. 1988); Monahan v. School Dist. No. 1 of Douglas County, 425 N.W.2d 624 (Neb. 1988).

[125] Mrs. C. v. Wheaton, 916 F.2d 69 (2d Cir. 1990).

[126] Big Beaver Falls Sch. Dist. v. Jackson *ex rel.* Nesmith, 615 A.2d 910 (Pa. Commw. Ct. 1992).

[127] Murphy v. Timberlane Regional Sch. Dist., 22 F.3d 1186 (1st Cir. 1994).

[128] Burlington Sch. Comm. v. Department of Educ., 471 U.S. 359 (1985).

[129] Florence County Sch. Dist. Four v. Carter, 114 S. Ct. 361 (1993). *Compare* Tucker v. Bay Shore Union Free Sch. Dist., 873 F.2d 563, 568 (2d Cir. 1989).

In *Burlington*, the child had been removed by his parents from an inappropriate placement and enrolled in a private program that was later found to be "proper." The Court had no difficulty ruling for the student and reasoned that Congress, in passing the IDEA, "intended to give handicapped children both an appropriate education and a free one . . . ."[130] The Court warned, however, that parents place themselves at financial risk when they unilaterally remove their children from publicly selected placements.[131] If the public program had been found appropriate, even if the private program were superior, the parents would have been responsible for the private school costs. The High Court also reasoned that retroactive reimbursement was not a form of damages; rather, it "merely requires the Town to belatedly pay expenses that it should have paid all along and would have borne in the first instance had it developed a proper IEP."[132]

In *Carter,* a student was removed by her parents from an inappropriate public placement and enrolled in an appropriate private school that specialized in educating children with disabilities. Given the above, it would appear that the case was sufficiently analogous to *Burlington* as to have it resolved at hearing, but not so. In the present case, reimbursement was denied by the district, because the private school was not state approved. A list of approved institutions was not made available to the public, where as the State of South Carolina chose to approve private school placements on a case-by-case basis. Accordingly, parents would "have no way to know" whether the school they selected met state standards and was therefore state approved.

The state's desire to determine private-school eligibility notwithstanding, the Supreme Court reasoned that since an appropriate program had not been offered by the district, and because one had been provided by the private school despite its lack of state approval, reimbursement would be required. Furthermore, insofar as FAPE standards were intended to apply to public supervised placements, not parental unilateral placements, barring reimbursement when an appropriate, but unapproved, program was provided would defeat

---

[130] Burlington Sch. Comm. v. Department of Educ., 471 U.S. 359, 372 (1985).
[131] *See* Hall v. Shawnee Mission Sch. Dist. (USD No. 512), 856 F. Supp. 1521 (D. Kan. 1994) (where the court denied reimbursement because the public placement was determined to have been appropriate).
[132] Burlington Sch. Comm. v. Department of Educ., 471 U.S. 359, 370-371 (1985).

the statutory purpose of the IDEA. Also, the Court maintained that full reimbursement must be provided, if the costs of the private education were found reasonable.

Attorney Fees

A plaintiff who prevails in an IDEA[133] case may recover attorney fees, but that has not always been the case.[134] In *Smith v. Robinson*,[135] the Supreme Court refused to grant attorney fees to prevailing parents. Subsequently, Congress essentially reversed *Smith* by enacting The Handicapped Children's Protection Act (HCPA) of 1986.[136] The HCPA not only allows parents who prevail the right to recover attorney fees, but it also permits them to seek redress "under the Constitution, title V of the Rehabilitation Act of 1973, or other federal statutes protecting the rights of children and youth with disabilities,"[137] subject to exhaustion of remedies.

Today, a court, in its discretion, may grant reasonable attorney fees under the IDEA to prevailing parents.[138] Fees may be based on time preparing for and representing the client during administrative hearings and for litigation. The hours submitted need to be reasonable for the work performed and the hourly rate must be within the range charged the local community. No bonus or multiplier may be used in calculating fee amounts.[139] Determining an appropriate fee settlement for administrative and judicial proceedings is not as simple as it may seem, for it is often difficult to determine who prevailed (primarily where multiple issues were contested and neither party "won"

---

[133] At one time, however, fees were collected under § 504 of the Rehabilitation Act, under 42 U.S.C. § 1988, or under the American Rule. *See, e.g.,* Laughlin v. School Dist. No. 1, 686 P.2d 385 (Or. Ct. App. 1984), *aff'd,* 689 P.2d 335 (Or. Ct. App. 1984), *review denied,* 695 P.2d 50 (Or. 1985) (where fees were allowed under § 504); Stuart *ex rel.* Stuart v. Nappi, 610 F. Supp. 90 (D. Conn. 1985) (where attorney fees were provided under § 1988); Diamond v. McKenzie, 602 F. Supp. 632 (D.D.C. 1985) (where attorney fees were provided under the American Rule).

[134] *See* Bonar *ex rel.* Bonar v. Ambach, 599 F. Supp. 945 (W.D.N.Y. 1984), *rev'd in part, vacated in part,* 771 F.2d 14 (2d Cir. 1985).

[135] Smith v. Robinson, 468 U.S. 992 (1984).

[136] P.L. 99-372, 101-796, codified at 20 U.S.C. § 1415(e)(4)(B). For a more detailed discussion of the rights of parties under the HCPA, *see* David L. Dagley, *Prevailing Under the HCPA,* 90 EDUC. L. REP. 547 (1994).

[137] 20 U.S.C. § 1415(f).

[138] 20 U.S.C. § 1415(e)((4)(B). See Marcus X *ex rel.* Jessica X v. Adams, 856 F. Supp. 395 (E.D. Tenn. 1994).

[139] 20 U.S.C. § 1415(e)(4)(C).

on all issues) or whether full fees are appropriate. Courts have addressed a variety of related issues. A few courts have reasoned that fees should be awarded when the plaintiff succeeds on some claims, even if they do not prevail on the major claim;[140] others have concluded that fees should be awarded if the plaintiffs prevailed on any major claim;[141] some provided percentage or reduced settlements where the plaintiffs failed to win all claims;[142] some awarded fees for work conducted prior to an official due process hearing;[143]most provided fees for expert witnesses;[144] a few even provided interest on the original fee amount;[145] others denied fees paid to nonlawyers who represented the prevailing plaintiffs in an action;[146] several denied fees to plaintiffs because their relief was no greater than the district's prior settlement offer;[147] others denied fees because the plaintiffs unreasonably protracted the process by commencing litigation;[148] several reduced the fees where time was spent pursuing unsuccessful claims;[149] some reduced the fees where the proposed rate or number

---

[140] *See, e.g.,* Krichinsky v. Knox County Sch., 963 F.2d 847 (6th Cir. 1992).

[141] *See, e.g.,* Wheeler v. Towanda Area Sch. Dist., 950 F.2d 128 (3d Cir. 1991) (where the plaintiffs failed to show that they prevailed on any of the major claims, however); Christopher P. v. Marcus, 915 F.2d 794 (2d Cir. 1990) (where the parent was found not to have prevailed).

[142] *See, e.g.,* Max M. v. Illinois State Bd. of Educ., 684 F. Supp. 514 (N.D. Ill. 1988), *aff'd sub nom.* Max M. v. New Trier High Sch. Dist., 859 F.2d 1297 (7th Cir. 1988) (where the HCPA was retroactively applied to allow a 50% award); Turton v. Crisp County Sch. Dist., 688 F. Supp. 1535 (M.D. Ga. 1988).

[143] *See, e.g.,* Barlow-Gresham Union High Sch. Dist. No. 2 v. Mitchell, 940 F.2d 1280 (9th Cir. 1991); Shelly C. *ex rel.* Shelbie C. v. Venus Indep. Sch. Dist., 878 F.2d 862 (5th Cir. 1989); Rossi v. Gosling, 696 F. Supp. 1079 (E.D. Va. 1988). But see Fischer *ex rel.* Fischer v. Rochester Community Sch., 780 F. Supp. 1142 (E.D. Mich. 1991); Child v. Spillane, 866 F.2d 691 (4th Cir. 1989).

[144] *See, e.g.,* Aranow v. District of Columbia, 791 F. Supp. 318 (D.D.C. 1992); Chang *ex rel.* Chang v. Board of Educ. of Glen Ridge Township, 685 F. Supp. 96 (D.N.J. 1988); Moore v. District of Columbia, 674 F. Supp. 901 (D.D.C. 1987).

[145] *See, e.g.,* Georgia Ass'n of Retarded Citizens v. McDaniel, 855 F.2d 794 (11th Cir. 1988).

[146] *See, e.g.,* Arons v. New Jersey State Bd. of Educ., 842 F.2d 58 (3d Cir. 1988), *cert. denied,* 488 U.S. 942 (1988).

[147] *See, e.g.,* Mr. L. *ex rel.* Matthew L. v. Woonsocket Educ. Dep't, 793 F. Supp. 41 (D.R.I. 1992); Hyden *ex rel.* Hyden v. Board of Educ. of Wilson County, 714 F. Supp. 290 (M.D. Tenn. 1989).

[148] *See, e.g.,* Johnson v. Bismarck Pub. Sch. Dist., 949 F.2d 1000 (8th Cir. 1991); Howey *ex rel.* Howey v. Tippecaneo Sch. Corp., 734 F. Supp. 1485 (N.D. Ind. 1990).

[149] *See, e.g.,* Puffer v. Raynolds, 761 F. Supp. 838 (D. Mass. 1988).

of hours was too high;[150] and others denied fees associated with IEP meetings, given that they were intended to be nonadversarial and informal.[151] In summary, the key to receiving fees is to prevail. Even the financial status of the parents is an irrelevant factor in determining entitlement.[152]

Conclusions

Rowley continues to be the single most important case interpreting the IDEA. Under this decision, districts are responsible for providing a FAPE that must be specially designed to meet the child's unique needs and to provide some educational benefit. Accordingly, districts are not required to provide "equal" or maximizing programs. Moreover, under the IDEA, they must select the LRE, and are not required to "mainstream" or to "fully include," but are responsible for determining placement on an individualized basis.

Given the events described above, the pendulum seems to have stopped somewhere between all or nothing; the IDEA does not require all things for all children with disabilities, but nor does it allow exclusion or inappropriate programming. The compromise that Congress made requires "appropriate" education, despite claims from some that the "best" should be provided as well as counterclaims that even appropriate is too expensive. Additionally, federal lawmakers and the courts require educators to involve parents in the decision-making process,[153] and to meet explicitly the identification, evaluation, IEP development, placement, and due process requirements of the IDEA.

---

[150] *See, e.g.,* Beard v. Teska, 31 F.3d 942 (10th Cir. 1994); Williams v. Boston Sch. Comm., 709 F. Supp. 27 (D. Mass. 1989); Neisz v. Portland Pub. Sch. Dist., 684 F. Supp. 1530 (D. Or. 1988).

[151] *See, e.g.,* Fenneman v. Town of Gorham, 802 F. Supp. 542 (D. Me. 1992).

[152] *See, e.g.,* Mitten *ex rel.* Mitten v. Muscogee County Sch. Dist., 877 F.2d 932 (11th Cir. 1989).

[153] Although parents have the right to participate during committee meetings, they are not "support personnel" as defined by the IDEA, and may not require the district to provide them with in-service training to help educate them regarding the handicaps of their children. *See* Rettig v. Kent City Sch. Dist., 720 F.2d 463, 465 (6th Cir. 1983).

Chapter 3
Related Services

Introduction

Under the IDEA, a child with a disability who qualifies for special education may be entitled to related services. This means that a school district must provide:

> transportation and such developmental, corrective, and other supportive services as are required to assist a child with a disability to benefit from special education, and includes speech pathology and audiology, psychological services, physical and occupational therapy, recreation, including therapeutic recreation, early identification and assessment of disabilities in children, counseling services,

including rehabilitation counseling, and medical services for diagnostic and evaluation purposes. The term also includes school health services, social work services in schools, and parent counseling and training.[1]

Over the years, the number of identifiable related services available to children with disabilities has continued to increase,[2] whether by school district acquiescence or judicial mandate. In addition, both federal and state courts have reviewed related disputes, with three such cases, *Board of Education of the Hendrick Hudson Central School District v. Rowley,*[3] *Irving Independent School District v. Tatro,*[4] and *Zobrest v. Catalina Foothills School District,*[5] having reached the Supreme Court. Related services cases are grouped by topic and are presented below.

Transportation

If a student with a disability is to attend school and receive a FAPE, it first may be necessary to provide him or her with transportation. Under IDEA regulations, this means transportation to and from school, between schools, and in and around school buildings; moreover, specialized equipment, such as adapted buses, lifts, and ramps may be needed.[6]

---

[1] 34 C.F.R. § 300.16(a).

[2] For example, when the EHA was recodified as the IDEA in 1990, rehabilitation counseling was added to the law while social work services, which previously had been identified under the regulations, was included in the statute.

[3] Board of Educ. of the Hendrick Hudson Cent. Sch. Dist. v. Rowley, 458 U.S. 176 (1982).

[4] Irving Indep. Sch. Dist. v. Tatro, 468 U.S. 883 (1984).

[5] Zobrest v. Catalina Foothills Sch. Dist., 113 S. Ct. 2462 (1993).

[6] 34 C.F.R. § 300.16(b)(14).

As long as transportation is for a qualified student in need of special education,[7] whether in a public[8] or a private facility,[9] or, under certain conditions, in a school outside of the district,[10] the courts have upheld the requirement that it be provided, even if it requires special adaptations.[11] However, the courts have placed some limits on the availability of transportation. For example, transportation has been denied where the nature of the disability does not require that the child be transported,[12] where a student would not have benefited from the placement,[13] where parents unilaterally placed their chil-

---

[7] Transportation has been denied to students who were not qualified under the IDEA. *See* A.A. *ex rel.* A.A., Jr. v. Cooperman, 526 A.2d 1103 (N.J. Super. Ct. App. Div. 1987); Dubois v. Connecticut State Bd. of Educ., 727 F.2d 44 (2d Cir. 1984).

[8] *See, e.g.,* Allen v. School Comm. of Boston, 508 N.E.2d 605 (Mass. 1987) (where the district was found in civil contempt for failing to transport special-need students during a bus driver strike); Taylor v. Board of Educ. of Copake-Taconic Hills Cent. Sch. Dist., 649 F. Supp. 1253 (N.D.N.Y. 1986) (where the family care provider was reimbursed for transportation expenses and baby-sitting fees incurred in transporting an EHA eligible child after the district failed to do so); Hurry v. Jones, 734 F.2d 879 (1st Cir. 1984) (where the parents acquired reimbursement from the public school for transportation costs, time, and effort, but not for physical and emotional hardship, because it failed to provide such service for their child).

[9] *See* Felter v. Cape Girardeau Sch. Dist., 810 F. Supp. 1062 (E.D. Mo. 1993); School Dist. of Philadelphia v. Commonwealth Dep't of Educ., 547 A.2d 520 (Pa. Commw. Ct. 1988) (where transportation to a learning center offering unisensory training was required); Pires *ex rel.* Pires v. Commonwealth Dep't of Educ., 467 A.2d 79 (Pa. Commw. Ct. 1983) (where reimbursement for transportation costs to a private school was required).

[10] *See, e.g.,* Pinkerton v. Moye, 509 F. Supp. 107 (W.D. Va. 1981) (where the school district was required to provide transportation to the school outside of the district that the child would have attended had she not had a disability). For a related case, see Alamo Heights Indep. Sch. Dist. v. State Bd. of Educ., 790 F.2d 1153 (5th Cir. 1986) (where the school district was required to provide out-of-district transportation for a child so that his working mother could rely on custodial care until she could pick him up).

[11] Macomb County Intermediate Sch. Dist. v. Joshua S., 715 F. Supp. 824 (E.D. Mich. 1989) (where special transportation was required for a student with a tracheostomy tube).

[12] McNair v. Oak Hills Local Sch. Dist., 872 F.2d 153 (6th Cir. 1989) (where the court held that the child's hearing impairment did not qualify her for transportation).

[13] Thomas v. Cincinnati Bd. of Educ., 918 F.2d 618, 627 (6th Cir. 1990) (where the court rejected a mainstreaming option for a child whose disabilities were "simply too severe").

dren,[14] where parents refused to accept the school district's placement,[15] and where parents were seeking transportation for themselves when their children were in residential care.[16] In addition, another court limited the number of trips home a child in residential placement could make at public expense. Where the school district already was paying for three round trips per year for the student.[17] The parents were demanding additional visitations for their child and coverage of their own transportation costs as well. These costs included airfare for the parents and two siblings, and hotel, food, and car expenses for the entire family. The court noted that despite the ambitious goal incorporated within the child's IEP stating that he would improve his interpersonal relationships within the home, the school board was "not required to foot the bill for family gatherings."[18]

Transportation may be provided directly by the district (in buses, vans, or cars), or through contract. Contracts may be with companies that specialize in providing such services for populations with disabil-

---

[14] McNair v. Cardimone, 676 F. Supp. 1361 (S.D. Ohio 1987), *aff'd sub nom.* McNair v. Oak Hills Local Sch. Dist., 872 F.2d 153 (6th Cir. 1989) (where a hearing impaired student did not qualify for transportation services after her parents unilaterally placed her in a private school). *But see* Tribble v. Montgomery County Bd. of Educ., 798 F. Supp. 668 (M.D. Ala. 1992) (where a school district was required to provide transportation, speech, physical, and occupational therapy for a student who was unilaterally placed in a private school by his parents because the court found that even under such circumstances the district was not relieved of its duty to provide related services off school grounds).

[15] *See* School Bd. of Pinellas County, Fla. v. Smith, 537 So. 2d 168 (Fla. Dist. Ct. App. 1989) (where a district was not required to transport a student to a geographically distant facility given that a facility within its service region was providing the student with a FAPE); Barwacz v. Michigan Dep't of Educ., 681 F. Supp. 427 (W.D. Mich. 1988) (where reimbursement for transportation was denied to a mother who had unilaterally removed her daughter from an appropriate placement and enrolled her in a total communication program); Work v. McKenzie, 661 F. Supp. 225 (D.D.C. 1987) (where reimbursement for transportation was denied to parents who had unilaterally withdrawn their child from an appropriate placement).

[16] Bales v. Clarke, 523 F. Supp. 1366 (E.D. Va. 1981) (where parents were denied reimbursement for their travel expenses while their child was placed in the Home for Crippled Children in Pittsburgh, Pennsylvania).

[17] Cohen *ex rel.* Cohen v. School Bd. of Dade County, Fla., 450 So. 2d 1238 (Fla. Dist. Ct. App. 1984).

[18] *Id.* at 1240.

ities, regular taxi companies,[19] or even parents. Depending upon the child's location within the district, the distance from the school, the number of additional children to be transported who are located near the child or along the route, and any special adaptation that is needed, it may prove cost efficient for the district simply to pay the parents to transport their own child. However, parents do not have the right to reimbursement when another form of transportation has been incorporated into the IEP,[20] although they always retain the right to transport their own children without being compensated by the district. Accordingly, the IDEA requires transportation services to be provided for qualifying students, but allows school districts to exercise discretion as to the form of the transportation, assuming, of course, that it is "appropriate." Where appropriate transportation has not been provided, the courts have not been reluctant to require reimbursement for actual costs, interest,[21] and time and effort.

Medical, Health, & Psychological Services

Under IDEA regulations, "medical services" are those that are "provided by a licensed physician to determine a child's medically related disability that results in the child's need for special education and related services."[22] Such services are for diagnostic and evaluative purposes only. In contrast, "school health services" are those

---

[19] The use of taxi companies has been permitted under the IDEA, but problems regarding efficiency, timeliness, and even safety have at times existed. *See, e.g.,* Tinkham v. Groveport-Madison Local Sch. Dist., 602 N.E.2d 256 (Ohio Ct. App. 1991) (where a developmentally disabled child was sexually assaulted by a taxi driver); Jane Doe "A" v. Special Sch. Dist. of St. Louis County, 682 F. Supp. 451 (E.D. Mo. 1988), *aff'd,* 901 F.2d 642 (8th Cir. 1990) (where, for § 1983 purposes, a district was found not to have acted with deliberate indifference or to have had requisite knowledge of a bus driver's actions in sexually and physically abusing students with disabilities).

[20] DeLeon v. Susquehanna Community Sch. Dist., 747 F.2d 149 (3d Cir. 1984) (where parents were unsuccessful in claiming that their child's IEP had been inappropriately changed when the decision to stop funding individual carriers was made).

[21] Fallon v. Board of Educ. of Scotch Plains—Fanwood Sch. Dist., 447 A.2d 607 (N.J. Super. Ct. Law Div. 1982) (where interest of 8% per year was provided to the plaintiffs for costs associated with tuition and transportation).

[22] 34 C.F.R. 300.16(b)(4).

provided by a qualified school nurse or other qualified person.[23] If these services are needed to assist a child to benefit from special education, they would qualify as "related services" under the IDEA and would be required to be provided. Although these definitions appear straightforward, there have been numerous complex, and often contradictory, court rulings. Some of the more relevant decisions are discussed below.

Psychological Services

The above definitions of medical and health services notwithstanding, the courts more often than not examine both the nature of the service as well as the qualifications of the provider in determining whether a particular service qualifies as a related service. These issues were discussed in a federal district court case involving psychotherapy, *Max M. v. Illinois State Board of Education*.[24] Here, although intensive psychotherapy was found to be essential to the development of an appropriate program for the student, the school district failed to incorporate it into his IEP. Subsequently, his parents privately obtained and paid for psychotherapy from a psychiatrist. When the parents requested reimbursement, the school district refused. The parents challenged the refusal and eventually filed suit. The federal district court ruled in favor of the parents.

In reaching its decision, the court relied heavily on an earlier federal trial court ruling from Connecticut which held that if psychological services are required to assist a student with an emotional disability to benefit from special education, then they qualify as related services and must be provided without cost to the parents.[25] The court in *Max M.* also found that the parents were entitled to reimbursement even though the services were provided by a psychiatrist rather than a psychologist. It reasoned that the nature of the service, rather than the credential of the provider, was the touchstone. Accordingly, the court held that since psychotherapy qualified as a related service, reimbursement could not otherwise be denied as a nonrelated med-

---

[23] 34 C.F.R. 300.16(b)(11).
[24] Max M. v. Illinois State Bd. of Educ., 629 F. Supp. 1504 (N.D. Ill. 1986). *See also* Doe v. Anrig, 651 F. Supp. 424 (D. Mass. 1987) (where reimbursement was granted for psychotherapy provided at a hospital).
[25] Papacoda v. Connecticut, 528 F. Supp. 68 (D. Conn. 1981).

ical service simply because it was provided by an individual with a medical degree.[26]

Along with *Max M.*, several other cases have, with mixed results, addressed the appropriateness of psychiatric services and psychotherapy as components of IEPs. For example, courts have held that psychotherapy provided by a nonphysician qualified as a health service even though it was supervised by a psychiatrist[27] and that psychotherapy provided to an emotionally disturbed child who was placed in a residential setting pursuant to his IEP was a related service even though the state board of education had promulgated regulations which considered psychiatric therapy to be outside the definition of related services.[28] On the other hand, courts have ruled that a public school was not required to fund the placement of a child with a disability in a private psychiatric hospital as a related service[29] and that where the psychotherapy provided in a hospital setting was primarily for medical and psychological reasons, it did not qualify as a related service for which the district was responsible.[30]

---

[26] Also, the court ruled that the amount of reimbursement could have been limited to an amount a qualified nonmedical district employee would have charged had the district provided such a service. However, since the district failed to provide data upon which the court could determine the appropriate amount of relief, the parents were found to be entitled to full reimbursement.

[27] *See* D.G. v. Board of Educ., 576 F. Supp. 420 (D.N.J. 1983) (where psychotherapy was provided by a staff member with "no more credentials than a Master's in Social Work"); T.G. v. Board of Educ. of Piscataway, 576 F. Supp. 420 (D.N.J. 1983), *aff'd*, 738 F.2d 425 (3d Cir. 1984), *cert. denied*, 469 U.S. 1086 (1984) (where psychotherapy services were included in the child's IEP and were provided in a facility for the emotionally disturbed).

[28] *In re* A Family, 602 P. 2d 157 (Mont. 1979).

[29] McKenzie v. Jefferson, 566 F. Supp. 404 (D.D.C. 1983) (where the placement at the private psychiatric hospital was found to be for medical rather than educational reasons). *See also* Darlene L. v. Illinois State Bd. of Educ., 568 F. Supp. 1340 (N.D Ill. 1983) (where the court held that the EHA did not require participating districts or states to provide medical services); Metropolitan Gov't of Nashville and Davidson County v. Tennessee Dep't of Educ., 771 S.W.2d 427 (Tenn. Ct. App. 1989) (where reimbursement for medical costs incurred at a psychiatric hospital was denied).

[30] Clovis Unified Sch. Dist. v. California Office of Admin. Hearings, 903 F.2d 635 (9th Cir. 1990).

Catheterization

Perhaps the most important health services case is the Supreme Court's decision in *Irving Independent School District v. Tatro*.[31] Here the plaintiff, Amber Tatro, had spina bifida and suffered from orthopedic and speech impairments along with a neurogenic bladder. In order to attend school, she required clean intermittent catheterization (CIC) every three to four hours; CIC can be performed by either a school nurse or a lay person with less than one hour of training. The IEP designed for Amber included early childhood development classes, as well as special services such as physical and occupational therapy, but did not include CIC. The district maintained that CIC was a medical service and therefore inappropriate for inclusion within her IEP.

After the Tatros unsuccessfully pursued administrative remedies, they filed suit in federal court. At trial, the court ruled a CIC was not a related service under the IDEA because it did not serve a need arising from the effort to educate. Furthermore, the court found that the district had not violated section 504 of the Rehabilitation Act because schools are not required to provide governmental health care for people seeking to participate in federally funded programs.[32] On appeal, the Fifth Circuit reversed and remanded. It found CIC to be a related service because Amber would not have been able to attend classes or benefit from special education without having CIC performed.[33] The court also ruled that by failing to provide CIC, the district effectively excluded Amber from a program receiving federal financial assistance, thereby violating section 504 as well.

On remand, the trial court noted that CIC could be performed by nonphysicians and as a result did not qualify as a medical service excludable under the IDEA. Accordingly, the district was ordered to modify Amber's IEP to include CIC and to pay compensatory damages. On further review, the Fifth Circuit affirmed,[34] and the Supreme Court granted certiorari.[35]

---

[31] Irving Indep. Sch. Dist. v. Tatro, 468 U.S. 883 (1984).

[32] Tatro v. Texas, 481 F. Supp. 1224, 1229 (N.D. Tex. 1979).

[33] Tatro v. Texas, 625 F.2d 557 (5th Cir. 1980) *(Tatro I)*.

[34] Tatro v. Texas, 703 F.2d 823 (5th Cir. 1983) *(Tatro II)*.

[35] Irving Indep. Sch. Dist. v. Tatro, 464 U.S. 1007 (1983).

The Supreme Court largely followed an earlier Third Circuit opinion and other lower court rulings which held that since CIC enables students to attend school, it would qualify as a related service if it needed to be performed during the school day.[36] The Court reasoned that "[a] service that enables a handicapped child to remain at school during the day is an important means of providing the child with the meaningful access to education that Congress envisioned."[37] Moreover, CIC was held to be a supportive service designed to assist the child to benefit from special education; to qualify as a health service (rather than as a medical service); and to be appropriately included within an IEP for other than diagnostic and evaluative purposes.

Nursing Care

The reasoning established in *Max M.* (i.e., that the nature of the service, rather than just the credentials of the provider, should be considered in determining whether a service qualifies as a related service) was later applied in rulings involving nursing care. In the first case, *Detsel v. Board of Education,*[38] a student with a severe physical disability required extensive care, including the administration of medication through a tube to the child's jejunum by means of a procedure known as a "P, D, and C." This process calls for ingesting a saline solution into the lungs, striking the person over the lungs for four minutes, and suctioning the mucus. To be administered safely, the provider must have the ability to perform cardio-pulmonary resuscitation due to potential complications that might arise as a result of a tracheotomy and to deal with respiratory distress. In *Detsel*, the child's doctor described her condition as potentially life-threatening. A physician was not required to provide these services

---

[36] Tokarcik v. Forest Hills Sch. Dist., 665 F.2d 443 (3d Cir. 1981), *cert. denied*, 458 U.S. 1121 (1982); Hairston v. Drosick, 423 F. Supp. 180 (S.D. W. Va. 1976) (where a child's right to attend school could not depend on her mother's presence, even if conditions and circumstances permitted such attendance). *Contra* Dady v. School Bd. of Rochester, 282 N.W.2d 328 (Mich. Ct. App. 1979) (where CIC was found to be a medical service under state law). *See also* Sherer v. Waier, 457 F. Supp. 1039 (W.D. Mo. 1978) (where the plaintiff failed to exhaust administrative remedies).

[37] Irving Indep. Sch. Dist. v. Tatro, 468 U.S. 883, 891 (1984).

[38] Detsel v. Board of Educ. of Auburn, 637 F. Supp. 1022 (N.D.N.Y. 1986), *aff'd*, 820 F.2d 587 (2d Cir. 1987), *cert. denied*, 484 U.S. 989 (1987).

however; they could be provided by a licensed practical nurse or a registered nurse, but not a school nurse.

The court began its analysis with a review of both congressional intent in enacting the IDEA and the nature of the requested services. It then ruled that the therapeutic health services sought by the plaintiff more closely resembled the medical services[39] specifically excluded by the IDEA. The court reasoned that even though the requested services did not fulfill the "physician" requirements set forth in the Act, the exclusion of the disputed services was in keeping with the spirit of the law.

Similarly, in *Bevin H. v. Wright,*[40] where maintenance of a tracheostomy tube, being fed and medicated by means of a gastronomy tube, and chest physical therapy were found to be so varied, intensive, time-consuming, and costly, a federal trial court in Pennsylvania ruled that they were not required to be included as related services for a seven-year-old girl who suffered from severe physical and mental disabilities. The court reasoned that in so far as the required services must be provided with constant vigilance rather than intermittent care by a nurse, they go far beyond the meaning of related services and are inconsistent with the meaning of the law.

These cases do not support the position that nonextensive nursing services that qualify as related services cannot be incorporated into IEPs, or that school districts need no longer feel compelled to hire and deploy qualified nursing and health care staff.[41] Rather, they maintain that such services can be essential components to an appropriate placement and must be included in IEPs as necessary.[42]

---

[39] *See also* Ellison v. Board of Educ. of Three Village Cent. Sch. Dist., 597 N.Y.S.2d 483 (App. Div. 1993) (where the court held that the district was not responsible for providing a specially trained nurse to assist a respirator-dependent quadriplegic child while at school as this was found to be akin to medical services for a purpose other than diagnosis or evaluation); Field v. Haddonfield Bd. of Educ., 769 F. Supp. 1313 (D.N.J. 1991) (where the district was not required to pay for a medical service—i.e., the student's enrollment in a drug treatment facility).

[40] Bevin H. v. Wright, 666 F. Supp. 71 (W.D. Pa. 1987).

[41] For a related case, *see* Kelly v. Parents United for the D.C. Pub. Sch., 641 A.2d 159 (D.C. Ct. App. 1994) (where parents challenged the district's nonenforcement of a statute requiring attendance of school nurses for a specified number of hours per week as well as attendance at athletic events).

[42] *See* Macomb County Intermediate Sch. Dist. v. Joshua S., 715 F. Supp. 824 (E.D. Mich. 1989) (where health care services were required to be provided during transport).

In a related case, *Neely ex rel. Neely v. Rutherford County Schools*, a seven-year-old child with congenital central hypoventalization syndrome (a rare condition that results in trouble breathing) was denied nursing care services while in school.[43] Such services include suctioning of a breathing tube which had been placed in an opening in the child's throat (i.e., a stoma), ventilation via an AMBU bag (a device that artificially pumps air into the lungs), and additional resuscitation methods. If the child were to be serviced inappropriately or if the response time were slow, she could foreseeably suffer brain damage or death. Furthermore, although the father averred otherwise, the care giver would have to devote virtually all attention to the plaintiff; accordingly, distractions and supplemental duties would have to be kept to a minimum.

In the past, each parent alternately had visited the school to provide the services themselves, but were no longer able to do so. The district then hired a person with a nursing assistant's license to provide the care and also intended to train selected teachers to provide services. The plaintiffs objected to this decision and removed their daughter from school. In developing its position, the district court noted that in Tennessee, only a licensed practical nurse, a registered nurse, a respiratory care specialist, certain relatives, or the patient may perform the services required. Accordingly, the choice of a nurse's assistant or a teacher to provide the services was clearly in conflict with state law. The court further reasoned that the plaintiff needed the requested services to allow her to attend school in the mainstream and therefore to benefit from instruction, and that the district should be responsible for related costs—projected to be $13,680. Interestingly, the court found the care requested to be "clearly medical,"[44] but the costs of the care not to be so burdensome that the service would fall within the medical exclusion.

Do Not Resuscitate (DNR) Orders

More than ever before, children with significant health care needs are attending public schools. This is due in part to the fact that medical technologies and medicine now enable many children who, in

---

[43] Neely *ex rel.* Neely v. Rutherford County Sch., 851 F. Supp. 888 (M.D. Tenn. 1994).

[44] *Id.* at 894.

the past, would have died or been hospitalized to persist to school age and beyond, and in part to mainstreaming and full-inclusion efforts to educate most children in regular classes. Assuming the child is not in a persistent vegetative state or comatose, it is likely that the district will be responsible for providing some type of education or service. To qualify for services, the child simply needs to reside within the district (see Chapter 1 for a related discussion) and to qualify for protection under the IDEA. Further, the child does not have to demonstrate the ability to benefit from services to be eligible for them,[45] and may be educated in or near the mainstream, if that is found to be least restrictive. In practice, medically fragile children are likely to be placed along the continuum of alternative placements with some in the mainstream and others in hospital and residential facilities.

In recent years, some parents of medically fragile children have given DNR orders to school officials, and have proclaimed that their children have a "right to die" on school grounds. They expect school officials to comply with their wishes and threaten suit if this "right" is violated. However, there is no such federal right (constitutional or statutory) to date, not even a "living will" mandate, that would require educators to allow a child to die on school·grounds and do nothing to assist.[46] In fact, it can be convincingly argued that failure to provide emergency care to a child with a disability would be discriminatory under section 504 (if the institution is a recipient of federal financial assistance) and the Americans with Disabilities Act (ADA). Moreover, if death is allowed to occur unchallenged, it is conceivable that tort suits could be filed by noncustodial parents as well as the parents of the other children in the classroom who were exposed to the tragedy. Additionally, from a nonlegal perspective, many educators would be morally and ethically opposed to such a practice, not to mention the public relations problems with the community that could evolve. Accordingly, most districts that have been confronted with DNR orders do not follow them and should not mistakenly incorporate them in IEPs as related services.

---

[45] Timothy W. v. Rochester, N.H., Sch. Dist., 875 F.2d 954 (1st Cir. 1989).

[46] *But see* Cruzan v. Director, Mo. Dep't of Health, 497 U.S. 261 (1990) (where under the Constitution a competent person may refuse life sustaining care); *In re* Gardner, 534 A.2d 947 (Me. 1987); *In re* Conroy, 486 A.2d 1209 (N.J. 1985).

Given the above, districts appear caught between the proverbial rock and a hard place. How, then, can the district respond to the parent in such a way as to resolve the controversy, yet ideally avoid litigation. The following procedures may prove helpful.

(1) Prepare a related policy consistent with these recommendations and the opinions of local legal counsel. (See Table 3-1 for an example.)

(2) Upon receipt of a DNR order, provide the parents with a copy of the policy and inform them that such orders do not apply to nonmedical personnel (check state law to be sure of this position) and that local policy does not allow district employees to comply.

(3) When an emergency arises, respond as you typically would (e.g., by calling 911 or an area emergency service or by directly providing emergency care).

(4) Once on the scene, provide the paramedics or other emergency care providers (ECPs) with the DNR; it will then be their responsibility to carry out the order or to provide services. Nearly all ECPs, however, will attempt to resuscitate given that laws or best practice in most states require that legal proof of intent be obtained.[47] Because this could take time, even with computerized systems, resuscitation measures generally are initiated in the interim.

The above procedure allows school officials to initially assist the child and it effectively shifts the life-and-death decision to medical personnel.

---

[47] HARVEY D. GRANT, ROBERT H. MURRAY, JR., & J. DAVID BERGERON, EMERGENCY CARE, 6th ed. 20 (1994).

Table 3-1: Sample Policy
Do Not Resuscitate Orders

Appropriately trained staff members whose responsibilities include the provision of life-sustaining emergency care shall take all reasonable steps to provide such care to any student on school grounds in need of life-sustaining emergency care, and shall attempt to contact an ambulance in accordance with regular school policies to secure the speedy transportation of the student to hospital facilities.

It is the policy of [the local school unit] not to comply with directives from parents or others that life-sustaining emergency care should not be provided to any particular student in need of such care while under the control and supervision of the school.

[The local school unit] shall consider requests for alternative forms of life-sustaining emergency care, but those requests must be supported by written medical substantiation by the child's doctor. Determinations shall be made on such requests by a team of persons at the school who are knowledgeable about the child. This team may seek additional outside information when necessary for a decision. Any determination made on such a request must be based on the likelihood that the chosen form of life-sustaining emergency care shall maintain the child's life until an ambulance arrives or the student is otherwise transported to the care of medical personnel.

For purposes of this policy, "life-sustaining emergency care" means any procedure or intervention applied by appropriately trained school staff that may prevent a student from dying who, without such procedure or intervention, faces a risk of imminent death. Examples of life-sustaining emergency care may include: efforts to stop bleeding, unblocking airways, mouth-to-mouth resuscitation, and cardio-pulmonary resuscitation ("CPR").

Source: Eric R. Herlan, Is There a Right to Die on School Grounds? How to Respond to "Do Not Resuscitate" (DNR) Orders in School 17-18 (1994) (unpublished manuscript).

Maintenance of Tracheostomy Tube

Another related service that has been the subject of litigation involves the maintenance of tracheostomy tubes. Suits brought on behalf of students in need of tracheostomy tube care have met with mixed results, depending on the extensiveness of their needs. In 1992, in *Granite School District v. Shannon M. ex rel. Myrna M.,*[48] a federal district court in Utah denied services. Here, a student who required constant tracheostomy care to attend school was provided with an IEP calling for home instruction which was found to have conferred some educational benefit. The court concluded that the care the student required fell within the "medical services" exclusion of the IDEA and that she could not satisfactorily be included in classes with children who were not disabled; accordingly, the school district was not required to provide such a service in order to enable her to attend school.[49]

By contrast, in the Ninth Circuit, in *Department of Education, Hawaii v. Katherine D.,*[50] the student suffered from cystic fibrosis and tracheomalacia, which caused her windpipe to be floppy instead of rigid. Consequently, a tracheostomy tube was implanted which allowed her to breathe and to expel mucus secretions from her lungs. If she were to attend school, this service had to be provided during the school day. However, based on the recommendation of her treating physician, the district concluded that such medical services could not be provided within a school setting and therefore proposed a homebound program. The parents appealed, and an administrative hearing officer concluded that the homebound program was not the LRE for the plaintiff, given that she "was clearly capable of participating in regular classes with nonhandicapped children."[51] The hearing officer then ordered the district to pay for her existing private placement. The district appealed and offered a public school place-

---

[48] Granite Sch. Dist. v. Shannon M. *ex rel.* Myrna M., 787 F. Supp. 1020 (D. Utah 1992).

[49] *See also* Thomas v. Cincinnati Bd. of Educ., 918 F.2d 618 (6th Cir. 1990) (holding that a child who had to breathe through a tracheostomy was properly placed on homebound instruction).

[50] Department of Educ., Haw. v. Katherine D., 531 F. Supp. 517 (D. Haw. 1982), *aff'd in part, rev'd in part,* 727 F.2d 809 (9th Cir. 1984), *cert. denied,* 471 U.S. 1117 (1985).

[51] *Id.* at 815.

ment in a setting where staff were to be trained to provide her with the necessary services. Yet, staff members were so "reluctant" to provide the services that they filed a related grievance seeking clarification of their contractual responsibilities. Consequently, the attitude of the staff, coupled with the recommendation of the child's physician, led to her remaining in the private placement.

The Ninth Circuit largely affirmed the trial court ruling. It held that homebound instruction was not an appropriate education within the meaning of the law and concluded that placement in a public school with properly trained staff was necessary.[52] But, because the state failed to offer an appropriate public placement, it was required to pay for one in the private sector.[53]

Medication Administration

Over the years, the administration of medication at school has become increasingly common. This is due not only to the growing number of medically fragile students in need of medication during school hours, but also to the rights of children under the IDEA and section 504—that is, medication generally can be provided by a school nurse or other trained individual and therefore qualifies as a health service. Therefore, many school districts are involved either in the administration of medication or in the supervision of self-administration by students. Note, however, that although appropriately trained educators and nursing staff may legally administer medication, they may not medically diagnose ailments or prescribe treatment or drugs, even for such nonprescription items as aspirin, antacid, or vitamins.

---

[52] *See* Macomb County Intermediate Sch. Dist. v. Joshua S., 715 F. Supp. 824 (E.D. Mich. 1989) (where a school district was required to provide transportation to a student who had a CIC in place).

[53] *See also* Hymes v. Harnett County Bd. of Educ., 664 F.2d 410 (4th Cir. 1981) (where the Fourth Circuit did not address the substantive issue of the appropriate public school placement of a student who had a tracheostomy tube inserted in his neck to facilitate his breathing and which required periodic suctioning of mucus secretions. However, in examining whether the student's parents could be awarded attorney fees, it noted the result of a state administrative hearing in their behalf. The district did not appeal that part of the administrative decision which determined that the student was entitled to a placement in a regular classroom rather than the homebound program it offered, since such a setting was found to be consistent with the dictates of the EHA).

The increase in dispensing medication also brings with it an increase in the potential for liability. The best way to avoid both injury and litigation is to adopt a draconian policy which prohibits the administration of medication during the school day, unless it is essential to the child's satisfactory education, well-being, or attendance.[54] The Supreme Court made this position clear in *Tatro* when it stated that:

> only those services necessary to aid a handicapped child to benefit from special education must be provided, regardless how easily a school nurse or lay person could furnish them. For example, if a particular medication or treatment may appropriately be administered to a handicapped child other than during the school day, a school is not required to provide nursing services to administer it.[55]

Where circumstances dictate that medication must be provided during the school day, public policy considerations dictate an obligation to ensure that it is competently rendered.[56] Although having sound school policies in place may not free a district from all liability, to the extent that they are followed, they can help in a district's defense if a related case is filed. Thus, the following suggestions are made.

(1) Written authorizations from both the parent and the physician should be kept on file, even if the medication is to be self administered (authorization from the physician is needed in order to verify that the medication was in fact prescribed).

(2) A description of any probable reactions or side effects to the medication and an explanation of emergency care also should be filed. This type of information is now commonly available from pharmacies.

(3) Individuals responsible for the administration of medication must be properly trained regarding proper dispensation, the effects of the specific drugs in use, and appropriate techniques in the handling of needles and syringes.

---

[54] *See* DeFalco *ex rel.* DeFalco v. Deer Lake Sch. Dist., 663 F. Supp. 1108 (W.D. Pa. 1987) (where a school district did not violate 42 U.S.C. § 1983 for a single incident of failing to provide medication to a student with diabetes).

[55] Irving Indep. Sch. Dist. v. Tatro, 468 U.S. 883, 894 (1984).

[56] O'Brien v. Township High Sch. Dist. 214, 392 N.E.2d 615, 618 (Ill. App. Ct. 1979).

(4) When students self-administer their medication, they should do so in the presence of the school nurse or trained lay person. In order to protect their privacy, they should not do so in front of other students.

(5) Although federal law does not require districts to hire physicians, psychiatrists, or LPNs to supervise the procedures,[57] such individuals should be consulted when policies are being prepared; this should ensure that appropriate medical procedures are used and that correct up-to-date information is shared.

(6) Students who self-administer should not be permitted to carry the medication,[58] and for security purposes all medication should be stored by school officials in a locked compartment.

(7) All medication should be delivered to school officials with labels intact. Each label should include the student's name, date of expiration, and directions for use (such as dosage; when it should be consumed; what, if anything, should be eaten or drunk when consuming).

(8) Also on file should be the student's home or emergency phone number; the name, strength, and serial number of the medication; the names and phone numbers of the physician and pharmacist; and storage instructions (e.g., avoid sunlight, store between thirty-five and sixty degrees). These files should be kept strictly confidential, with access limited to school personnel with a legitimate "need to know." General access would result in a violation of a student's privacy rights and could be potentially stigmatizing.[59]

(9) A student's file should also include notations of the receipt, use, return, and disposal of drugs, syringes, and needles.

(10) A record should be maintained regarding observations of what are thought to be unforeseen medication-related changes in behavior.

(11) Finally, a comprehensive policy regarding medication administration should include a statement indemnifying those employees who are responsible for administration, while school districts should carry adequate commercial insurance or establish a self-insurance plan sufficiently large to cover possible suits.

---

[57] *See, e.g.,* 507 EHLR 121.

[58] *But cf.* Bertens v. Stewart, 453 So. 2d 92 (Fla. Dist. Ct. App. 1984) (where a school board's code of conduct rule that students not personally possess "medicine," when applied to a fifth grade student's possession and distribution of nonprescription vitamin pills, was so vague that it failed to meet due process requirements).

[59] *See* Roe v. Ingraham, 403 F. Supp. 931 (S.D.N.Y. 1975).

Climate Control

In an unusual case, *Espino v. Besteiro*, the school district placed a seven-year-old student who could not adequately regulate his body temperature in an air-conditioned plexiglass cubicle within a regular classroom that was not air-conditioned.[60] Due to the child's inability to dissipate or conserve heat it was essential that he be provided with a climate controlled environment if he was to attend school. To meet this need, the superintendent, rather than air-condition an entire school or classroom, chose to have the cubicle constructed and placed in the classroom without consulting either the placement committee or the child's parents. The superintendent was of the opinion that such an arrangement would meet the child's unique needs, and would not open up a "Pandora's box" by encouraging parents of other children to complain that their children were not being educated in air-conditioned classrooms. The district's director of special services also supported the use of the cubicle, but for a different reason. The director maintained that it would be easier to control the temperature in the cubicle than in the classroom.

The use of the cubicle not only made it difficult for the child to interact with his peers but, at times, made it impossible for him to understand instructions provided by his teacher. Initially, the cubicle lacked a sound system, and a one-way radio receiver proved less than satisfactory due to background noise, the loudness of the air-conditioner, interference from a radio station, and the child's "fiddling with the controls." Yet, despite these difficulties, the child performed well in school and appeared to get along with his classmates even though they had their limited opportunities to interact.

When the school district insisted on maintaining this arrangement, the child's parents succeeded in obtaining an injunction. The court stated that "[w]ith the possible exception of a child whose immunological system requires that he . . . be kept within a sterile atmosphere, education within a cubicle will hardly ever be appropriate."[61] Accordingly, it ordered the district to provide an air-conditioned environment within which the student could both interact with his peers and obtain educational benefits commensurate with his classmates.

---

[60] Espino v. Besteiro, 520 F. Supp. 905 (S.D. Tex. 1981).
[61] *Id.* at 914.

Assistive Technology Devices & Services

Under the IDEA, assistive technology devices include any commercial, modified, or customized item, piece of equipment, or product system used to increase, maintain, or improve the functional capabilities of children with disabilities.[62] Similarly, assistive technology services include those that assist a child in selecting, acquiring, or using assistive technology.[63] Such devices and services are required to be made available to all IDEA students if required as special education, related services, or supplementary aids and services within the child's IEP.[64] Today there is a significant number of devices and services available to children. (See Table 3-2 for a partial list.)

Table 3-2
Selective Assistive
Technology Devices & Services

Devices	Services
Any item, piece of equipment or product system, whether acquired commercially off the shelf, modified, or customized, that is used to increase, maintain, or improve functional capabilities of individuals with disabilities.	Any service that directly assists an individual with a disability in the selection, acquisition, or use of an assistive technology device.
Augmentative Communication: Communication Board WOLF TouchTalker DynaVox Say-It-All Looptapes	The evaluation of the needs of an individual with a disability, including a functional evaluation of the individual in the individual's customary environment.

---

[62] 34 C.F.R. § 300.5.
[63] 34 C.F.R. § 300.6.
[64] 34 C.F.R. § 300.308.

Devices (continued)	**Services** (continued)
<u>Computer Access/Instruction:</u> Alternative Keyboard Speech Synthesizer Switches Word Prediction Software Wrist Rests Software	Purchasing, leasing, or otherwise providing for the acquisition of assistive technology devices by individuals with disabilities.
<u>Visual Aids:</u> Magnifying Devices Closed Circuit Television Large Print Books Brailled Material	Selecting, designing, fitting, customizing, adapting, applying, maintaining, repairing, or replacing of assistive technology devices.
<u>Seating and Positioning:</u> Standing Frames Walkers Chair Inserts Cushions	Coordinating and using other therapies, interventions, or services with assistive technology devices, such as those associated with existing education and rehabilitation plans and programs.
<u>Assistive Listening:</u> Hearing Aids Personal FM Units Closed Caption TV	Training or technical assistance for an individual with disabilities, or, where appropriate, the family of an individual with disabilities.
<u>Physical Education, Recreation, Leisure, and Play:</u> Drawing Software Adapted Puzzles Beeping Balls Game Rules in Braille or on Audio Cassette	Training or technical assistance for professionals (including individuals providing education and rehabilitation services), employers, or other individuals who provide services to, employ, or are otherwise substantially involved in the major life functions of individuals with disabilities.
<u>Self Care/Environmental Control:</u> Adapted Utensils Electric Feeders Remote Control Switches Pointer Sticks to Access On/Off Switches	

Source: Preschool Technology Training Project, Assistive Technology for Preschoolers with Disabilities: Collected Resources (1995) at 6-8.

Sign-language Interpreter

The premier case involving the use of sign-language interpreters as related services was *Board of Education of the Hendrick Hudson Central School District v. Rowley*,[65] discussed in detail in Chapter 2. The bottom line for that case was that because Amy Rowley did not require an interpreter to incur some educational benefit and to be provided a FAPE, one was not necessary. That decision did not foreclose future opportunities for the use of interpreters, however. It is clear today that where an IEP requires the services of a sign-language interpreter to appropriately serve the child, one must be provided at no cost to the family.[66]

Speech, Language, Physical, & Occupational Therapy

Clearly, speech,[67] language, physical,[68] and occupational[69] therapies can qualify as related services when ever they are needed to

---

[65] Board of Educ. of the Hendrick Hudson Cent. Sch. Dist. v. Rowley, 458 U.S. 176 (1982).

[66] For a related case regarding the rights of deaf parents, *see* Rothschild v. Grottenthaler, 725 F. Supp. 776 (S.D.N.Y. 1989), *aff'd in part, vacated and remanded in part,* 907 F.2d 286 (2d Cir. 1990) (where the district was required to provide deaf parents with a sign-language interpreter at school initiated functions such as parent-teacher conferences. However, the parents were required to provide their own interpreter for graduation ceremonies and other extra-curricular activities). For related higher education cases, *see* Jones v. Illinois Dep't of Rehabilitation Servs., 504 F. Supp. 1244 (N.D. Ill. 1981), 689 F.2d 721 (7th Cir. 1982) (where the Department was held responsible under § 504 for providing an interpreter to a college student); Barnes v. Converse College, 436 F. Supp. 635 (D.S.C. 1977) (where an interpreter was required under § 504).

[67] "Speech pathology" includes identification of children with speech or language impairments; diagnosis and appraisal of specific speech or language impairments; referral for medical or other professional attention necessary for the habilitation of speech or language impairments; provision of speech and language services for the habilitation or prevention of communicative impairments; and counseling and guidance of parents, children, and teachers regarding speech and language impairments. 34 C.F.R. 300.16(b)(13).

[68] "Physical therapy" means services provided by a qualified physical therapist. 34 C.F.R. 300.16(b)(7).

[69] "Occupational therapy" includes improving, developing or restoring functions impaired or lost through illness, injury, or deprivation; improving ability to perform tasks for independent functioning when functions are impaired or lost; and preventing, through early intervention, initial or further impairment or loss of function. 34 C.R.F. 300.16(b)(5).

enable the child to obtain educational benefit.[70] Related cases have
dealt with (1) whether any of the aforementioned must be provided
within an IEP, (2) whether compensatory services were required
when such services had not been appropriately provided,[71] (3) the
amount, manner, type, or duration of services,[72] and (4) where the
services were to be provided (e.g., public or private; home or
school).[73]

Providing Services in Private Religious Schools

Federal regulations require education agencies to continue to
make special education and related services available to children who
have been placed by their parents in private schools, even those that
are religious. Generally, such services are made available in a public
school, neutral facility, or mobile trailer. Only a few services, however, can be constitutionally delivered in private religious
schools/facilities to eligible children. For example, diagnostic speech
and hearing services[74] and sign-language interpreters[75] may be provided to all children in their school of attendance. However, the provision of instructional equipment, materials, teachers, and guidance
counselors are prohibited.[76]

---

[70] For a related article, *see* Mary Jane K. Rapport, *Laws that Shape Therapy
Services in Educational Environments,* 15 PHYSICAL AND OCCUPATIONAL THERAPY
IN PEDIATRICS (1995).

[71] Pittsburgh Bd. of Educ. v. Commonwealth Dep't of Educ., 581 A.2d 681 (Pa.
Commw. Ct. 1990).

[72] Johnson v. Lancaster-Lebanon Intermediate Unit 13, Lancaster City Sch. Dist.,
757 F. Supp. 606 (E.D. Pa. 1991); Howell *ex rel.* Howell v. Waterford Pub. Sch.,
731 F. Supp. 1314 (E.D. Mich. 1990); School Dist. of Philadelphia v.
Commonwealth Dep't of Educ., 547 A.2d 520 (Pa. Commw. Ct. 1988).

[73] Dreher v. Amphitheater Unified Sch. Dist., 22 F.3d 228 (9th Cir. 1994); Tribble v.
Montgomery County Bd. of Educ., 798 F. Supp. 668 (M.D. Ala. 1992); *In re*
Children Residing at St. Aloysius Home, 556 A.2d 552 (R.I. 1989); Kattan *ex rel.*
Thomas v. District of Columbia, 691 F. Supp. 1539 (D.D.C. 1988).

[74] Wolman v. Walter, 433 U.S. 229 (1977).

[75] *See* Zobrest v. Catalina Foothills Sch. Dist., 113 S. Ct. 2462 (1993) (where the use
of a sign-language interpreter at a private religious school was determined not to
be unconstitutional). *But see* Goodall v. Stafford County Sch. Bd., 930 F.2d 363
(4th Cir. 1991) (where the request for a cued-speech interpreter at a private religious school was denied).

[76] *See* Meek v. Pittenger, 421 U.S. 349 (1975); School Dist. of Grand Rapids v. Ball,
473 U.S. 373 (1985).

The key case in this area is *Zobrest v. Catalina Foothills School District*,[77] where a deaf high school student was unilaterally placed for religious reasons in a private religious school by his parents. While in public schools, the child received a variety of services, including the use of a sign-language interpreter. Had he remained in public schools, he would have received an interpreter; accordingly, there was no debate that such a service was needed by the plaintiff. The primary dispute then was whether providing such a service would violate the First Amendment Establishment Clause.[78] In reversing in favor of the plaintiff, the Supreme Court reasoned that the IDEA provides services that are distributed neutrally to any child qualifying as disabled; that no funds are given directly to the sectarian school; and that an interpreter is different than a teacher in that he or she neither adds to nor subtracts from the educational environment.[79]

Third-party Liability[80]

The per pupil costs of special education are generally two to three times greater than for regular education, with individual IEPs sometimes costing as much as $160,000.[81] Although Congress may not have anticipated current levels of funding, it is clear that it did not intend that educational agencies be the sole source of revenue. Federal regulations stipulate that states may use whatever government or private sources are available to them and that the IDEA did not relieve insurers or other third parties of the obligation to pay for services.[82] Third parties have not rushed forward demanding to pay their fair share, however, and legislative acts and judicial pressure have been needed before Medicaid, private insurance companies, or others have "volunteered" payment.

---

[77] Zobrest v. Catalina Foothills Sch. Dist., 113 S. Ct. 2462 (1993).

[78] For a related article *see* Dixie Snow Huefner, *Zobrest v. Catalina Foothills School District: A Foothill in Establishment Clause Jurisprudence?* 87 EDUC. L. REP. 15 (1994).

[79] Zobrest v. Catalina Foothills Sch. Dist., 113 S. Ct. 2462, 2467-2469 (1993).

[80] This section is adapted from an article by Kathy Dye Spaller & Stephen B. Thomas, *A Timely IDEA: Third Party Billing for Related Services*, 86 EDUC. L. REP. 581, 581-592 (1994).

[81] *In re* Smith, 926 F.2d 1027 (11th Cir. 1991).

[82] 34 C.F.R. § 300.301.

Medicaid

In 1988, Congress amended title XIX of the Social Security Act (Medicaid)[83] stipulating, in part, that the Secretary of Health and Human Services (HHS) could not refuse to pay for covered services for eligible[84] children with disabilities, even if the services were incorporated into their IEPs. Interestingly, the amendments to title XIX were passed only three days after the Supreme Court affirmed a lower court ruling concluding that special education services could not be excluded from Medicaid reimbursement.[85]

In 1990, the Second Circuit addressed a related case, *Detsel v. Sullivan*.[86] In *Detsel,* the plaintiff had previously been denied medical-related services under the IDEA because they were viewed as too extensive to qualify as health services, even though none was provided directly by a physician.[87] This current litigation did not involve the school, however; instead, the parents sued Medicaid, because the HHS Secretary had refused payment based on a regulation requiring private duty nursing services to be provided at home or in a hospital. The court ruled for the plaintiffs and reasoned that the Secretary's decision was based on an out-dated assumption that a person needing a private duty nurse would be in either a home or hospital setting.

Over the years, even after it became clear that Medicaid would share the financial responsibility for related services for eligible children, it remained difficult for school practitioners to determine which specific services would be funded, for they varied by state, and by what reimbursement rate would be used. Mandatory services now include inpatient and outpatient hospital services, physician services, and Early and Periodic Screening, Diagnosis, and Treatment Services for Children (EPSDT); optional services include physical and occupational therapy, speech and language pathology, audiology,

---

[83] 42 U.S.C. § 1396 (1992).

[84] Eligible individuals include those who are receiving aid to families with dependent children, qualified low-income pregnant women and their children, people age 65 or older whose income and resources are below specific levels, and others who are blind or disabled and are receiving Supplemental Security Income (SSI). *See* 42 C.F.R. §§ 435.110-435.170 (1992).

[85] Bowen v. Massachusetts, 487 U.S. 879 (1988).

[86] Detsel v. Sullivan, 895 F.2d 58 (2d Cir. 1990).

[87] Detsel v. Board of Educ. of Auburn, 637 F. Supp. 1022 (N.D.N.Y. 1986), *aff'd,* 820 F.2d 587 (2d Cir. 1987), *cert. denied,* 484 U.S. 989 (1987).

and psychological services. Furthermore, reimbursement rates range from a theoretical low of 50% (several states) to a theoretical high of 83% (Mississippi had the highest reimbursement rate in 1990, 80%), based on state per capita income. (See Table 3-3.) The formulas for determining the state and federal shares are as follows:

State share $= [(\text{state per capita income})^2 / (\text{national per capita income})^2] \times 45\%$

Federal share $= 100\%$ minus the state share (with a minimum of 50% and a maximum of 83%)

Table 3-3
Federal Medical
Assistance Percentage (1990)

State	FMAP	State	FMAP	State	FMAP
Alabama	73%	Louisiana	73%	Ohio	60%
Alaska	50%	Maine	65%	Oklahoma	68%
Arizona	61%	Maryland	50%	Oregon	63%
Arkansas	75%	Massachusetts	50%	Pennsylvania	57%
California	50%	Michigan	53%	Rhode Island	55%
Colorado	52%	Minnesota	53%	South Carolina	73%
Connecticut	50%	Mississippi	80%	South Dakota	71%
Delaware	50%	Missouri	59%	Tennessee	70%
Florida	55%	Montana	71%	Texas	61%
Georgia	62%	Nebraska	61%	Utah	75%
Hawaii	55%	Nevada	50%	Vermont	63%
Idaho	73%	New Hampshire	50%	Virginia	50%
Illinois	50%	New Jersey	50%	Washington	54%
Indiana	64%	New Mexico	72%	West Virginia	77%
Iowa	63%	New York	50%	Wisconsin	59%
Kansas	56%	North Carolina	67%	Wyoming	66%
Kentucky	73%	North Dakota	68%		

Source: Roberta A. Kreb, *Third Party Payment for Funding Special Education and Related Services*, 3:1-3:20, LRP PUBLICATIONS (1991).

Insurance

In addition to Medicaid, there may be occasions when school districts can tap private insurance companies (e.g., Aetna), not-for-profit corporations (e.g., Blue Cross/Blue Shield), and Health Maintenance Organizations (HMOs) to help pay related costs. At the same time, there are numerous obstacles to remove or avoid before payment can be realized: parental permission is generally required; there can be no costs, hidden or direct, to the parents; parents may not suffer a financial loss (e.g., a decrease in available lifetime coverage or any other benefit;[88] an increase in premiums; the discontinuation of the policy; or an out-of-pocket expense such as a co-payment[89] or deductible). Furthermore, once an insurance group realizes that specific costs can be covered by either Medicaid or the IDEA, it may often exclude such services from its policy.[90] Under existing law neither government nor the courts can require a private insurer to include within its policy items it chooses not to insure.

Given the limited ability of state governments to mandate the substance of private insurance policies, it is unlikely that private insurance will prove to be a significant source of revenue or reimbursement, particularly compared to Medicaid. However, where reimbursement remains possible, related claims should be filed.

Conclusion

Related services have become more available over the last twenty years due, in part, to the case law discussed above, but also to an increased awareness of educators and parents as to what may be required to provide appropriate programs for special-needs children. Yet, there are limitations as to what must and will be provided (e.g., restrictions on services performed by medical doctors, psychiatrists, and nurses). Nevertheless, those related services that permit a child to attend school and to benefit from special education appear to have firm support both in the legislature and in the courts.

---

[88] Shook v. Gaston County Bd. of Educ., 882 F.2d 119 (4th Cir. 1989).

[89] *See, e.g.,* Seals v. Loftis, 614 F. Supp. 302 (E.D. Tenn. 1985).

[90] *See, e.g.,* Chester County Intermediate Unit v. Pennsylvania Blue Shield, 896 F.2d 808 (3d Cir. 1990) (where a group of parents unsuccessfully sued to require Blue Cross/Blue Shield to accept financial responsibility for physical therapy services).

Chapter 4
Disease

Introduction

It goes without saying that vaccines do not exist for all diseases and that not all children have taken those vaccines currently in existence.[1]

---

[1] For a discussion of the legal issues regarding immunization, *see* STEPHEN B. THOMAS, HEALTH RELATED LEGAL ISSUES IN EDUCATION 7-15 (1987); Susan G. Clark, *The National Childhood Vaccine Injury Act*, 94 EDUC. L. REP. 671 (1994).

Moreover, vaccines for such diseases as chicken pox are not widely used,[2] while those for other maladies such as cytomegalovirus are not fully developed.[3] Furthermore, the origin of some diseases, such as Crohn's is still unknown, or is not fully understood, as is the case with the common cold. As a result, there are times when students contract a disease and difficult decisions have to be made regarding admission, continued attendance, or placement. In light of the need to better understand the mandates of the IDEA and other related laws on disability, this Chapter identifies selected diseases contracted by school children and discusses their legal implications.

Disease Summary

Acquired Immune Deficiency Syndrome (AIDS)

The AIDS virus, HIV, was first recognized in 1979 and was established as a separate disease entity in 1981. There is no known vaccine or cure for AIDS. The disease results in severe and irreversible damage to the body's immune system, thereby causing a person to become vulnerable to a variety of uncommon infections; it also leaves individuals susceptible to rare types of cancer (e.g., Karposi's sarcoma) and pneumonia (e.g., Pneumocystis carinii). Most of these infections would have been repelled had the immune system been operating properly.[4]

There are no proven cases where HIV was transmitted through casual contact.[5] Moreover, experts believe that the virus is not air-

---

[2] C.Y. Hong & L.G. Goh, *Routine Immunization Against Chickenpox. Is It Time?* 34 J. SINGAPORE PEDIATRICS SOCIETY (1-2) 57-66 (1992).

[3] Anne A. Gershon, *Immunizations for Pediatric Transplant Patients*, 43 KIDNEY INTERNATIONAL, SUPPLEMENT 43, § 87-90 (October 1993).

[4] SCIENTIFIC AMERICAN MEDICINE, *Acquired Immunodeficiency Syndrome*, 7: XI: 1-24 at 1 (Edward Rubenstein & Daniel D. Federman, eds. 1994).

[5] In fact, in 1986, the then United States Surgeon General, Dr. C. Everett Koop, attempted to allay fears by reiterating the medical position that:

There is no known risk of non-sexual infection in most situations which we encounter in our daily lives. We know that family members living with individuals who have the AIDS virus do not become infected except through sexual contact. There is no evidence of transmission (spread) of [the] AIDS virus even though these family members shared food, towels, cups, razors, even toothbrushes and kissed each other . . . . Everyday living does not present any risk of infection. You cannot get AIDS from casual social contact[s] . . . such as shaking hands, hugging, social kissing, crying, coughing, or sneezing . . . . Nor has AIDS been contracted from swimming in pools or

borne (like colds), nor transmitted through fecal contamination of food (such as hepatitis A), nor carried by insects (as with malaria). Rather, they believe that it is transmitted through the blood (like hepatitis B). Accordingly, blood or contaminated semen must be passed directly into another person's blood system if the virus is to be transmitted. The virus also is present in other body fluids (e.g., saliva), but is in an attenuated condition and apparently is not transmissible in that state.[6]

Data from the National Center for Health Statistics indicate that between 1985 and 1993, the vast majority of men who contracted HIV did so through "homosexual activity" (63.7% of cases), "injecting drug use" (19.6% of cases), and "homosexual activity and injecting drug use" (7.1% of cases). Furthermore, during the period, 4.3% of those infected could not determine the source of transmission. Accordingly, that left only 5.3% for all other causes, including heterosexual contact, which accounted for only 2.2% of all cases during the period. For men, the category that decreased the most in percent of total was "homosexual activity," while the category that increased the most was "injecting drug use."

The pattern was different for women with only two high incidence areas: "injecting drug use" (49.2% of cases) and "heterosexual activity" (33.2% of cases). Additionally, 8.5% had undetermined sources. That left only 9.1% for all other causes. For women, clearly the largest decreases were in the categories of "injecting drug use," and "transfusion," while the category that increased the most was "heterosexual activity."

---

hot tubs or from eating in restaurants (even if a restaurant worker has AIDS or carries the AIDS virus). AIDS is not contracted from sharing bed linens, towels, cups, straws, dishes, or other eating utensils. You cannot gets AIDS from toilets, doorknobs, telephones, office machinery, or household furniture.

From the Surgeon General, 256 JAMA, 2785-68 (1986). Furthermore, the Americans with Disabilities Act, 42 U.S.C. § 12113(d) requires the Health and Human Services Secretary to publish a list of the diseases that are food-borne. Neither AIDS nor HIV is included on the list, 57 Fed. Reg. 174, Sept. 8, 1992.

[6] The AIDS virus has also been discovered in the saliva of victims, yet appears not to be very infectious in that state. Researchers speculate that antibodies deactivate the virus in the saliva, so that it does not infect others. The fact that there are no reported cases to date where either kissing or lesbian activities have resulted in transmission supports this claim. SCIENTIFIC AMERICAN MEDICINE, *Acquired Immunodeficiency Syndrome*, 7:XI: 1-24 (Edward Rubenstein & Daniel D. Federman, eds. 1994).

As is apparent, there is little positive from the aforementioned. Although the areas in decline, like "transfusion" (males and females) and "hemophilia/coagulation disorder" (females only), represent lower percentages than in the past, occurrences are still common, with actual numbers considerably higher in 1993 than in 1985 and 1990 (e.g., male transfusion victims increased from 111 in 1985, to 460 in 1990, to 528 in 1993). Part of the problem is that there still is no test for this deadly virus; the existing test detects antibodies. Accordingly, blood donated by an individual who had contracted HIV, but had not developed antibodies, might then transmit the disease to the recipient.

Table 4-1

AIDS Cases in the United States (1985-93)

Sex and Transmission Category	Number of Persons Infected 1985-93	% of Total Infected 1985-93	% Total 1985	% Total 1993
Male	285,063	100.0%	100.0%	100.0%
Homosexual activity	181,468	63.7%	71.9%	56.9%
Injecting drug use	55,900	19.6%	14.7%	22.7%
Homosexual activity and injecting drug use	20,376	7.1%	7.9%	6.5%
Hemophilia/ coagulation disorder	2,855	1.0%	1.0%	1.3%
Born in Caribbean/African countries	2,596	.9%	1.4%	.8%
Heterosexual activity	6,169	2.2%	.4%	3.1%
Sex with injecting drug user	(3,317)	(1.2%)	(.3%)	(1.3%)
Transfusion	3,496	1.2%	1.5%	.8%
Undetermined	12,203	4.3%	1.3%	7.8%
Female	38,684	100.0%	100.0%	100.0%
Injecting Drug use	19,037	49.2%	54.4%	46.8%
Hemophilia/ coagulation disorder	71	.2%	.4%	.2%
Born in Caribbean/African countries	1,160	3.0%	5.9%	2.2%
Heterosexual activity	12,847	33.2%	22.2%	34.5%
Sex with injecting drug user	(7,541)	(19.5%)	(15.5%)	(16.0%)
Transfusion	2,283	5.9%	11.3%	3.4%
Undetermined	3,286	8.5%	5.7%	12.9%

Source: Percents were calculated from data in Health United States 1993, National Center for Health Statistics, United States Department of Health & Human Services.

Expect the numbers of children affected to remain fairly stable or to decline slightly. Of the more than 300,000 cases of AIDS reported between 1985 and 1993, 4,645 were pediatric cases of children thirteen or younger. Given the known forms of transmission, these numbers are particularly high. However, the figures for children have stabilized in recent years (i.e., in 1985 there were only 129 new pediatric cases, while by 1990 the number increased to 718, but declined slightly to 629 by 1993)—the range between 1988 and 1993 was 565 to 744.[7]

Symptoms. AIDS has a long incubation period, generally ranging from six months to two years, although it can vary beyond this range—possibly as long as ten years.[8] A person with AIDS typically experiences weight loss of more than ten pounds in less than two months; fever that has persisted more than a week; swollen glands; enlarged lymph nodes in the neck, armpit, or groin; night sweats that persist for several weeks; diarrhea or bloody stools; dry cough; blotches or bumps on or under the skin, inside the mouth, nose, eyelids, or rectum; fatigue; and white patches in the mouth.

Chicken Pox

Chicken pox, or varicella zoster, is caused by the herpes zoster virus. It chiefly affects the skin and the lining of the mouth and throat. It is both infectious and contagious, but is generally mild when compared to other childhood diseases. A vaccine for chicken pox is now in limited use with generally good results.[9]

Symptoms. A child with chicken pox will have a skin rash, which later dries out, and a slight fever. Children typically do not appear sick beyond their rash, and require only about seven to ten days to recuperate. Adults generally have a more severe reaction with flu-like symptoms, and they need more time for recovery.

---

[7] National Center for Health Statistics, Health United States 1993, United States Department of Health & Human Services (1993).

[8] *Id. See also* Centers for Disease Control, Morbidity and Mortality Weekly Report No. 41, No. RR-18 (Dec. 25, 1992) at 4.

[9] SCIENTIFIC AMERICAN MEDICINE, *Herpesvirus Infections,* 7:XXVI: 4-6 (Edward Rubenstein & Daniel D. Federman, eds. 1994). *See also* Philip A. Brunell, *Varicella-Zoster Infection,* 1587-1591. TEXTBOOK OF PEDIATRIC INFECTIOUS DISEASES, VOL. II (Ralph D. Feigin & James D. Cherry, eds., 3d ed., 1992).

Crohn's Disease

Crohn's disease is a chronic condition of unknown origin which is characterized by inflammation of the bowel. The bowel wall and supporting membrane enlarge, resulting in a narrowing of the intestinal lumen. Small bowel obstruction occurs in 25% to 30% of patients, while perianal disease occurs in approximately 80% of those infected. In severe cases, surgery may be required. The disease can be disabling in cases where surgery is needed or where recuperation time is lengthy.[10]

Symptoms. A person with Crohn's disease ordinarily has a history of abdominal pain, diarrhea, and perianal disease and may also complain of fever and weight loss.

Cytomegalovirus (CMV)

Cytomegalovirus is a member of the herpes group and, although common, is virtually unknown to the general public because it is harmless to most people. While it was not isolated until the mid-1950s, health care professionals are becoming increasingly familiar with its symptoms and its potential danger.[11] For example, CMV can cause injury to the fetus of a woman who contracts it for the first time during pregnancy. In this case, the virus may cause hearing loss, mental retardation, or developmental delays. Approximately 5,000 children born each year in the United States are mentally retarded as a result of CMV. This disease is also dangerous to adults who have a suppressed immunity, such as those who receive chemotherapy treatments for cancer, undergo organ transplants, or have an immune deficiency disease (e.g., AIDS). However, if the body is capable of resisting CMV, antibodies will develop in the blood. The virus does not die, it simply goes dormant and remains in the cells of the body. At times it may reactivate but, in most situations, the reaction is so mild that a person may exhibit no symptoms.

Cytomegalovirus is spread by contact with body secretions including urine, saliva, feces, blood and blood products, semen, breast milk, respiratory secretions, and cervical secretions. The CDC has

---

[10] SCIENTIFIC AMERICAN MEDICINE, *Inflammatory Bowel Disease,* 4:IV: 10-15 (Edward Rubenstein & Daniel D. Federman, eds. 1994).

[11] SCIENTIFIC AMERICAN MEDICINE, *Herpesvirus Infections,* 7:XXVI: 7-8, at 7 (Edward Rubenstein & Daniel D. Federman, eds. 1994).

noted that because the risk to school personnel, particularly to women of childbearing age, is not fully known, it is important to inform them when infected children are present. Moreover, the CDC recommends that care for any infant or child include hygienic measures such as washing hands after contact with secretions, diapers, catheters, or other contaminated articles.

Symptoms. Symptoms for CMV are similar to those for mononucleosis: fever, sore throat, fatigue, and swollen glands. Also, it may cause pneumonia or enlargement of the liver or spleen.

Hepatitis A & B

Hepatitis A is a disease caused by a virus and was probably described by Hippocrates when he used the term epidemic jaundice. This disease is transmitted via food, water, milk, clothing, eating utensils, and other objects contaminated by feces. Raw shellfish from sewage-contaminated water is also a common source of the disease. Inadequate sewage disposal and unsanitary latrines may contaminate water used for bathing or dish washing; dirty bathrooms and improperly laundered towels are other possible sources of contamination. Hepatitis A is highly contagious, even before symptoms appear. Family members can be immunized against the disease for a short time by having gamma globulin injections, although to require injections for an entire student body is typically impractical.

Hepatitis B, or serum hepatitis, is caused by a different virus and is more serious than is the A strain, but is not spread as easily. Similar to AIDS, hepatitis B is transmitted by contaminated blood or by sexual contact. Ear piercing, tattooing, acupuncture, or any medical or dental procedures that cut or puncture the skin can pass the virus. Cirrhosis of the liver can result in chronic cases.[12]

Symptoms. Hepatitis A typically starts with intestinal flu-like symptoms: fever, headache, aching muscles, loss of appetite, nausea, and vomiting. These symptoms generally do not appear until two to six weeks after exposure to the virus, which travels through the blood stream and lodges in the liver. The patient may have swelling, tenderness, and sharp pain in the upper right abdomen. Bile formed by

---

[12] SCIENTIFIC AMERICAN MEDICINE, *Acute Hepatitis*, 4:VII: 1-11 (Edward Rubenstein & Daniel D. Federman, eds. 1994).

the liver backs up into the blood stream, causing the patient's skin and eye-whites to turn yellowish. The breath develops a sickly sweet odor, and the urine turns brown due to abnormally high amounts of bile being excreted through the kidneys. The symptoms for hepatitis B are generally the same as for hepatitis A, but often last longer and are more severe.

Herpes Simplex 1 & 2

Approximately 75% of the population is infected by the herpes simplex 1 virus, which generally occurs early in childhood. This virus causes cold sores or fever blisters. While the blisters are present the virus is highly contagious and is easily transmitted, but it is not likely to be passed on in the latent stage. Furthermore, the virus is not cured simply when the sores heal, although it does go dormant. Antibodies develop which make future occurrence less severe, but they do not prevent recurrence, which is unpredictable and can be caused by overexposure to sunlight, certain foods or drugs, and stress.

Herpes simplex 2 is a sexually transmitted virus that cannot be cured. It generally infects the genitalia, buttocks, and thighs with painful sores and blisters, and is the most common venereal disease in America today, affecting over twenty million persons. The disease is highly contagious through direct contact of infected areas. Recent studies have found that simplex 2 can survive for short periods on toilet seats, towels, and the like, although experts doubt that the disease is likely to be transmitted by contact with such sources.[13]

Symptoms. Usually before the blisters caused by simplex 1 appear, there is a burning or itching sensation. A few days after the sores erupt, the blisters enlarge, burst, and begin to dry out. They usually heal on their own within two to three weeks and seldom leave a scar. A major concern with simplex 1 is that the virus may be transmitted to the eye and cause ulceration of the cornea or blindness. In young children, the primary infection often goes unnoticed, although it can result in a loss of appetite, fever, and considerable ulceration in the mouth; in adults the disease may result in severe illness if a pri-

---

[13] SCIENTIFIC AMERICAN MEDICINE, *Fungal, Bacterial, and Viral Infections of the Skin*, 2:VII: 14-16, and *Human and Animal Herpesvirus*, 7:XXVI:1-4 (Edward Rubenstein & Daniel D. Federman, eds. 1994).

mary infection occurs. In a school setting, children should be instructed in proper hygiene in order to prevent transfer to the carrier's eyes or to other persons.

Persons with herpes simplex 2 will have an itching or tingling sensation in the genitalia, followed by the eruption of sores or blisters. In the first attack, the sores customarily appear two days to two weeks after exposure and last two to three weeks. Subsequent attacks, which may occur in a few weeks or not for years, generally last about five days and are less severe. Fever, malaise, and headaches may accompany the outbreak. In severe cases, the virus can go to the brain and cause a serious form of encephalitis, or pass to the eye and result in blindness. As with herpes simplex 1, school children should be instructed in proper hygiene and be directed to cover all exposed sores.

Mononucleosis

Mononucleosis is caused by the Epstein-Barr virus, an organism in the herpes-virus group. Nearly 85% of preadolescents have been infected. For young children, the disease can be so mild that it is mistaken for a cold, but, for late teens or adults, it can be serious. When the virus enters the body, it causes changes in a category of disease-fighting white blood cells known as B lymphocytes which are crucial for fighting infection. In a small percentage of cases, liver involvement may be considerable and jaundice may occur. Also, the person may have an enlarged spleen or prolonged fever. This disease should be of particular concern to educators because it is spread by oral contact, hence its nickname as "the kissing disease."[14]

Symptoms. A week or two following exposure the lymph nodes in the neck, or possibly armpit or groin, become swollen and sore. The patient may experience aching joints, fever, sore throat, difficulty in swallowing, fatigue, or skin rash. Because the symptoms may not be very specific, accurate diagnosis usually requires a blood test to confirm the high level and irregular appearance of B lymphocytes.

---

[14] SCIENTIFIC AMERICAN MEDICINE, *Herpesvirus Infections,* 7:XXVI: 7-9 (Edward Rubenstein & Daniel D. Federman, eds. 1994).

Tuberculosis (TB)

Tuberculosis, the "white plague of the nineteenth century," is a reportable, communicable, infectious, inflammatory, acute or chronic disease that may occur in almost any part of the body. Pulmonary infection is the most common result of TB, although it can spread to any other organ through the blood stream and lymphatics. The disease occurs most commonly by inhalation of the tubercle bacilli. It is rarely transmitted through ingestion, due to the development of the pasteurization of milk and tuberculin skin testing programs for cattle, or through direct infection such as a cut in the skin or mucous membrane. Tubercle bacilli are present in the air as a result of coughing, sneezing, and expectorating by infected persons; accordingly, TB is essentially an air-borne infection. Primary TB infections are often not recognized since they are usually asymptomatic; however, secondary infections can be more severe. Moreover, TB is 200 to 500 times more common in patients who are HIV positive than in HIV negative individuals.[15]

Symptoms. Symptoms can include coughing, sputum production, fatigue, night sweats, irritability, rapid pulse rate, low-grade fever, weight loss, vomiting, anorexia, indigestion, and pallor.

Related Case Law

The remaining portion of this Chapter provides a discussion of relevant case law dealing with disease in the schools. These cases are typically based on section 504 although a few also allege a violation of either the IDEA or the Fourteenth Amendment. As discussed in Chapter 1, the Fourteenth Amendment requires compliance by public schools. If a claim is based on facially discriminatory practices (e.g., segregation based on disease or disability within school), rational basis scrutiny would be applied, unless the child is functionally excluded. In that case, middle tier scrutiny would be used. Also, the IDEA may be selected as a basis for a related suit if the child qualifies as other health impaired and is in need of special education, while section 504 would apply to recipients of federal financial assis-

---

[15] SCIENTIFIC AMERICAN MEDICINE, *Infections Due to Mycobacteria*, 7: VII: 1-14 (Edward Rubenstein & Daniel D. Federman, eds. 1994).

tance where a disease results in a physical or mental impairment that substantially limits a major life activity (e.g., learning or working) of an otherwise qualified person. Moreover, there would be a possible section 504 violation where the individual had a record of impairment, or was treated as though she or he had an impairment.

The seminal case interpreting the appropriateness of claiming a disease as a disability under section 504 involved a teacher, rather than a student, although the application to student admission/retention cases is clear. In *School Board of Nassau County, Florida v. Arline*,[16] the contract of a teacher with thirteen years of experience was terminated following three relapses of TB. After the teacher was denied relief in state administrative proceedings, she filed suit in federal court. The teacher asserted that her susceptibility to TB qualified her as an individual with a disability and that her dismissal violated section 504. She further contended that her disability did not create a barrier to continued employment because the risk of transmission was minimal. As an alternative to termination, she urged that the district offer a reasonable accommodation by assigning her to a teaching or administrative position working with persons less susceptible to the disease. The trial court ruled in favor of the school board, but the Eleventh Circuit reversed and remanded in favor of the teacher.

The school board appealed to the Supreme Court, which ruled that a disease could, under certain conditions, qualify as a disability, and remanded the case to determine if Arline was otherwise qualified at the time of her termination.[17] The Court reasoned that:

> The fact that *some* persons who have contagious diseases may pose a serious health threat to others under certain circumstances does not justify excluding from the coverage of the Act *all* persons with actual or perceived contagious diseases. Such exclusion would mean that those accused of being contagious would never have the opportunity to have their condition evaluated in light of medical evidence

---

[16] School Bd. of Nassau County v. Arline, 772 F.2d 759 (11th Cir. 1985), *rev'd*, 480 U.S. 273 (1987).

[17] *See* Arline v. School Bd. of Nassau County, 692 F. Supp. 1286 (M.D. Fla. 1988) (where the teacher was otherwise qualified at the time of her discharge, she was entitled to reinstatement and back pay).

and a determination made as to whether they were 'otherwise qualified.'[18]

Additionally, the Court reasoned that the test to determine whether to employ an individual with a contagious disease should include findings of facts based on reasonable medical judgments about "(a) the nature of the risk (how the disease is transmitted), (b) the duration of the risk (how long is the carrier infectious), (c) the severity of the risk (what is the potential harm to third parties), and (d) the probabilities the disease will be transmitted and will cause varying degrees of harm."[19]

The remaining cases in this Chapter are grouped under three major headings: AIDS, Crohn's, and hepatitis B.

AIDS

Perhaps the most publicized case of a student with AIDS was *In re Ryan White.*[20] Ryan was a child with hemophilia who contracted AIDS through a blood transfusion and later was denied admission to public school. A homebound program, which included audio and video communications and a tutor, was prepared for him. However, Ryan's mother wanted him to be able to attend public schools even though he faced the increased probability of contracting other diseases due to his immune deficiency.

Despite his family's repeated requests, Ryan initially was denied admission when school officials reasoned that the risk of transmission to other children was too great. Health officials disagreed, as did the impartial hearing officer who held that Ryan's current homebound placement was inappropriate because it was not least restrictive, in light of his ability to perform in a mainstream setting, and because his presence did not represent a danger to others. Accordingly, the hearing officer ordered Ryan admitted to regular classrooms when his health allowed, and provided for homebound education during the times when he was unable to attend. Based on this decision, Ryan was readmitted to school, only to be excluded by a court order before the end of his first day. The court order kept Ryan out of

---

[18] School Bd. of Nassau County v. Arline, 772 F.2d 759 (11th Cir. 1985), *rev'd*, 480 U.S. 273, 285 (1987) (emphasis in original).

[19] *Id.* at 288.

[20] *In re* Ryan White, 507 EHLR 239 (1986).

school for over one and one half months until a state appellate court threw out the previous order, thereby permitting him once again to attend school.

Following Ryan White's case, numerous additional cases were filed from coast to coast, most of which were based on section 504, with the majority holding for the plaintiff children. Selected cases are presented below in chronological order within category.

State & Local Policy Disputed. *District 27 Community School Board v. Board of Education of New York*[21] involved a controversy that arose after officials in New York City announced a policy concerning the admission of children with AIDS to public schools. The policy stated that such children would not be automatically excluded, but would be reviewed on an individual basis to determine whether their health and development permitted them to attend school in an unrestricted setting. Following this announcement, a four-member panel was convened to review the cases of school-aged children reported to have AIDS.

One of the panel's initial reviews involved a seven-year-old child who had been diagnosed as having AIDS. It recommended that the child be allowed to remain in a regular educational placement. Subsequently, two local community school boards sought a temporary restraining order and a permanent injunction prohibiting educational officials from admitting any child with AIDS to any public school in the city if the school was attended by students who did not have AIDS and if the school was not designed to accommodate the needs of such children.

The court denied relief, holding that a blanket exclusion of students with AIDS would be arbitrary and capricious. It concluded that a student with AIDS is clearly physically impaired as defined under section 504, and that students may also be covered by the IDEA (if their condition deteriorates to the point of needing special education and related services). Moreover, it ruled that the Fourteenth Amendment was violated when the district proposed to exclude students with AIDS, but not those with AIDS-related complex (ARC) or asymptomatic carriers who represented an equal risk of contagion.

---

[21] District 27 Community Sch. Bd. v. Board of Educ. of N.Y., 502 N.Y.S.2d 325 (Sup. Ct. 1986).

Board of Education of Plainfield v. Cooperman[22] involved a challenge to state policy guidelines for the admission to school of children with AIDS, ARC, or HTLV-III antibodies. The guidelines provided for a Medical Advisory Panel to review local school board decisions to exclude children with diseases and required the admission of any such child unless either of two conditions was present: (1) the student was not toilet trained, was incontinent, or was otherwise unable to control drooling; or (2) the student was unusually physically aggressive, with a documented history of biting or harming others.[23] The appellate court ruled that the state regulations, which had not been adopted in compliance with statutory rule-making procedures, were null and void. It also required the Commissioner of Education to provide the school boards with a hearing at which time witnesses and evidence might be examined. The court concluded that there was sufficient evidence of a "potential risk of exposure" to warrant immediate hearings prior to the admission of each involved child.

In dissent, Judge Gaulkin argued that little evidence supported the majority opinion and concluded that "[t]he [b]oards have made no showing at all, much less a sufficient one, to justify the continued infringement of the constitutional rights of these children. On this record, to bar the children from school until 'appropriate procedural requirements' . . . are satisfied is to turn due process on its head."[24]

On appeal, the Supreme Court of New Jersey found several issues moot due to the admission of one child to a class for the neurologically impaired and the out-of-district change of residence for the other.[25] However, the court acknowledged that due process requires adequate protection for individuals as well as for the public at large, but then upheld the challenged practices. The court reasoned that the amended state regulations allowed for a fair hearing with all parties having the right to present evidence, to provide witnesses, and to cross examine witnesses. Additionally, the power to regulate such matters was found to reside in the state rather than in local school boards.

---

[22] Board of Educ. of Plainfield v. Cooperman, 507 A.2d 253 (N.J. Super. Ct. App. Div. 1986).

[23] *Id.* at 257-58.

[24] *Id.* at 279 (Gaulkin, J., concurring in part and dissenting in part).

[25] Board of Educ. of Plainfield v. Cooperman, 523 A.2d 655 (N.J. 1987).

Exhaustion Under the IDEA & Section 504. In *Doe v. Belleville Public School District No. 118*,[26] a six-year-old boy with hemophilia who contracted HIV was denied admission to the first grade. When suit was brought on his behalf, the district sought to dismiss for failure to exhaust administrative remedies under the IDEA. The court ruled that the IDEA did not apply because the physical condition of the child did not adversely affect his ability to learn, and that exhaustion under the IDEA was therefore not required. Even if the IDEA did apply, the court reasoned, exhaustion still would not have been necessary, given that further administrative appeals would have been futile due to defective procedures. The defendant's motion to dismiss was then denied, in part because exhaustion of remedies was not required under section 504.

Exhaustion also was a central issue in *Robertson v. Granite City Community Unit School District No. 9*,[27] where a seven-year-old with hemophilia was assigned to a "modular" classroom after he was diagnosed as having an AIDS-related complex. When his mother discovered that he was the only pupil in the "modular" classroom, she requested his removal from this setting and placement in a regular first grade classroom with other students. After the mother's requests were denied, she filed suit. The court found that since the child's learning and behavioral problems were not a result of his health condition, he was not covered under the IDEA, and that his mother was therefore not required to exhaust administrative remedies. Furthermore, since he was otherwise qualified under section 504, the court provided a preliminary injunction ordering his return to a regular classroom setting. In developing its position, the court noted that it could imagine nothing more traumatic than for a child to go to school and then to be "placed in a classroom by himself, not being allowed to play with other children, [or] . . . to eat with his classmates."[28]

IDEA-based Decision. One of the few AIDS-related cases that was resolved under the IDEA originated in Oklahoma when the Wagoner school system refused to place an HIV positive child with

---

[26] Doe v. Belleville Pub. Sch. Dist. No. 118, 672 F. Supp. 342 (S.D. Ill. 1987).
[27] Robertson v. Granite City Community Unit Sch. Dist. No. 9, 684 F. Supp. 1002 (S.D. Ill. 1988).
[28] *Id.* at 1005.

an emotional disorder in a special education classroom. *In Parents of Child, Code No. 870901W v. Coker,* the court held that the child was entitled to a placement under the IDEA on the basis of his emotional disorder.[29] It also ruled that he could not be barred from school by a state law regarding contagious diseases. The Concerned Parents Association had hoped that the law would have barred the child's attendance.

Biters & Children Not in Control of Bodily Fluids. *Thomas v. Atascadero Unified School District*[30] involved a child with AIDS who, shortly after being admitted to kindergarten, bit a classmate but failed to break the skin. The school board, upon receiving a psychologist's report that the child would probably continue his aggressive behavior, removed him from the regular classroom and provided home instruction. In a suit brought by the parents, the court determined that there were "no reported cases of the transmission of the AIDS virus in a school setting" and that the "overwhelming weight of medical evidence [was] that the AIDS virus is not transmitted by human bites, even bites that break the skin."[31] Because the child qualified as disabled under section 504, he was "otherwise qualified" to attend regular kindergarten and there was no evidence that he posed a significant risk to others, the court ordered his readmission.

Martinez v. School Board of Hillsborough County, Florida,[32] concerned a trainable mentally handicapped (TMH) kindergarten-aged student with AIDS who was incontinent, often had blood in her saliva, and sucked her fingers. Due to these conditions, she was excluded from a regular class for children who were TMH. The trial court initially reasoned that the plaintiff had "been dealt a hand not to be envied by anyone"[33] and that it would add "insult to injury"[34] to deny her the opportunity to lead as normal an educational and social

---

[29] Parents of Child, Code No. 870901W v. Coker, 676 F. Supp. 1072 (E.D. Okla. 1987).

[30] Thomas v. Atascadero Unified Sch. Dist., 662 F. Supp. 376 (C.D. Cal. 1987).

[31] *Id.* at 380.

[32] Martinez v. School Bd. of Hillsborough County, Fla., 675 F. Supp. 1574 (M.D. Fla. 1987), *vacated and remanded,* 861 F.2d 1502 (11th Cir 1988), *on remand,* 711 F. Supp. 1066 (M.D. Fla. 1989). *See also* Martinez v. School Bd. of Hillsborough County, 692 F. Supp. 1293 (M.D. Fla. 1988) for a related case.

[33] *Id.* at 1582.

[34] *Id.*

life as possible, unless she posed a real and present risk to others. The court then found, however, that the child's presence in the classroom represented a specific potential harm to others that clearly outweighed her interests in a more integrated placement. The court based its decision in part on CDC guidelines which state that children who lack control of body secretions may need a more restricted school environment.

The Eleventh Circuit vacated the lower court decision and remanded since it found that the youngster was otherwise qualified to attend regular classes for children who were TMH. On remand, in light of the low overall risk of her transmitting the HIV virus, the trial court ordered the district to admit her to a regular TMH classroom and to have a school nurse available to consult should there be a question as to the advisability of the child being in the classroom on a given day.[35]

General Exclusion/Homebound Placement. In *Ray v. School District of DeSoto County*,[36] three children from a single family with hemophilia tested HIV-positive. After enrolling in elementary school, they were removed from their regular classrooms and were provided with homebound instruction. The parents filed suit and were granted an injunction, allowing the children to attend public school. In its conclusions of law, the court noted that it

> recognizes the concern and fear which is flowing from this small community, particularly from parents of school age children . . . . However, the [c]ourt may not be guided by such community fear, parental pressure, and the possibility of lawsuits. 'These obstacles, real as they may be, cannot be allowed to vitiate the rights . . .' [of the Ray children].[37]

As a result, the court provided a preliminary injunction admitting the children, "unless and until" it was established that they represented a "real and valid" threat to others within the school setting. The court

---

[35] For an in-depth case study of Eliana Martinez's legal battles, *see* MONTE L. BETZ, THE KINDERGARTNER WITH AIDS AND THE CLASSROOM BARRIER (1992).

[36] Ray v. School Dist. of DeSoto County, 666 F. Supp. 1524 (M.D. Fla. 1987).

[37] *Id.* at 1535.

also required the district to provide an educational program to better inform the parent population about AIDS/HIV and its transmissibility.[38]

An Illinois case, *Doe v. Dolton Elementary School District No. 148*,[39] involved a twelve-year-old child who had apparently contracted HIV from blood transfusions while undergoing open heart surgery. He was subsequently excluded from the school's regular classrooms and extracurricular activities on the basis of his illness. In a suit brought by the child's parents, the court, relying on testimony from the school superintendent, ruled that the homebound instruction provided by the district was inferior to what children received in the regular classroom setting. Also, the court held that the plaintiff was otherwise qualified to attend school in that he did not pose a significant risk of infecting others, and ordered his admission to curricular and extracurricular activities, with the exception of contact sports.

Phipps v. Saddleback Valley Unified School District[40] involved an eleven-year-old with hemophilia who had been exposed to the HIV virus and was denied admission to school on the basis that the district was in the process of formulating its policy. An appellate court affirmed a permanent injunction on his behalf, subject to periodic reevaluation of his medical condition. The appellate tribunal reasoned that since the student had been attending school regularly without incident, there was no reason for him to be excluded.

The weight of these cases, coupled with the realization that there have been no reported cases on point for five years, should make it clear that absent exigent circumstances, students with AIDS, or who are HIV positive, must be admitted to public/federal recipient schools based either on the IDEA, section 504, or both, as appropriate. Thus, administrators and other educators must take the neces-

---

[38] *See also* Ware v. Valley Stream High Sch. Dist., 551 N.Y.S.2d 167 (1989); Fink v. Board of Educ. of Tully Cent. Sch., 542 N.Y.S.2d 918 (Sup. Ct. 1989) (where school district residents unsuccessfully challenged a local board's implementation of a state regulation regarding AIDS instruction).

[39] Doe v. Dolton Elementary Sch. Dist. No. 148, 694 F. Supp. 440 (N.D. Ill. 1988).

[40] Phipps v. Saddleback Valley Unified Sch. Dist., 251 Cal. Rptr. 720 (Ct. App. 1988).

sary steps to devise and implement policies[41] insuring the rights of children with AIDS or HIV to receive a FAPE.

Crohn's

In *County of Los Angeles v. Kling*,[42] an applicant who was denied admission to a nursing school on the basis that the program would have been too stressful filed suit alleging that she had been discriminated against on the basis of her disability, Crohn's disease. The district court disagreed, concluding that she was properly denied admission due to academic deficiencies. On appeal, the Ninth Circuit Court of Appeals reversed and ruled that Kling was an otherwise qualified individual with a disability within the meaning of section 504 who was denied admission solely on the basis of her disability. The court noted that the physician had assumed that because of Crohn's disease Kling would be unable to complete the school's program, but that he had not evaluated her on an individual basis. Moreover, the physician had testified that if he had known more about the appellee's medical history, he would have "swayed very strongly toward acceptance." The court then concluded that it was "precisely this type of general assumption about a handicapped person's ability that section 504 was designed to avoid."[43]

On further appeal, the Supreme Court reversed and remanded without comment from the majority.[44] Justice Stevens dissented strongly from the summary disposition and maintained that:

> Presumably, the Court's reversal is not based on a view that the Court of Appeals misapprehended the governing standard . . . . Apparently, the Court disagrees with the Ninth Circuit's application of that standard. However, the Court's reversal is not accompanied by a review of the [d]istrict [c]ourt's factual findings or a determination that they are not, in fact, "clearly erroneous."[45]

---

[41] For an excellent treatment of policies in this area, *see* MATTHEW J. WELKER & SARAH J. PELL, THE FORMULATION OF AIDS POLICIES: LEGAL CONSIDERATIONS FOR SCHOOLS (1992).

[42] County of Los Angeles v. Kling, 769 F.2d 532 (9th Cir. 1985).

[43] *Id.* at 534.

[44] County of Los Angeles v. Kling, 474 U.S. 936 (1985) (mem.).

[45] *Id.* at 938-939. On remand from the Supreme Court, the Ninth Circuit, in turn, returned the action to the district court, 782 F.2d 1510 (9th Cir. 1986).

Although the plaintiff was unsuccessful in this case, it should not be assumed that persons with Crohn's disease will not qualify for protection under section 504, the IDEA, or both. Other plaintiffs who meet statutory requirements could very well prevail.

Hepatitis B

In *New York State Association for Retarded Children v. Carey*,[46] children with hepatitis B were excluded from classes by the board of education, although the Department of Health had recommended their isolation within their respective schools. After an injunction was issued to prevent their exclusion, numerous students with hepatitus B who were mentally retarded were admitted, but most were assigned to new classes, teachers, or schools. No effort was made to isolate or reassign children with hepatitis B who were not mentally retarded. School district officials agreed that the exclusion of children who were not disabled was unnecessary because their behavior was not likely to result in the transmission of the disease in so far as they were not prone to bite and had control of their body fluids.

The district court in *Carey* ruled that with simple prophylactic and classroom management measures, the presence of the children did not represent a substantial risk to others, and that by excluding the children, the district violated section 504, the IDEA, and the Fourteenth Amendment. On appeal, the Second Circuit affirmed, concluding that the district had failed to prove more than a remote possibility of a health hazard and that isolating the children would have a foreseeably detrimental effect.

Community High School District 155 v. Denz[47] involved a TMH child with Down's syndrome who carried hepatitis B and who repeatedly tested positive for an "e antigen," indicating a high degree of infectivity. After the school district denied a requested change of placement from a homebound program to a regular special education setting, a hearing ensued. The hearing officer disagreed with the district's action and, in ordering the placement, required the assignment of a teacher's aide to guard against the infection of other children or staff. The hearing officer found that relatively inexpen-

---

[46] New York State Ass'n for Retarded Children v. Carey, 466 F. Supp. 479 (E.D.N.Y. 1978), *aff'd*, 612 F.2d 644 (2d Cir. 1979).

[47] Community High Sch. Dist. 155 v. Denz, 463 N.E.2d 998 (Ill. App. Ct. 1984).

sive preventative procedures would minimize any risk to others. The
state superintendent of education, relying on medical testimony indicating the low risk of transmission, affirmed, as did a trial court. A
state appeals court held that the child's good hygiene and a teacher's
aide could guard against conditions which might pose a risk of transmission. As a result, the homebound program was not "least restrictive," and the lower court order mandating the special education
placement was upheld.

The most recent case, *Jeffrey S. ex rel. Ernest S. v. State Board of
Education of Georgia*,[48] concerned a fifteen-year-old with an I.Q. of
less than fifty who was classified as having a mild to moderate mental
disability. In addition, the youngster was in the final stages of renal
disease, requiring an ileostomy bag and dialysis twice a week, and
suffered from a metabolic bone disease. When the district learned
that the student was also a carrier of hepatitis B, he was placed on
homebound instruction. A federal magistrate ordered Jeffrey reinstated on the basis that he was otherwise qualified to attend school
pursuant to section 504, that he was excluded solely due to his disability, and that there was no evidence that he posed a threat to other
students. A federal district court adopted the recommendation that
he be permitted to attend school, but the Eleventh Circuit reversed.
It ruled that in so far as the district court failed to provide a *de novo*
review, a trial on the merits was required due to potential harm to
both parties.

Conclusion

Case law to date indicates that students with physical or mental
disabilities due to contagious disease may well be covered under section 504. Furthermore, claims may also be filed under the IDEA if

---

[48] Jeffrey S. *ex rel.* Ernest S. v. State Bd. of Educ. of Ga., 896 F.2d 507 (11th Cir.
1990). *See also* Kohl *ex rel.* Kohl v. Woodhaven Learning Center, 672 F. Supp.
1226 (W.D. Mo. 1987), *rev'd and remanded*, 865 F.2d 930 (8th Cir. 1989), *cert.
denied*, 493 U.S. 892 (1989) (reversing an injunction ordering the admission to a
residential placement of a 32-year-old man who was mentally retarded, bilaterally
blind, and an active carrier of hepatitis B even though he was otherwise qualified
under § 504 and excluded solely on the basis of his disability; the limited inocula-
tion plan for staff members who would be in direct contact with him posed an
unreasonable risk to staff members who would not have been immunized).

the disease impairs the child's ability to learn in the classroom to the degree that special education and related services are needed. Only when the child's presence represents a danger to others is the district permitted to require a more restrictive placement. The determination of whether the child poses a risk to others should be left to medical professionals based on current medical knowledge. Whether a special education student attends school in the regular classroom, in special settings, in segregated schools, or has home instruction will continue to be the responsibility of the IEP team, assuming, of course, that medical facts and the aggregate abilities and behaviors of the student are used to determine placement, and not any bias, prejudice, or unfounded fear of educators or members of the community. Related policies should be direct, clear, and unambiguous.

Chapter 5
Student Records

Introduction

Prior to 1974, it was common for educators to deny parents the right to review their child's school records. Granting access was a time-consuming and costly affair that involved such responsibilities as explaining and interpreting records, establishing access and complaint procedures, maintaining files, and the like. Many educators were undoubtedly apprehensive that access would increase their accountability by further opening up the education process to public scrutiny. They were concerned that some items in the records would be misleading, inaccurate, or even defamatory, and that complaints or court actions would follow. Moreover, educators were worried that increased public awareness would be sure to result in more clerical and administrative responsibilities to manage, more controversies to resolve, more hearings to provide, more forms to prepare, and more records to maintain.

In 1974, a year prior to the enactment of the Education for All Handicapped Children Act (EAHCA/part B of the IDEA), the United States Congress enacted the Family Educational Rights and Privacy Act (FERPA), also known as the Buckley Amendment.[1] Congress was aware of the responsibility that it was placing on educators, but it believed that, on balance, the rights of parents and students to know and to understand the content of school records, as well as to restrict access of third parties to those records, were paramount.

---

[1] 20 U.S.C. § 1232g.

The Buckley Amendment applies to all students attending institutions receiving federal financial assistance, not just to pupils with disabilities. However, while FERPA is broader in scope and coverage than the IDEA, the relationship between the two has particular importance for parents of students with disabilities, since typically these children are subject to more evaluations, tests, and observations than are those students without disabilities. Furthermore, whether an appropriate education is indeed being provided may substantially be verified by school records. Accordingly, parental access to such records is essential if the rights of children with disabilities are to be guaranteed. Thus, since the IDEA requires states and local educational agencies to develop policies consistent with FERPA,[2] this Chapter focuses on how the IDEA, its accompanying regulations, and FERPA interact as well as what they collectively require. More specifically, this Chapter examines topics such as records, access rights, the amendment of records, the destruction of records, and penalties for noncompliance.

Records Covered

The confidentiality provisions of FERPA include all records, files, documents, and other materials containing personally identifiable information directly related to a student that are maintained by an educational agency or by a person acting for such agency.[3] Among the materials classified as educational records are a number of reports, surveys, studies, summaries, and the like, that include information on more than one student. Parents wishing to view their child's records have access to all individualized data that are not otherwise excluded, but may examine only that portion of group information that is specific to their child.[4] All other data must be obliterated or withheld. Yet another form of records often maintained by educators is directory information, which may include a student's name, address, telephone number, date and place of birth, major field of study, participation in officially recognized activities and sports, weight and height of members of athletic teams, dates of

---

[2] 20 U.S.C. § 1417(c).
[3] 20 U.S.C. § 1232g(a)(4)(A).
[4] 34 C.F.R. § 300.564.

attendance, degrees and awards received, and the most recent previous educational agency or institution attended.[5] While written consent is not required for the release of directory information, before data are made available, an educational agency must not only provide public notice of the categories of information that it has designated as directory, but it must also allow a reasonable period of time for parents to request that that information not be released without their consent.[6] However, it should be noted that federal laws do not "require" recipients to provide directory information and many have chosen not to do so.[7]

Each year an agency must notify parents of students with disabilities[8] of their right to inspect and review, request amendment of, and consent to disclosure of covered records. Typically, all of the aforementioned information is placed in a single notice to parents and may be provided by any means that is reasonably likely to inform them of their rights.[9] Notice may be publicized in a public newspaper, a school paper, a student handbook, a note to parents to be carried by their children, or by other methods (or combination of means) that would guarantee adequate circulation to notify involved parents.[10] In addition, upon request, an agency must provide parents with a list of the types and locations of educational records that it collects, maintains, or uses.[11]

The comprehensiveness of IDEA and FERPA regulations notwithstanding, not all school records qualify as educational records subject to disclosure. In fact, three exceptions in FERPA are impor-

---

[5] U.S.C. § 1232g(a)(5)(A). *See* Hathaway v. Joint Sch. Dist. No. 1 of Green Bay, 329 N.W.2d 217 (Wis. Ct. App. 1982) (where access to a computer-generated list of names and addresses was permitted under state statute); Oregon County R-IV Sch. Dist. v. LeMon, 739 S.W.2d 553 (Mo. Ct. App. 1987) (where the disclosure of names, addresses, and phone numbers was not barred by FERPA). *But see* Kestenbaum v. Michigan State Univ., 294 N.W.2d 228 (Mich. Ct. App. 1980), *aff'd,* 327 N.W.2d 783 (Mich. 1982) (where release of a magnetic tape containing the names and addresses of students was ruled to violate state law).

[6] 20 U.S.C. § 1232g(a)(5)(B). *See* Sauerhof v. City of New York, 438 N.Y.S.2d 982 (Sup. Ct. 1981) (where notice was required prior to the release of medical and personal student records).

[7] *See, e.g.,* Krauss v. Nassau Community College, 469 N.Y.S.2d 553 (Sup. Ct. 1983).

[8] *See* Mattie T. v. Johnston, 74 F.R.D. 498 (N.D. Miss. 1976).

[9] 34 C.F.R. § 99.7.

[10] *See* Rios v. Read, 73 F.R.D. 589 (E.D.N.Y. 1977).

[11] 34 C.F.R. § 300.565.

tant to special education. Records excluded from the disclosure requirements are those (1) made by educational personnel that are in the sole possession of their maker and are not accessible by or revealed to any other person except a temporary substitute; (2) maintained separately by the law enforcement unit of an educational agency that are used only for their own law enforcement purposes;[12] and (3) pertaining to a student who is eighteen years of age or older, or who is in an institution of postsecondary education, which are made by a physician, psychiatrist, psychologist, or other professional or para-professional person for use in the treatment of eligible students and are not available to other persons, except at the request of the student.[13] In addition, distribution of information that is not derived from school sources is not regulated by FERPA.[14]

Access Rights

Pursuant to FERPA, parents have the right to inspect and review records containing personally identifiable information related to the education of their child.[15] Furthermore, absent a court order or applicable state law, a noncustodial parent has the same right of access to these records as does the custodial parent.[16] The agency maintaining the records must also provide reasonable interpretations and explanations of information contained in the file.[17]

---

[12] *But see* Belanger v. Nashua, N.H. Sch. Dist., 856 F. Supp. 40 (D.N.H. 1994) (where the court held that juvenile records qualified as educational records).

[13] 20 U.S.C. § 1232g(a)(4)(B)(i)(ii)(iv). A fourth exception, 20 U.S.C. § 1232g(a)(4)(B)(iii) applies to personnel records pertaining exclusively to an individual employed by an educational agency but not in attendance there which are made in the ordinary course of business and are not available for any other purpose.

[14] Frasca v. Andrews, 463 F. Supp. 1043 (E.D.N.Y. 1979). *See also* Arkansas Gazette Co. v. Southern State College, 620 S.W.2d 258 (Ark. 1981) (where records of a state athletic organization did not qualify as educational records under FERPA); Klein Indep. Sch. Dist. v. Mattox, 830 F.2d 576 (5th Cir. 1987) (where FERPA did not apply to employment records).

[15] 20 U.S.C. § 1232g(a)(1)(A).

[16] 34 C.F.R. § 300.562(c). *See, e.g.,* Page v. Rotterdam-Mohonasen Cent. Sch. Dist., 441 N.Y.S.2d 323 (Sup. Ct. 1981) (where the natural father was permitted to view his child's records, despite a signed statement by the custodial mother requesting that such access be denied).

[17] 34 C.F.R. § 99.10(c).

Under FERPA, parental permission or consent is transferred to eligible students who reach their eighteenth birthday or who are attending postsecondary institutions.[18] However, the related IDEA regulation qualifies this right of access as it applies to students with disabilities. It maintains that the policies and procedures can take a student's age and the type or severity of the disability into consideration.[19]Other restrictions include limits on students' access to financial records of parents, and letters of recommendations where a right of access has been waived.[20]

An educational agency is not required to comply with a request if the records being sought pertain to an individual who is neither a student, nor has ever been a student, at that particular school/district.[21] For example, a parent or eligible student would not have access to records maintained by institutions to which the student applied, but was not admitted. Access to school records, other than to directory information, by third parties generally is permitted only if written consent of the parent is provided.[22] Major exceptions to the disclosure provisions apply to: other school officials with legitimate educational interests; officials representing schools to which the student has applied for admission, assuming proper notice to parents has been provided; persons responsible for determining a student's eligibility for financial aid; organizations conducting certain studies; authorized representatives of the United States Comptroller General, the Secretary of the Department of Education, and certain state and local education authorities; individuals carrying out the functions of accrediting organizations; and, in emergency situations, persons who can protect the health and safety of the student or other persons.[23] Also, written permission is not necessary if the parents of

---

[18] 20 U.S.C. § 1232g(d).

[19] 34 C.F.R. § 300.574.

[20] 20 U.S.C. § 1232g(a)(1)(B)(C).

[21] 20 U.S.C. § 1232g(a)(6).

[22] 20 U.S.C. § 1232g(b)(1). *But see* Aufox v. Board of Educ. of Township High Sch. Dist. No. 113, 588 N.E.2d 316 (Ill. App. Ct. 1992) (where the district's attorney and court clerk were permitted under state law to view a student's records without parental consent).

[23] 20 U.S.C. § 1232g(b)(1)(A-G, I). *But see* Board of Educ. of N.Y. v. Regan, 500 N.Y.S.2d 978 (Sup. Ct. 1986) (where the state comptroller was not entitled to a list of students, because such information was confidential under FERPA).

a dependent eligible student request access,[24] or if records have been subpoenaed or otherwise obtained through judicial order except that the parents and student must be notified in advance of the district's compliance.[25] However, prior to ordering the release of information, a court will weigh the need for access against the privacy interests of the student.

If disclosure of aggregated data is warranted, the information may have to have all identifiable data obliterated and put in a scrambled order to lessen the likelihood that individual data could be identified.[26] Where consent is not acquired but the records are released anyway, IDEA and Fourteenth Amendment violations may exist.[27]

Where written consent is required, the specific records being requested must be identified, the proposed use of the information must be specified, and the methods of acquiring the data must be explained. In addition, parents have the right to request a copy of the material to be released.[28] Furthermore, it is the responsibility of the educational unit to maintain a record of all individuals or groups, except exempted parties, that request or obtain access to a child's records.[29] This record must state the legitimate interests of those provided with access and must be kept with the student's other records.[30]

---

[24] 20 U.S.C. § 1232g(b)(1)(H).

[25] 20 U.S.C. § 1232g(b)(2)(B). *See* Reeg v. Fetzer, 78 F.R.D. 34 (W.D. Okla. 1976); and Mattie T. v. Johnston, 74 F.R.D. 498 (N.D. Miss. 1976).

[26] Bowie v. Evanston Community Consol. Sch. Dist. No. 65, 538 N.E.2d 557 (Ill. 1989) (where masked and scrambled test scores were made available under the State Freedom of Information Act); Western Serv. v. Sargent Sch. Dist., No. RE-33J, 719 P.2d 355 (Colo. Ct. App. 1986) (where disclosure was permitted after names were omitted, the order was scrambled, and ethnic origin was coded); Kryston v. Board of Educ., East Ramapo Cent. Sch. Dist., 430 N.Y.S.2d 688 (App. Div. 1980) (where the court ordered disclosure of scrambled test scores); Board of Educ., Island Trees Union Free Sch. Dist. v. Butcher, 402 N.Y.S.2d 626 (App. Div. 1978) (where the court ordered the disclosure of student records after all identifying data were obliterated).

[27] Sean R. *ex rel.* Dwight R. v. Board of Educ. of Woodbridge, 794 F. Supp. 467 (D. Conn. 1992).

[28] 20 U.S.C. § 1232g(b)(2)(A).

[29] 34 C.F.R. § 300.563; 20 U.S.C. § 1232g(b)(4)(A).

[30] 20 U.S.C. § 1232g(b)(4)(A).

The educational unit that maintains student records must comply with a legitimate request for review without unnecessary delays and before any meeting or hearing regarding the identification, evaluation, IEP, or educational placement of a child. Unless the parents agree otherwise, the delay in providing access should be no longer than forty-five days.[31]

An agency that has received a parental request for access to records may not charge a fee to search for or to retrieve information. Once records are located, parents may be charged for copies as long as payment does not effectively prevent them from exercising their rights to review those records.[32] Additionally, if parents request permission to tape-record parent-teacher conferences or placement meetings, federal courts have upheld their right to do so.[33] In fact, one federal trial court even required a school district to provide a written transcript (at an estimated cost of $4,700), despite the availability of a verbatim electronic record.[34] The First Circuit disagreed, however, concluding that an electronic transcript of an administrative hearing was sufficient to meet due process requirements.[35]

Amending Records

Parents who disagree with the content of an educational record may request that it be amended.[36] If officials refuse to comply with the request, the parents are entitled to a hearing at which time a hearing officer will determine whether the challenged material is

---

[31] 20 U.S.C. § 1232g(a)(1)(A); 34 C.F.R. § 500.562(a); 34 C.F.R. § 300.562.

[32] 34 C.F.R. § 300.566.

[33] *See* Gardner v. School Bd. Caddo Parish, 958 F.2d 108 (5th Cir. 1992) (where the district court had concluded that the parents had the right to tape-record parent-teacher conferences, but the circuit court held that the plaintiffs failed to prove that exhaustion would have been futile); E.H. v. Tirozzi, 735 F. Supp. 53 (D. Conn. 1990) (where Danish parents were allowed to tape-record placement meetings); V.W. v. Favolise, 131 F.R.D. 654 (D. Conn. 1990) (where parents were allowed to tape-record parent-teacher meetings). *See also* Caroline T. v. Hudson Sch. Dist., 915 F.2d 752 (1st Cir. 1990) (where the court upheld the authority of the district to have a court reporter present at a hearing).

[34] Militello v. Board of Educ. of Union City, 803 F. Supp. 974 (D.N.J. 1992).

[35] Edward B. v. Paul, 814 F.2d 52 (1st Cir. 1987).

[36] 34 C.F.R. § 300.567.

accurate and appropriately contained within the file.[37] The hearing officer must render a decision within a reasonable time.[38] If the officer rules that the contested material is inaccurate or serves no educational purpose, it should be removed immediately. On the other hand, if the material is found not to be inaccurate, misleading, or otherwise in violation of the student's right to privacy, it need not be removed or otherwise amended. Parents who remain concerned over the content of any file may prepare a statement explaining their objections; that statement must then be placed with or attached to the contested information.[39] The parent's rebuttal or qualifying statement must be maintained with the original document for as long as the record or contested portion is retained by the agency.[40]

Destruction of Records

When an agency that maintains personally identifiable information no longer needs the records, it is required to notify the parents. The parents may ask for copies of the file, or may simply request that it be destroyed. The agency must then destroy the information, but may retain a permanent record of the student's name, address, telephone number, grades, attendance record, classes attended, grade level completed, and year completed.[41] State statutes and regulations that are not inconsistent with federal regulations may then be followed as to when unnecessary records may be destroyed.

Noncompliance

Where parents are denied the right to inspect and review the records of their child, or if nonexempt third parties are allowed to view a child's record without parental permission, a FERPA violation has been committed, assuming the institution is a recipient of federal financial assistance. As a result, an action by the Secretary of Education may be taken to terminate aid if it is determined that com-

---

[37] 34 C.F.R. § 300.568.
[38] 34 C.F.R. § 99.22(e).
[39] 34 C.F.R. § 500.569; 20 U.S.C. § 1232g(a)(2).
[30] 34 C.F.R. § 300.569(c).
[41] 34 C.F.R. § 300.573.

pliance could not be secured by voluntary means.[42] It is the majority view, however, that no independent private right of action exists under FERPA.[43] The above limitations notwithstanding, suit still is possible under the appropriate portions of the IDEA. In such a case, administrative appeals must be exhausted prior to filing suit in a court of appropriate jurisdiction.

Conclusions

Complaints under FERPA and lawsuits under the IDEA or possibly section 1983 can be easily avoided with regard to student records. School district policy should be direct and clear. The types of records maintained by the district, parental/student rights to access, notice and consent requirements, third-party access, and the procedures used to challenge the content of records should be specified in writing and explained when necessary. Parents need to know where records are kept, how specifically to gain access, and what costs they will incur, if any. "Informed consent" to access, to testing, or to placement cannot be acquired when parents have limited information available to them, or when limited efforts are made to explain records in terms understood by parents.

---

[42] 20 U.S.C. § 1232g(f).

[43] *See* Daniel B. v. Wisconsin Dep't of Pub. Instruction, 581 F. Supp. 585 (E.D. Wis. 1984); Price v. Young, 580 F. Supp. 1 (E.D. Ark. 1983); Girardier v. Webster College, 563 F.2d 1267 (8th Cir. 1977). *But see* Fay v. South Colonie Cent. Sch. Dist., 802 F.2d 21 (2d Cir. 1986) (where a FERPA violation could be the basis for allowing a noncustodial father to bring suit under 42 U.S.C. § 1983 where a school district wrongfully denied him access to the educational records of his children).

Chapter 6
Discipline

Introduction

School officials are responsible for maintaining an environment that is both safe and conducive to learning for all students. Consequently, to carry out this duty, educators must devise, promulgate, and enforce reasonable rules and regulations. Any such precepts are assumed to be established in good faith and to be essential to meet the school's legitimate educational objectives. At the same time, because the obligation of school personnel to oversee student behavior is similar to the task performed by parents as they care for their own children, educators, to some extent, act in loco parentis.

Insofar as the legal construct of in loco parentis presumes voluntary parental consent in granting school officials control over their children during school hours, an inherent conflict arose with the passage of compulsory attendance laws. That is, it is presumed that parents voluntarily consent to subjecting their children to the schools. Yet, conversely, they may be subject to adverse legal consequences if they do not follow the law.[1] It follows, then, in balancing the need of the state to ensure that all of its citizens receive an education on the one hand, and the right of parents to be free to direct the lives of their children on the other, that educators do not, and cannot, exercise absolute control over the lives of students. Moreover, since pupils are "persons" under the Constitution who "do not shed their rights at the school house gate,"[2] they are entitled to equal protection and due process as schools enforce their legitimate disciplinary codes.

Students' rights notwithstanding, when children violate school rules, they may properly be subject to discipline. Among the options available, school officials have the authority to use suspensions, expulsions, transfers, in-school suspensions, and withdrawals from extracurricular programs in dealing with violators. A primary consideration in the application of discipline is whether potential sanctions infringe upon Fourteenth Amendment protected property or liberty interests. If so, a public school student is entitled to procedural safeguards prior to the imposition of a penalty.

The guidelines for student suspensions were, in large part, clarified by the Supreme Court's 1975 ruling in *Goss v. Lopez*.[3] In *Goss*, for the first time, the Court ruled that a student's right to a public education is a protected property interest that may not be withdrawn without minimum procedural due process; furthermore, the student's liberty interest in his or her reputation and good name is similarly protected. The Court held that while short-term suspensions of up to ten days do not require a formal hearing, a student is entitled to an informal conference to guard against the possibility of unfair, mistaken, or arbitrary decisions. During this meeting, the student must be informed of the basis for the allegations and be allowed the right to respond to the evidence. A student may be suspended immediately, without an informal hearing, only when he is a danger to him-

---

[1] *See* DAVID TYACK, THOMAS JAMES, & AARON BENAVOT, LAW AND THE SHAPING OF PUBLIC EDUCATION, 1785-1954 (1987), David Tyack, *Toward a Social History of Law and Public Education,* in SCHOOL DAYS, RULE DAYS: THE LEGALIZATION AND REGULATION OF EDUCATION, 212-237 (David L. Kirp & Donald N. Jensen, eds. 1986).

[2] Tinker v. Des Moines Sch. Dist., 393 U.S. 503, 506 (1969).

[3] Goss v. Lopez, 419 U.S. 565, 581 (1975).

self or to others, or when he causes a substantial disruption of the school environment. However, even where a pupil can be excluded temporarily on the basis of disruptive behavior, the student must be given an informal hearing as soon after the removal as possible, typically within three days.

In *Goss,* the Court established that a student is not entitled to a formal due process hearing for a suspension of up to ten days. The essential elements of a formal hearing (usually applicable for expulsions) include notice, an opportunity to be heard, the chance to present evidence, and a decision on the record by a fair and impartial third-party decision maker.[4] Moreover, students with disabilities who may be subject to discipline have protection in addition to that provided by *Goss.* In fact, in so far as discipline may impact upon their rights to a free appropriate public education, substantive and procedural due process protections are activated. Accordingly, it is necessary and helpful to review the parameters of relevant federal statutes, regulations, judicial opinions, and administrative decisions.

Suspension & Expulsion

Early Developments

Mills v. Board of Education of the District of Columbia[5] is one of the seminal cases concerning the educational rights of children with disabilities. In addition to helping establish some of the basic principles that are now embedded in the IDEA, the court included a reference to the due process rights of students with disabilities since many of the children involved had been identified as having behavioral problems or as being emotionally disturbed. Relying on earlier case law,[6] the court held that the exclusion, suspension, reassignment, or transfer of exceptional students from public schools without afford-

---

[4] For a more thorough discussion of due process hearings, *see* Chapter 2.
[5] Mills v. Board of Educ. of D.C., 348 F. Supp. 866 (D.D.C. 1972).
[6] *See, e.g.,* Hobson v. Hansen, 269 F. Supp. 401 (D.C.S.C. 1967); Vought v. Van Buren Pub. Sch., 306 F. Supp. 1388 (E.D. Mich. 1969); Williams v. Dade County Sch. Bd., 441 F.2d 299 (5th Cir. 1971).

ing them at least a prior hearing or a periodic review thereafter was a violation of the Due Process Clause.[7]

Hearings pursuant to the adoption of the IDEA indicated that Congress was well aware of *Mills* and the need to protect students from improper exclusion for behavior that was a manifestation of their disabilities.[8] Consequently, not long after the IDEA and its accompanying regulations went into effect, a substantial body of litigation involving closely interrelated questions concerning the disciplining of protected students began to accumulate. These cases culminated in 1988 with the Supreme Court's ruling in *Honig v. Doe*,[9] which offered guidance and clarification of many of the concerns surrounding discipline. Although *Honig* is clearly the most significant case to date, several *pre-Honig* cases merit discussion.

Stuart v. Nappi,[10] decided three months after the promulgation of the IDEA regulations, was the first case under its auspices to address the imposition of disciplinary sanctions. The dispute involved the suspension, and recommended expulsion, of a high school student in Connecticut with a history of behavioral problems compounded by her deficient academic skills which were due to a variety of learning disabilities and limited intelligence. After the student was involved in school-wide disturbances, she received a ten-day suspension pending a further hearing based on the superintendent's recommendation that she be expelled for the remainder of the school year.

The student and her mother successfully enjoined the district's attempt to expel her from school. The court ruled that while educators may take swift disciplinary action against a disruptive student by such means as a short-term suspension of up to ten days, which is not considered a change in placement,[11] they are prohibited from using

---

[7] Furthermore, although Pennsylvania Ass'n for Retarded Children v. Pennsylvania, 334 F. Supp. 1257 (1971), 343 F. Supp. 279 (1972) was concerned with children who were mentally retarded, some also were described as hard to handle.

[8] *See* S. REP. NO. 168, 94th Cong., 1st Sess. at 6 (1975). *See also* Honig v. Doe, 484 U.S. 305, 324 (1988).

[9] Doe *ex rel.* Gonzales v. Maher, 793 F.2d 1470 (9th Cir. 1986), *aff'd as modified sub. nom.* Honig v. Doe, 484 U.S. 305 (1988).

[10] Stuart v. Nappi, 443 F. Supp. 1235 (D. Conn. 1978).

[11] *See also* Board of Educ. of Peoria v. Illinois State Bd. of Educ., 531 F. Supp. 148 (C.D. Ill. 1982) (where the suspension of an eleventh grade student with a learning disability for five days for intolerable verbal abuse of a teacher was upheld *Goss* procedures were followed).

the expulsion proceedings to alter the placement of a disruptive student with a disability. Moreover, in holding that students with disabilities are neither immune from discipline nor have a right to participate in programs if they misbehave, the court noted that as long as school officials comply with the procedural due process provisions within the IDEA, they can initiate an IEP meeting to request a change in the placement of a child who is disruptive.[12]

Almost two years later, in *Sherry v. New York State Education Department*,[13] another federal district court examined the indefinite suspension of a child from a residential state school for the blind who was deaf, blind, and suffered from brain damage and an emotional disorder that made her self-abusive. As a result of injuries that she inflicted upon herself, the child was hospitalized for medical treatment. Eight days later, the Superintendent of the school notified the mother that her daughter would not be able to return to the school until such time as her condition improved or more staff was hired. The following week, the superintendent informed the student's mother that her daughter would be formally suspended if she insisted on the child's return to the school. When the school refused to return the student to her residential placement, the mother brought suit for injunctive and declaratory relief. After another eight

---

[12] *See also* Concerned Parents and Citizens for the Continuing Educ. at Malcolm X (PS 79) v. New York City Bd. of Educ., 629 F.2d 751 (2d Cir. 1980), *cert. denied*, 449 U.S. 1078 (1981) (the transfer of a child from one school to another was not a change of placement); Doe v. Koger, 480 F. Supp. 225 (N.D. Ind. 1979) (a district may transfer a disruptive student to an appropriate, more restrictive environment but, under the IDEA, may not expel such a student whose disability gives rise to the disruptive behavior); Victoria L. *ex rel.* Carol A. v. District Sch. Bd., 741 F.2d 369 (11th Cir. 1984) (affirming the denial of an injunction that would have prevented the transfer of a student with a mild learning disability from a high school to a more restrictive placement in an alternative learning center); Jackson v. Franklin County Sch. Bd., 765 F.2d 535 (5th Cir. 1985) (refusing to order a district to readmit a student with a learning disability who had been assigned to a state hospital after he had engaged in inappropriate sexual conduct with female classmates; in light of his disruptive behavior, the court agreed that the district's proffered placement in a private school was more appropriate). However, the Fifth Circuit later ruled that the district violated the student's rights to due process under both the IDEA and the Fourteenth Amendment when it refused to provide him with notice and a hearing concerning his continued exclusion from public school. Jackson v. Franklin County Sch. Bd., 806 F.2d 623 (5th Cir. 1986).

[13] Sherry v. New York State Educ. Dep't, 479 F. Supp. 1328 (W.D.N.Y. 1979).

days, the Superintendent advised the mother that her daughter could return to the school in four days.

The court rejected the school's defense of mootness and ruled on the merits of the case. It held that the child's initial eight-day, short-term suspension on an emergency basis was not a change of placement. However, it also concluded that the superintendent's decision to suspend the child indefinitely amounted to an impermissible change of placement absent a hearing before an impartial third-party decision maker.

The earliest post-IDEA federal appellate court ruling, and leading case on point prior to *Honig*, is *S-1 ex rel. P-1 v. Turlington*.[14] At issue in *Turlington* was whether a school's attempted expulsion of nine children with disabilities who had engaged in a variety of misbehaviors was a violation of the children's rights. Affirming in favor of the students, the Fifth Circuit laid out three important principles. First, consistent with the earlier trial court rulings on point, it held that a child with a disability cannot be expelled for misbehavior that is a manifestation of his or her disabling condition. Second, it ruled that the burden of determining whether a child's behavior is a manifestation of his or her disability rests upon the school and that this decision must be made by an individual or a group of individuals who have the requisite expertise to reach such a decision. Third, it concluded that even though a student may be expelled from school if his or her behavior is not a manifestation of a disability, the school could not terminate all educational services.

Although the above cases were helpful to practitioners in formulating the rights of students with disabilities, the impact of the cases was generally limited to their respective federal districts/circuits, since the Supreme Court was yet to rule on a related case. Much judicial agreement, in the midst of some conflict,[15] existed. Thus, it was time for the High Court to help clarify related matters.

---

[14] S-1 *ex rel.* P-1 v. Turlington, 635 F.2d 342 (5th Cir. 1981), *cert. denied,* 454 U.S. 1030 (1981).

[15] For example, courts disagreed as to whether removal for more than ten days constituted a change of placement. *Cf.* Stuart v. Nappi, 443 F. Supp. 1235 (D. Conn. 1978) with Doe *ex rel.* Gonzales v. Maher, 793 F.2d 1470 (9th Cir. 1986).

Honig v. Doe

The issue of disciplining students with disabilities finally came to a head in the Supreme Court's 1988 ruling in *Honig v. Doe*.[16]   In *Honig*, two students with emotional disabilities received indefinite suspensions pending their expulsions for violent and disruptive conduct that was disability-related. Both John Doe, who had been suspended for choking another student and for kicking out a classroom window, and Jack Smith, who was removed for a variety of offenses including making lewd comments to female classmates, verbal provocations, hostility, stealing, and extorting money from fellow students, had a history of inappropriate behavior in the schools.

In an opinion that was originally unpublished,[17] the district court permanently enjoined the school district from expelling or from indefinitely suspending any child for disability-related misconduct, and from authorizing a unilateral change in the placement. Additionally, the court not only ordered the district to enact guidelines to deal with the discipline of children with disabilities, but it also directed the state to provide services directly to any children whom the local educational agency was either unable or unwilling to serve. The Ninth Circuit affirmed with minor modifications, agreeing that an *indefinite* suspension is a change of placement in violation of the IDEA's stay-put provision and that the statute did not provide for a "dangerousness" exception. However, the appeals court concluded that a *fixed* suspension of up to thirty school days was permissible under the IDEA.

The Supreme Court affirmed, but modified slightly, the decision of the Ninth Circuit. The first of three issues examined by the Court—whether the case as it applied to Doe, who was then twenty-four, and to Smith, who was then twenty, was moot—arose for the first time during oral arguments. The court held that since the IDEA applied only to children between the ages of three and twenty-one, the case indeed was moot with regard to Doe. It further ruled that

---

[16] Honig v. Doe, 484 U.S. 305 (1988).
[17] The ruling of the trial court was subsequently added as an appendix to the Ninth Circuit's opinion. Doe *ex rel.* Gonzales v. Maher, 793 F.2d 1470, 1496 (9th Cir. 1986).

since there was a reasonable likelihood that Smith's complaint was capable of repetition, yet evading review, the suit was not moot with respect to his allegations.[18]

The Court next addressed the merits of Smith's case by reviewing the "stay-put" provision of the IDEA. It construed the language of the statute, which mandates that a child remain in his or her then current placement pending any proceedings to change the placement,[19] as prohibiting a school from unilaterally excluding a child with a disability from a classroom for dangerous or disruptive behavior caused by the disability. In its discussion, the Court clearly and unequivocally rejected the suggestion of Bill Honig, California's Superintendent of Public Education, that a dangerousness exception ought to be read into the law.[20] Instead, it reasoned that Congress clearly sought to strip school officials of the unilateral authority they traditionally had exercised to exclude students, especially those with emotional disabilities, because even an emergency exception for dangerous students was conspicuously absent from the IDEA. The Court maintained that this omission was intentional. Accordingly, the Court did not believe that it was "at liberty to engraft onto the statute an exception Congress chose not to create."[21]

Despite its refusal to redraft the IDEA, the Court hastened to add that its decision did not leave educators powerless. In fact, the Court explicitly pointed out that school officials were free to continue using normal disciplinary procedures when dealing with students who endangered themselves or others. The Court made specific reference to the use of study carrels, time-out,[22] detention, the restriction of privileges, and even short-term suspensions of up to ten days. Moreover, the majority noted that its decision not only allowed educators promptly to remove students who were most dangerous, but it

---

[18] *Contra* Honig v. Doe, 484 U.S. 305, 332 (1988) (Scalia, J. dissenting).

[19] 20 U.S.C. § 1415(e)(3).

[20] *See* Jackson v. Franklin County Sch. Bd., 765 F.2d 535, 538 (5th Cir. 1985); Victoria L. v. District Sch. Bd. of Lee County, Fla., 741 F.2d 369, 374 (11th Cir. 1984); S-1 *ex rel.* P-1 v. Turlington, 635 F.2d 342, 348, n.9 (5th Cir. 1981), *cert. denied,* 454 U.S. 1030 (1981).

[21] Honig v. Doe, 484 U.S. 305, 325 (1988).

[22] For a more recent case, *see* Hayes *ex rel.* Hayes v. Unified Sch. Dist. No. 377, 877 F.2d 809 (10th Cir. 1989) (since placing a child in a time-out room for an in-school suspension fell within the purview of the IDEA, parents were required to exhaust administrative remedies before filing suit on other causes of action).

also provided a cooling off period during which they could initiate IEP reviews and/or negotiate changes of placement with the children's parents. Finally, the Court noted that schools, which would bear the burden of proof as to the need to circumvent the requirement to exhaust administrative remedies,[23] could seek judicial relief to change the placement of a child who presented a real threat.[24] The Court thus opined that since the lower courts properly balanced the needs of the students against those of the schools, it would affirm the judgment of the Ninth Circuit. However, it ruled that a suspension in excess of ten days constituted a change of placement, thereby striking that part of the Ninth Circuit decision which held that a suspension in excess of ten school days (i.e., a thirty-day fixed suspension) was not a change in placement.

Turning briefly to the third, and final issue, an equally divided Court affirmed the Ninth Circuit's order directing the State of California to provide services directly to a child with a disability when the local educational agency fails to do so. As a result of the split decision, the order remains good law within the circuit, but not within the country at large.

---

[23] The IDEA also requires parents to exhaust administrative remedies prior to filing suit, unless administrative review would prove futile. *See, e.g.*, Carey *ex rel.* Carey v. Maine Sch. Adm. Dist. #17, 754 F. Supp. 906 (D. Me. 1990) (where the plaintiff failed to exhaust administrative remedies regarding his expulsion for bringing an automatic weapon and ammunition to school); Waterman v. Marquette-Alger Intermediate Sch. Dist., 739 F. Supp. 361 (W.D. Mich. 1990) (where exhaustion was required when parents claimed excessive and abusive discipline); H.R. v. Hornbeck, 524 F. Supp. 215 (D. Md. 1981) (where students were required to exhaust remedies prior to mounting a judicial challenge to the attempted exclusion of students with disabilities).

[24] *See, e.g.*, East Islip Union Free Sch. Dist. v. Andersen, 615 N.Y.S.2d 852 (Sup. Ct. 1994) (where granting a preliminary injunction allowing the district to continue a home-bound placement pending appropriate proceedings for a dangerous student with a learning disability); Texas City Indep. Sch. Dist. v. Jorstad, 752 F. Supp. 231 (S.D. Tex. 1990) (where school officials' request for a preliminary injunction was granted to prevent a student with an emotional behavior disability from attending regular classes and limiting him to behavior management classes, or home care, at his parents' election, where he constituted a severe and on-going threat of imminent danger to himself and others). *See also In re* Thomas W., 560 N.Y.S.2d 227 (Fam. Ct. 1989) (where the IDEA did not divest the Family Court of subject matter jurisdiction in truancy proceedings involving a child who was alleged to have an educational disability).

Remaining Questions

Although in *Honig v. Doe* the Supreme Court clarified several issues related to discipline, a number of significant questions were not addressed.[25] Who is required to determine whether a student's misbehavior is related to his disability? May a child with a disability be expelled (i.e., removed from his or her placement for more than ten days) for behavior that is not a manifestation of his disability? Must any services continue during a permissible expulsion? Are students who have not yet been identified, referred, or evaluated protected by the IDEA or section 504? Does the ADA play a role in future discipline cases? Do cumulative suspensions (in-school or out-of-school) that total more than ten days in a school year constitute a change in placement? May other forms of discipline, such as corporal punishment, be used with children with disabilities? The remaining portions of this section addresses these concerns.

Responsibility for Determining Disability Relatedness. Identifying which party is responsible for assessing whether a student's misbehavior is related to his or her disability can be critical, not only in determining the eventual outcome of the case, but also in determining whether the case is even filed. If plaintiffs were responsible for related costs, it is unlikely that many would seek to vindicate their rights through administrative review, or later through the filing of a suit, even if their rights had been violated. Furthermore, most parents simply do not have either the expertise to perform the necessary evaluations or the financial resources to have them performed by independent professionals. Accordingly, if proving disability relatedness were the responsibility of parents, the procedural protection provided for in federal law would be virtually meaningless. As a result, courts have consistently reached the conclusion that the bur-

---

[25] For a related discussion of the issues involved, *see* Gail Sorenson, *Update on Legal Issues in Special Education Discipline*, 81 EDUC. LAW REP. 399 (1993). *See also* Gail Paulus Sorenson, *Special Education Discipline in the 1990s*, 62 EDUC. LAW REP. 387 (1990); Eugene A. Lincoln, *Disciplining Handicapped Students: Questions Unanswered in Honig v. Doe*, 51 EDUC. LAW REP. 1 (1989).

den of proof is on educational officials, should they claim that a student's misbehavior is not causally related to his disability.[26]

Behavior Unrelated to Disability. The next question asks whether a student may be expelled for behavior that is not a manifestation of his disability. The majority of courts have concluded that expulsion (i.e., the removal from an existing IEP and the provision of home instruction or tutoring)[27] is a permissible option if there is no relationship between the behavior and the disability.[28] However, in practice, these same courts also tend to give every benefit of doubt to the student and have rendered decisions contrary to opinions not just of administrators, but also of IEP teams.[29] Despite the difficulty of proving nonrelatedness, several districts have successfully met the burden of proof at state administrative proceedings. Thus, where school officials showed that students who shot an arrow at a school bus[30] distributed illegal drugs[31] exhibited behaviors that were not disability related, they were able to expel them.

---

[26] *See* S-1 *ex rel.* P-1 v. Turlington, 635 F.2d 342 (5th Cir. 1981), *cert. denied,* 454 U.S. 1030 (1981). For an early state case, *see also* Southeast Warren Community Sch. Dist. v. Department of Pub. Instruction, 285 N.W.2d 173 (Iowa 1979) (where a school district erred in expelling a student without first reevaluating him to consider the appropriateness of an alternative placement). Also, for a discussion of the relationship test, *see* David L. Dagley, Michele D. McGuire, & Charles Evans, *The Relationship Test in the Discipline of Disabled Students,* 88 EDUC. LAW REP. 13 (1994).

[27] Because the total cessation of services for children on IEPs does not appear permissible at this time, the term "expulsion" means the removal of the student from the current IEP; it does not mean the total withdrawal of services. Rather, home instruction or tutoring is substituted for the previous IEP. The student's record, at district discretion, could reflect that the student has been expelled, as compared to simply receiving a change in placement.

[28] For a case discussing many of the issues involved in disciplining students with disabilities, *see* Webster Groves Sch. Dist. v. Pulitzer Publishing Co., 898 F.2d 1371 (8th Cir. 1990) (where a school expelled a 14-year-old student with a disability for bringing a gun to school and threatening another child with the weapon, the youngster's grandmother/legal guardian initiated a challenge to the IEP committee's determination that the student's misbehavior was not a manifestation of the disability; a newspaper covering the story was not entitled to attend courtroom proceedings, to review the file, or to intervene since restricting access would protect the confidentiality of the information under FERPA).

[29] School Bd. of County of Prince William, Va. v. Malone, 762 F.2d 1210 (4th Cir. 1985) (where the student's involvement in drug trafficking was found to be disability related).

[30] *Elk Grove Unified Sch. Dist.,* 16 EHLR 622 (SEA CA 1990).

[31] *In re Child with Disabilities,* 18 IDELR 1318 (SEA MI 1992).

Continuation of Services. An important related question considers the extent to which services must be continued for students with disabilities who have been legally excluded from school. In *S-1 ex rel. P-1 v. Turlington*, the Fifth Circuit held that although a school may expel a student for misbehavior unrelated to his disability, it cannot terminate all educational services. This position was also taken by the Office of Special Education and Rehabilitation Services (OSERS) in its 1989 letter to Frank New, the Director of Special Education for the Ohio Department of Education.[32] Later, in 1991, OSERS reaffirmed its position when it rejected dicta to the contrary in *Doe ex rel. Gonzales v. Maher*[33] and again proposed that even if a student were permissibly expelled, all educational services could not be terminated.[34]

Most recently, the Seventh Circuit, in *Metropolitan School District of Wayne Township v. Davila*,[35] offered further support for OSERS' position. In *Davila*, the court held that a letter from the OSERS (i.e., the New letter[36]), requiring the continuation of services for students who are subjected to long-term suspensions or expulsions, was not a legislative rule requiring notice and comment under the Administrative Procedures Act (APA).[37] Rather, the court found that since Davila's letter was an interpretive rule announcing OSERS' construction of the IDEA, it did not trigger the APA's requirements. The effect of the court's decision was to render the letter valid and binding within the Seventh Circuit upon its release. Consequently, in the absence of controlling Supreme Court prece-

---

[32] *New*, EHLR 213:258 (OSERS 1989).

[33] Doe *ex rel.* Gonzales v. Maher, 793 F.2d 1470, 1482 (9th Cir. 1986), *aff'd as modified sub nom.* Honig v. Doe, 484 U.S. 305 (1988).

[34] *Symkowick*, 17 EHLR 469 (OSERS 1991). *Cf.* Board of Trustees of Pascagoula Mun. Separate Sch. Dist. v. Doe, 508 So. 2d 1081, 1086 (Miss. 1987) (if a student's inappropriate behavior was not related to his disability, school officials may then be responsible for providing educational services during the expulsion period).

[35] Metropolitan Sch. Dist. of Wayne Township v. Davila, 969 F.2d 485 (7th Cir. 1992), *rev'g*, 446 F. Supp. 1331 (S.D. Ind. 1991), *cert. denied*, 113 S. Ct. 1360 (1992).

[36] The letter was from Robert R. Davila, Assistant Secretary of the OSERS to Frank E. New, the Director of Special Education in the Ohio Department of Education. *New*, EHLR 213:258 (OSERS 1989).

[37] 5 U.S.C. § 553 (1994).

dent,[38] it appears prudent to provide services that are consistent with the IEP during an expulsion period for children who are protected by the IDEA.[39] At the same time, it should be noted that neither the Seventh Circuit nor OSERS requires all services identified within the IEP to be continued. Rather, any services that are provided should be consistent with the IEP.

Pre-referral Protection. Assume that a regular education student has violated school rules for the third time regarding both fighting and the use of alcohol on school grounds. Also assume that the student is temporarily suspended from school pending his expulsion hearing which is to take place in three days. The evidence against the student clearly will support expulsion. After reviewing the evidence, the parents may realize that their only hope for keeping their son in school is to claim that his behavior is a disability that went unrecognized prior to this incident. No previous referral had been made, nor had the student been evaluated for having a severe behavior disability or for having an attention deficit disorder or any other disability. Under these circumstances, there appear to be two primary options for educators who are trying to balance their concerns about drugs, alcohol, violence, and costly litigation with the student's rights and needs.

The first option is immediately to reinstate the student until such time as an evaluation has been completed and his IDEA/section 504 eligibility status has been determined. If the student is found to have a disability, and his behavior is shown to be disability related, he would then be provided with an appropriate placement, one specially designed to meet his unique needs. However, if he is found not to qualify for services or statutory protection, or if he qualifies but no relationship is found between the disability and the behavior, he may then be expelled. Note, however, that if the student qualified under the IDEA, services consistent with the IEP should be provided during the period of exclusion.

---

[38] The Supreme Court has not accepted a case on point and chose to deny certiorari in *Metropolitan. See* Metropolitan Sch. Dist. of Wayne Township v. Davila, 113 S. Ct. 1360 (1992).

[39] The rights of children who qualify as disabled only under § 504 are less clear. It appears that based on a memorandum from the Office of Civil Rights (OCR), OCR Senior Staff Memorandum, 3 EHLR 307:05 (1988), students covered only by § 504 may not be entitled to continuing services during an expulsion.

The second alternative is to treat the student as any other regular education pupil. In other words, the administration could proceed with the disciplinary hearing and if it is determined that the student committed the offense, he may be subject to expulsion or to some other appropriate sanction. Even if this option is selected, school personnel must still proceed with the referral and evaluation processes within statutory time lines.[40] If the student is eventually found to be disabled and if his behavior is found to be disability related, he should be reinstated (assuming his expulsion period has not already expired) and provided an appropriate placement. If, on the other hand, his behavior is not disability related, he may be expelled, but, as in the first alternative, services consistent with the IEP should be provided, typically in the home environment. And finally, if he is not found to be disabled, his expulsion would proceed on schedule.

Note that in the second alternative there was no prior knowledge of a disability nor any indication that the district was attempting to avoid providing appropriate services by excluding the student. Had that been the case, a clear violation of the IDEA,[41] section 504,[42] and possibly the ADA would have resulted. A word of caution: in so far as this area of the law is not well-settled, practitioners are advised to seek legal counsel before selecting alternative one, alternative two, or any other locally conceived option.

Cumulative Suspensions. Another area in need of clarification concerns cumulative suspensions. It now appears clear that under the IDEA, the removal of a child from his or her IEP for an aggregate of more than ten days during the school year constitutes a change of placement. If cumulative suspensions of more than ten days represents a "pattern of suspension," then section 504 may also have been violated.[43] In spite of the above, questions still remain: Do in-school suspension days count toward the ten-day total? Does the ten-day limitation begin anew following a change of placement, or is the number fixed for the school year?

---

[40] *See* Alvord Unified Sch. Dist., 17 EHLR 1021 (SEA CA 1990).

[41] Hacienda La Puente Unified Sch. Dist. v. Honig, 976 F.2d 467 (9th Cir. 1992).

[42] For cases involving § 504, *see Lumberton (MS) Pub. Sch. Dist.,* 18 IDELR 33 (OCR 1991); *Ohio County (KY) Sch. Dist.,* 17 EHLR 528 (OCR 1990); *Mineral County (NV) Sch. Dist.,* 16 EHLR 668 (OCR 1990).

[43] *OCR Memorandum,* 14 EHLR 307:05 (1988).

First, the IEP should help determine whether in-school suspension days may be counted toward the ten permitted prior to a change of placement. If the IEP allows for the in-school removal of the student from his or her regular classroom (typically in time-out or an alternative learning center) no change of placement is to have likely occurred. Conversely, if the student is removed only as a form of discipline and is not provided services consistent with the IEP, a change of placement will occur once the aggregate number of days for in-school[44] plus out-of-school[45] suspension surpasses ten. The key, then, is not whether the child is removed from school, but whether he or she has been withdrawn from his or her IEP.[46]

Second, the issue of whether the ten-day clock begins anew following each change of placement must be considered. Again, little direction has been provided by the courts or the legislature. The Office of Special Education Programs (OSEP), in an opinion letter to the Kansas State Department of Education, stated that under the IDEA, the ten-day suspension clock is re-set following a change in placement.[47] But, if a district changes the placement only to permit additional suspension days, a pattern of exclusion could exist that would violate the IDEA and section 504. As with the above, since this issue is not yet settled and possible scenarios seem countless, local districts would be wise to consult legal counsel when confronted with related matters.

Future Role of the ADA. It is unlikely that the ADA will play a significant role in most discipline cases. Where a student is enrolled in a program operated by an IDEA or other federal fund recipient, the IDEA and/or section 504 will be used as a basis for suit. The

---

[44] *See also* Big Beaver Falls Area Sch. Dist. v. Jackson, 624 A.2d 806 (Pa. Commw. Ct. 1993) (where the continued in-school suspension of a student for more than 15 days after it became clear that she would choose to leave school rather than submit to this form of discipline violated both the IDEA and state regulations as it substantially interfered with her right to a FAPE).

[45] *See York (SC) Sch. Dist. #3,* 17 EHLR 475 (OCR 1990); *Anderson County (TN) Sch. Dist.,* 16 EHLR 760 (OCR 1990).

[46] *E.g.,* where a district imposed an in-school suspension in excess of 10 days, OCR determined that because the pupils involved had been provided with virtually the same educational programs that they would have received in their regular classrooms, their rights had not been violated. *Chester County (TN) Sch. Dist.,* 17 EHLR 301 (OCR 1990).

[47] *Rhys,* 18 IDELR 217 (OSEP 1991).

future role of the ADA, if it is to have one, will primarily be with private schools that receive no IDEA funds, and possibly no federal financial assistance of any type.

The only published case to date involving the ADA concerns a seventeen-year-old high school senior with idiopathic thrombocytopenic purpura (a serious autoimmune disorder) who was expelled for a verbal outburst.[48] She had become "extremely agitated" after she had cut herself and had uttered two expletives during her hysteria. The student's level of anxiety was unusually high because even though her cut was minor, to her it was extremely serious due to her illness and related health problems. Moreover, although not an IDEA fund recipient, the private school was a recipient of federal financial assistance for section 504 purposes and conceded that it was required to make public accommodations within the meaning of the ADA. Accordingly, the court found that the student was otherwise qualified, had been discriminated against due to her disability, and was not provided with reasonable accommodations.[49] As a result, the court held that she was entitled to a preliminary injunction to prevent the school from proceeding with her expulsion.

Corporal Punishment & Other Forms of Discipline

There have been only a few lawsuits dealing with corporal punishment since the practice was upheld by the Supreme Court in *Ingraham v. Wright*.[50] The dearth of litigation is especially apparent when dealing with children with disabilities. The earliest relevant case, *Cole ex rel. Cole v. Greenfield-Central Community Schools*,[51] relied on language in *Stuart v. Nappi*[52] stating that children with dis-

---

[48] Thomas v. Davidson Academy, 846 F. Supp. 611 (M.D. Tenn. 1994).

[49] In the alternative, the school at one time offered the student three options: removal of driving privileges; taking away exam exemptions she had earned as a result of having an "A" average; or taking away her privilege of participating in extracurricular activities. Any of these options would have represented a reasonable accommodation. *Id.* at 619.

[50] Ingraham v. Wright, 430 U.S. 651 (1977). For a general overview of recent developments in the area, *see* John Dayton, *Corporal Punishment in Public Schools: The Legal and Political Battle Continues*, 89 EDUC. LAW REP. 729 (1994).

[51] Cole *ex rel.* Cole v. Greenfield-Cent. Community Sch., 657 F. Supp. 56 (S.D. Ind. 1986).

[52] Stuart v. Nasppi, 443 F. Supp. 1235, 1243 (D. Conn. 1978).

abilities are neither immune from school rules nor "entitled to any unique exemption or protections from a school's normal disciplinary procedures."[53] Consequently, a federal trial court held that the civil rights of a child who was hyperactive and emotionally disturbed were not violated when he was subjected to a variety of forms of discipline. The court upheld the school's use of paddling as a last resort, isolation seating (i.e., placing the child/student in an isolated area), and the placement of a one-inch strip of masking tape vertically upon the child's lips (viewed as symbolic rather than punitive physical punishment), because the educators did not treat him any differently than other pupils in the school. In reaching its conclusion, the court reasoned that an "elementary school [should not] be subjugated by the tyrannical behavior of a nine-year-old child."[54]

The first federal appellate corporal punishment case involving a child with a disability was resolved in a similar fashion. In *Fee v. Herndon*[55] the Fifth Circuit, relying in part on *Ingraham*, held that the alleged excessive corporal punishment of a sixth grade student who had an emotional disability was not a violation of 42 U.S.C. section 1983. The court reasoned that where the child's mother had signed a form permitting the use of corporal punishment, and where the school's reasonable use of the practice did not constitute arbitrary state action, his parents should have relied on remedies available under state law.

In *Waechter v. School District*,[56] a case that borders on the incredulous, parents of a fifth grade boy who suffered from a congenital heart defect, an orthopedic impairment, and a learning disability brought suit where the child died after he was forced to run a 350-yard sprint in less than two minutes for talking in line. Prior to this incident, district officials were aware of his condition, were informed by his doctor that he should not take part in competitive sports, and knew that the recess supervisor who ordered the punishment routinely employed this form of discipline.

---

[53] Cole *ex rel.* Cole v. Greenfield-Cent. Community Sch., 657 F. Supp. 56, 59 (S.D. Ind. 1986).

[54] *Id.* at 63.

[55] Fee v. Herndon, 900 F.2d 804 (5th Cir. 1990), *cert. denied*, 498 U.S. 908 (1990).

[56] Waechter v. School Dist., 773 F. Supp. 1005 (W.D. Mich. 1991).

The parents' claims under the Fifth and Fourteenth Amendments were denied on the ground that a mere lack of care cannot trigger a violation of constitutional proportions. They also were unsuccessful in alleging discrimination based on disability under section 504 because monetary damages were held not to be available in such an action. However, the parents' suit was permitted to proceed on the basis that the school officials failed to provide substantive due process in not taking steps to prevent the recess supervisor from engaging in the practices that ultimately led to the child's death. Although not directly involving corporal punishment, this case should serve as one more reminder for educators to exercise caution when dealing with any form of physical discipline.

Based on these cases, it appears that to the extent that corporal punishment, and other forms of discipline, are not prohibited by state law or school board policy and do not violate the behavior management provisions of a student's IEP, they are permissible, but remain subject to the child's ability to withstand the sanction.[57]

Search & Seizure

In *New Jersey v. T.L.O.*,[58] the Supreme Court upheld the warrantless search of a student's purse by the school's assistant principal and, in so doing, enunciated the rules governing search and seizure in the schools.[59] After holding that the Fourth Amendment's prohibition against unreasonable searches and seizures did apply to public school officials, the Court set out the guidelines under which a search is reasonable, noting that the reasonableness of the search depends upon the context within which it takes place.

---

[57] For an interesting case along these lines, *see* Chris D. v. Montgomery Bd. of Educ., 743 F. Supp. 1524 (M.D. Ala. 1990) (where a school's use of corporal punishment on a student with a disability destroyed his trust in the school's staff and instilled in him a strong desire for revenge, the court used this, in part, to reject the district's proposal that he return to the same placement).

[58] New Jersey v. T.L.O., 469 U.S. 325 (1985).

[59] For recent developments in the area, *see* Joseph R. McKinney, *The Fourth Amendment and the Public Schools: Reasonable Suspicion in the 1990s*, 91 EDUC. L. REP. 455 (1994); Eugene C. Bjorklun, *School Locker Searches and the Fourth Amendment*, 92 EDUC. L. REP. 1065 (1994).

The Court recognized that while a search of a student's purse is a substantial invasion of an individual's privacy, educators have a significant interest in maintaining order and discipline in the schools. As a result, it ruled that school officials are neither required to obtain a warrant before searching a student under their authority nor are they held to the requirement that searches be based on probable cause. Rather, the legality of the search depends upon a two-part test. First, the search must be justified at its inception, based on the totality of the circumstances which led the official to have reasonable suspicion that a student is, has, or is about to violate a school rule or the law.[60] Second, the search must be "reasonably related in scope to the circumstances which justified the interference in the first place."[61]

Eight years after *T.L.O.*, the first reported case, appellate or otherwise, involving the search of a student with a disability was *Cornfield ex rel. Lewis v. Consolidated High School District No. 230*.[62] In *Cornfield*, a seventeen-year-old high school student in a program for youngsters with behavior disorders who was observed as having an unusually large bulge in his pants was suspected of "crotching" drugs. School officials telephoned the student's mother and, despite her refusal to consent to a search, a teacher and a dean took him into a locker room, had him remove his clothes, and visually inspected his naked body. No evidence of drugs or other contraband was uncovered on his person or in his clothes. The mother filed suit under the Fourth, Fifth, and Fourteenth Amendments as well as under 42 U.S.C. section 1983, claiming that school officials violated his civil rights. After the trial court granted summary judgment in favor of the school, the Seventh Circuit affirmed. The court reasoned that, in so far as the educators had reasonable suspicion at its inception and were permissible in scope, the search was valid. Not surprisingly, the court devoted little attention to the student's disability, apparently

---

[60] Among the circumstances to be weighed are a student's age, the seriousness of the charge, the reliability of the informant, and the intrusiveness of the search.

[61] New Jersey v. T.L.O., 469 U.S. 325, 341 at n.7 (1985). For example, the search of a student's book bag might be justified for a hand gun but not for a rifle.

[62] Cornfield *ex rel.* Lewis v. Consolidated High Sch. Dist. No. 230, 991 F.2d 1316 (7th Cir. 1993).

discounting Cornfield's suggestion that he was suspected of being involved with drugs on the basis of his behavioral disorders.[63]

Gun-free Schools Act of 1994

Unfortunately, far too many American public schools will experience a knifing, shooting,[64] rape, or other violent act this year. Many, if not most, high schools will have to deal with drug use, drug sales, fights, and gangs. Students are at times at risk, not only because of disadvantaged backgrounds, but because many schools simply are not safe. Eliminating or at least reducing crime in our schools will, no doubt, be one of the major issues in the coming decade, as it has been in recent years, although so far little progress seems to have been made.

One legislative effort targeted to help reduce violence and return greater disciplinary discretion to administrators is the recent passage of amendments to, and the reauthorization of, the Elementary and Secondary Education Act, Improving America's Schools Act of 1994. As proposed, this Act would have had a profound impact on the stay-put provision of the IDEA and the rights of students with disabilities.[65] The Gun-Free Schools Act of 1994, in relevant part, permitted the forty-five day exclusion from school of any IDEA student who had brought a weapon to school. When expulsion occurred, the child could be placed in an interim alternative educational setting to be determined by the IEP team. Furthermore, if a parent or guardian of the student requested a due process hearing, the child was required to remain in the alternative educational set-

---

[63] For an update on strip searches generally, *see* Jacqueline A. Stefkovich, *Strip Searching After Williams: Reactions to Concern for School Safety?*, 93 EDUC. L. REP. 1107 (1994).

[64] Leffall v. Dallas Indep. Sch. Dist., 28 F.3d 521 (5th Cir. 1994) (where parents unsuccessfully sued following the shooting death of their child which had been caused by random gunfire in the parking lot of a high school after a school dance).

[65] P.L. 103-383, title III [Amendments to Other Acts], Part A [Amendments to the Individuals with Disabilities Education Act] § 314, 108 Stat. 3518 (1994). The motivation for this Amendment came from a situation in California where school officials were unable to expel a child with attention-deficit disorder who brought a gun to school in his car. *See* M.P. by D.P. v. Governing Bd. of the Grossmont Union High Sch. Dist., 858 F. Supp. 1044, 1050 (S.D. Cal. 1994); Lynn Schnaiberg, *E.S.E.A. Gives Schools New Disciplinary Tool,* EDUC. WEEK, Nov. 30, 1994, at 14.

ting during the pendency of any proceeding conducted pursuant to this Act, unless the parents and the local educational agency agreed otherwise. The Act also included an important limitation noting that nothing in the IDEA could supersede its provisions if a child's behavior was unrelated to his or her disability.

The extent to which this Act would have impacted the disciplining of students remains unknown, however, as the Supreme Court recently declared the Act to violate the Commerce Clause.[66] It may require further litigation to resolve this issue because the Act was part of the reauthorization of the ESEA.

Conclusions

In light of the IDEA, its regulations, and a variety of judicial and administrative decisions, the following standards have emerged.[67]

(1) A suspension (i.e., removal for ten days or less) is not a change of placement;[68] an expulsion (i.e., long-term suspension or removal for more than ten days) is a change of placement.[69]

---

[66] United States v. Lopez, No. 93-1260, 1995 WL 238424 (U.S. Sup. Ct. Apr. 26, 1995).

[67] For a related, yet different list, *see* Gail Sorenson, *Update on Legal Issues in Special Education Discipline*, 81 EDUC. L. REP. 399, 409-410 (1993).

[68] *See* Stuart v. Nappi, 443 F. Supp. 1235 (D. Conn. 1978); Sherry v. New York State Educ. Dep't, 479 F. Supp. 1328 (W.D.N.Y. 1979); Board of Educ. of Peoria v. Illinois State Bd. of Educ., 531 F. Supp. 148 (C.D. Ill. 1982). *See also* Mrs. A.J. v. Special Sch. Dist. No. 1, 478 F. Supp. 418 (D. Minn. 1979) (where an eighth grader, who had not yet been evaluated for special education under the EHA, had no cause of action under 42 U.S.C. § 1983 for receiving three consecutive five-day suspensions; however, her suspensions were unlawful pursuant to state law); Reineman v. Valley View Community Sch. Dist. # 365-U, 527 F. Supp. 661 (N.D. Ill. 1981) (the 10 day suspension of a student who had not yet been classified as having a disability under the EHA).

[69] *See* Howard S. v. Friendswood Indep. Sch. Dist., 454 F. Supp. 634 (S.D. Tex. 1978) (preliminary injunction to a student who had been expelled in violation of § 504 and the Fourteenth Amendment); Kaelin v. Grubbs, 682 F.2d 595 (6th Cir. 1982) (where an expulsion was a change of placement under the EHA); Adams Cent. Sch. Dist. v. Deist, 334 N.W.2d 775 (Neb. 1983), *modified and reh'g denied,* 338 N.W.2d 591 (Neb. 1983) (where the court held that local school officials were prohibited by the EHA from expelling a student whose disruptive behavior was caused by his disability); Lamont X. v. Quisenberry, 606 F. Supp. 809 (S.D. Ohio 1984) (that while a district may temporarily suspend a violent and disruptive

(2) A student with a disability cannot be unilaterally expelled from school for misbehavior that is a manifestation of his or her disability.

(3) The burden of determining that a child's behavior is not a manifestation of the disability rests upon the school.

(4) The IDEA does not recognize a dangerousness exception to permit the unilateral expulsion of a child with a disability.

(5) Even when a student may be expelled from school for behavior that is not a manifestation of his disability, a school must still provide services consistent with the IEP.

(6) Cumulative and indefinite suspensions exceeding ten days result in a change of placement.

(7) In-school suspension days may count toward the ten-day cap unless provisions are made within the IEP to allow such removal, or unless services continue to be provided during the in-school suspension (i.e, actually a varnation of time-out rather than in-school suspension.

(8) At this time it appears that the ten-day cap begins anew following each change in placement, unless some form of bad faith is shown to exist.

(9) Subject to state law, board policy, or a student's IEP, corporal punishment, other forms of discipline, and searches of the person or possessions of a student with a disability are legal to the same extent that other pupils may be subjected to these measures.

---

student, once the expulsion exceeds 10 days it is a change of placement); School Bd. of Prince William County v. Malone, 762 F.2d 1210 (4th Cir. 1985) (an expulsion was a change of placement for a student involved in the distribution of drugs); Doe *ex rel.* Gonzales v. Maher, 793 F.2d 1470 (9th Cir. 1986), *aff'd as modified sub. nom.* Honig v. Doe, 484 U.S. 305 (1988) (disability related conduct, even if dangerous or disruptive, did not justify the unilateral removal of an EHA-protected student); Doe v. Rockingham County Sch. Bd., 658 F. Supp. 403 (W.D. Va. 1987) (that the district was not allowed to place a student in a lengthy disciplinary suspension pending an administrative hearing).

In sum, educators should give serious consideration to these standards and, in establishing discipline policies for students, regardless of whether they have disabilities, officials should weigh the school's need to maintain a safe and orderly learning environment against pupils' rights to be free from unreasonable disciplinary sanctions.

Chapter 7
Minimum Competency Testing

Introduction

The publication of *A Nation at Risk* more than a decade ago[1] has not only led to widespread calls for reform but has also spawned a great deal of criticism of the American public education system. Parents, politicians, and policy makers are chagrined by poor student performances on standardized tests, by the inadequate writing and speaking skills displayed by many high school graduates, and by the perception that the curriculum is inundated with frills at the expense of the basics.[2] Business, industry, and even the military often require new personnel or recruits to complete special training because their prior education was insufficient.[3] Moreover, many states (e.g., Ohio, Wisconsin) are considering vouchers and additional private school support to provide more families with options other than public schools.[4] In response to these concerns over public education, there

---

[1] NATIONAL COMMISSION FOR EXCELLENCE IN EDUCATION, A NATION AT RISK: THE IMPERATIVE FOR EDUCATION REFORM (1983).

[2] For an overview of how public schools are viewed, *see* Stanley M. Elam, Lowell C. Rose, and Alec M. Gallup, *The 25th Annual Phi Delta Kappa/ GALLUP POLL of the Public's Attitudes Toward the Public Schools*, 75 PHI DELTA KAPPAN 98, 137 (1993).

[3] For a brief discussion of these and related issues, *see* Jonathan Weisman, *Skills in the Schools: Now It's Business' Turn*, 74 PHI DELTA KAPPAN 367 (1993).

[4] Expect this trend to continue over the remaining portion of this decade, given the overwhelming Republican victory in the November 1994 elections. Many incumbent Governors, like George Voinovich in Ohio, who support "educational choice" will now have legislative support to effectuate change (e.g., vouchers, tax credits, tax deductions). For a discussion of choice as it impacts upon special education, *see* Joseph R. McKinney, *Special Education and Parental Choice: Oxymoron in the Making*, 76 EDUC. L. REP. 667 (1992).

have been increasing demands for improved student assessment, the establishment of higher standards, and the provision of quality (if not excellent) programs.[5] One of the more controversial legislative and administrative responses to the call for accountability and improvement has been the development and use of minimum competency tests (MCTs).[6] Such tests were commonly used in the 1970s in response to "accountability" and became almost universal in the 1990s.

Supporters of MCTs offer several related arguments to buttress their position.[7] Some of these arguments are that MCTs: restore meaning to a high school diploma rather than having graduation determined by a mere measure of "seat time;" establish explicit standards needed to combat social promotion; help in diagnosing student weaknesses and in prescribing learning experiences; ensure that students attain minimum proficiency; provide an incentive to learn; give the public a standard to assess the efficacy of schools; and improve the image of public education. Critics of MCTs, on the other hand, raise a number of cautions.[8] Included among their concerns are: the unsound psychometric practice of basing a decision on a single variable; the use of test items that may not be adequately covered in the curriculum; the subjective nature of establishing minimum scores; the likelihood that teachers will tend to teach the content of the test and thereby narrow the curriculum; the excessive cost of test devel-

---

[5] One need only take a quick look at leading educational journals to see how much attention is devoted to this important topic. For example, in a two-year period three issues of *Educational Leadership* were themed "The Quest for Higher Standards" (Feb. 1991), "Using Performance Assessment (May 1992), and "The Challenge of Higher Standards" (Feb. 1993).

[6] At least 28 states have statutes allowing or requiring minimum competency testing of students: Arizona, Arkansas, California, Colorado, Connecticut, Delaware, Florida, Illinois, Indiana, Kansas, Kentucky, Louisiana, Maryland, Minnesota, Mississippi, Missouri, New Jersey, New Mexico, North Carolina, Ohio, Oklahoma, Rhode Island, South Carolina, Tennessee, Texas, Virginia, Washington, and Wisconsin. *See* JAMES A. RAPP, 4 EDUCATION LAW Table T4A (1993). For a general discussion of MCTs, *see* Peter W. Airasian, *Symbolic Validation: The Case of State-Mandated, High Stakes Testing,* 10 EDUC. EVALUATION & POLICY ANALYSIS 251, 310 (1988). *See also* Jackie Vaughn, *State Mandated Competency Testing: Can it Meet Fourteenth Amendment Standards?* 1988 DET. C.L. REV. 17 (1988).

[7] *See, e.g.,* W. James Popham, *The Merits of Measurement-Driven Instruction,* 68 PHI DELTA KAPPAN 650, 679 (1987).

[8] *See, e.g.,* Gerald W. Bracey, *Measurement-Driven Instruction: Catchy Phrase, Dangerous Practice,* 68 PHI DELTA KAPPAN 650, 683 (1988).

opment, administration, and grading; the practice of identifying the student as the person solely responsible for academic deficiencies; and the disproportionate impact MCT-based diploma sanctions have on minority students and students with disabilities.[9]

In examining related cases, courts have considered four primary issues: whether a state or school district has the authority to use MCTs to deny or to adversely affect a property right (e.g., promotion from grade to grade, receipt of a diploma and the provision of differentiated diplomas and certificates of attendance); whether impermissible discrimination results from the use of test scores; whether test reliability and validity are legally required; and whether adequate notice has been given students to prepare for the tests.

State Authority

The plenary power of the state over public education has long been acknowledged by the courts.[10] Clearly, a state has a legitimate interest in improving public schools and in ensuring the value and credibility of a high school diploma. Concomitantly, a state is free to establish educational policy regarding exit criteria, the curriculum, and matters of pedagogy.[11] When challenges are raised, the courts generally are reluctant to intervene in educational affairs and show great deference to the expertise of professional educators unless school policies or decisions are arbitrary.[12] There are several related reasons why judges are reluctant to act in matters related to instructional policy: they acknowledge that their involvement may encumber the operation of schools and may deteriorate many beneficial aspects of the student-teacher relationship; they realize that they are

---

[9] Steven Schriber, Case Comment, *High School Exit Tests and the Constitution: Debra P. v. Turlington*, 41 Ohio St. L.J. 1113, 1116-8 (1980); Mary G. Commander, Comment, *Minimum Competency Testing: Education or Discrimination*, 14 U. Rich. L. Rev. 769, 772-3 (1980).

[10] *See, e.g.*, Brown v. Board of Educ., 447 U.S. 483, 493 (1954) (reasoning that "education is perhaps the most important function of state and local governments . . . .").

[11] *See, e.g.*, Swany v. San Ramon Valley Unified Sch. Dist., 720 F. Supp. 764 (N.D. Cal. 1989) (holding that school officials acted reasonably when they withheld a diploma from a student who had not turned in logs to show his completion of an independent study in physical education).

[12] *See, e.g.*, James v. Board of Educ. of N.Y., 397 N.Y.S.2d 934 (1977).

unqualified to deal with many of the more technical areas of education (e.g., student assessment, IEP development, program evaluation); they understand that judicial involvement through litigation may encourage the filing of a myriad of related complaints; and they are concerned that judicial intervention may usurp the authority of legislatures and educators to design educational policies, standards, and requirements.

Many courts dealing with MCT issues have had "nothing but praise"[13] for efforts to improve the quality of education. In recognizing the authority of school officials to establish appropriate performance criteria, an intermediate appellate court in New York observed that the establishment of "a standard that would make a high school diploma . . . a meaningful credential . . . [was] clearly within the authority and power of [the board]."[14] Similarly, the Seventh Circuit ruled that a "[s]chool [d]istrict's desire to ensure the value of its diploma by requiring graduating students to attain minimal skills is admirable and the courts will interfere with educational policy decisions only when necessary to protect individual statutory or constitutional rights."[15] Likewise, a district court in Texas reasoned that citizens "have a right to expect that a high school diploma is not a meaningless piece of paper."[16] In sum, federal and state courts overwhelmingly recognize the rights of states to develop reasonable means, including MCTs, to determine the effectiveness of their educational programs with respect to all students to whom they issue a diploma.[17]

Discrimination

As a group, students with disabilities tend to perform less well on MCTs than students who do not have disabilities and are more often

---

[13] *See, e.g.,* Debra P. *ex rel.* Irene P. v. Turlington, 644 F.2d 397, 402 (5th Cir. 1981).

[14] Board of Educ. of Northport-East Northport Union Free Sch. Dist. v. Ambach, 458 N.Y.S.2d 680, 684 (App. Div. 1982).

[15] Brookhart v. Illinois State Bd. of Educ., 697 F.2d 179, 182 (7th Cir. 1983).

[16] Williams v. Austin Indep. Sch. Dist., 796 F. Supp. 251, 256 (W.D. Tex. 1992).

[17] *See, e.g.,* Brady v. Turlington, 373 So. 2d 1164 (Fla. Dist. Ct. App. 1979). For a more recent case, *see* Rankins v. Louisiana State Bd. of Elementary and Secondary Educ., 637 So. 2d 548 (La. Ct. App. 1994) (upholding the authority of the state board to require students to pass a graduate exit examination before obtaining a state high school diploma).

ineligible for a diploma or promotion. As a result, students have claimed that they were discriminated against in violation of the Equal Protection Clause and/or section 504. However, complaints under the IDEA are generally inappropriate, given that MCTs do not affect a student's opportunity to acquire a FAPE.[18]

Fourteenth Amendment

Depending upon the facts surrounding a particular claim under the Fourteenth Amendment, the standards of either intent or rational basis could apply. For example, where MCTs are used as a basis for promotion or diploma denial, any resulting disparate impact or alleged discrimination would be facially neutral, rather than facially discriminatory, and the appropriate standard would be intent. In contrast, if students with disabilities were denied opportunities to take MCTs, or if the testing conditions were not modified to accommodate their physical limitations, such practices would facially discriminate and would require the application of rational basis scrutiny.[19] To date, no state has been found liable of intentional discrimination in its use of MCTs, while claims of failure to accommodate are more likely filed under section 504, rather than the Fourteenth Amendment.

Section 504

Claims under section 504 for MCT-based discrimination are also rare for two primary reasons. First, students with disabilities are not required to take the tests in many states, and therefore are not retained in a particular grade or denied a standard diploma. Accordingly, they lack standing absent any form of discrimination or the loss of a property interest (i.e., they would be unable to show that

---

[18] The above notwithstanding, it is possible for the IDEA to be the basis of an MCT suit where the parents demand that the IEP be based upon the content of the competency test—rather than student ability and need—and administrative review has been exhausted.

[19] Rational basis scrutiny was applied in Rankins v. Louisiana State Bd. of Elementary and Secondary Educ., 637 So. 2d 548 (La. Ct. App. 1994); however, disability issues were not involved. Rather, a claim that exempting students in nonpublic schools, students in home schools, and persons acquiring general education development diplomas from taking the state graduate exit examination was discriminatory was denied.

they were victims of discrimination simply because they were identified as being in need of remedial assistance). Second, in those states where taking the test is prerequisite to receiving a diploma, students with disabilities who fail the test are often unable to qualify as "otherwise qualified," given that they are unable to meet state and district requirements even with reasonable accommodations.[20] Moreover, educational institutions are not required to lower or substantially modify their standards to accommodate students with disabilities;[21] although physical disabilities must be accommodated (e.g., the administration of a test in braille to a person with vision impairment), while tests may not reflect a student's impaired sensory, manual, or speaking skills. Furthermore, if the student has specific learning disabilities, test directions may need to be read to him or her, or additional time may be allowed for completion. However, tests need not be validated to each IEP (or section 504 service plan for students who do not qualify under the IDEA), although they must have demonstrated reliability and validity in regard to the mainstream curriculum.

Reliability and Validity

Once it is determined that a state has the authority to require students to pass a competency test prior to graduation or promotion, it is necessary to develop or select a test with acceptable levels of reliability and validity. Absent such psychometric qualities, an instrument may not accurately measure the desired skill or knowledge; rather, it may reflect varying degrees of error in addition to any true measure of achievement or aptitude.

Reliability is the accuracy or precision of the measuring instrument; the less error in the measurement, the greater the reliability. Lacking reliability, relations between variables cannot be measured accurately and, therefore, results are not dependable either as a stan-

---

[20] For a discussion of related issues, *see* S.E. Philips, *Testing Condition Accommodations for Disabled Students*, 80 EDUC. L. REP. 9 (1993).

[21] For example, to alter the content of an MCT has been ruled to be a substantial modification, and has not been mandated by either the legislature or the courts. *See* Brookhart v. Illinois State Bd. of Educ., 697 F.2d 179, 184 (7th Cir. 1983).

dard for graduation or as a guide for remediation.[22] High reliability is not a guarantee of useful test results (other factors such as validity must be considered), but without it, there can neither be dependable results nor defensible use of test scores where either property or liberty rights are implicated.[23] On the other hand, if a test has validity, it measures what it purports to measure (e.g., I.Q., math achievement, literacy, abstract reasoning).

There are numerous types of validity depending upon the inferences drawn from test scores. The type of validity mentioned above, instructional validity, is a form of content validity and is of particular importance to this discussion—it is a gauge of whether educators are providing instruction in the areas measured by the test. Establishing instructional validity does not require educators to expose students to the exact questions of a test. Rather, it mandates that students have the opportunity to acquire the skills, and that they be exposed to the information and provided with the experiences that will enable them to answer related test items.[24]

Perhaps the most significant ruling regarding reliability and validity is *Debra P. ex rel. Irene P. v. Turlington*,[25] apparently the first case to place the burden of proof for validity squarely upon the shoulders of school officials. The controversy in *Debra P.* arose when African-American students disproportionately failed the Florida assessment test mandated by the state legislature. In prohibiting the use of the test, the court found an implied property right based on the students' reasonable expectation of receiving a diploma if they satisfied attendance requirements and passed required courses. Additionally, the Fifth Circuit rejected the state's contention that the test covered material taught in the classroom, and found the basic skills test to be "fundamentally unfair." The court then concluded that although the

---

[22] For example, if a student were to take an I.Q. test and score say 50, 110, and 70 respectively, the instrument would lack reliability and its results would have no educational value.

[23] For a discussion of reliability, *see,* Chapter 26 in FRED N. KERLINGER, FOUNDATIONS OF BEHAVIORAL RESEARCH (3d ed. 1986).

[24] For a discussion of validity, *see id.,* Chapter 27.

[25] Debra P. *ex rel.* Irene P. v. Turlington, 474 F. Supp. 244 (M.D. Fla. 1979), *aff'd,* 644 F.2d 397 (5th Cir. 1981), *remanded,* 564 F. Supp. 177 (M.D. Fla. 1983), *aff'd,* 730 F.2d 1405 (11th Cir. 1984).

test could be used for remediation, it could not be used to deny a diploma until validity was established.

On remand, the trial court in *Debra P.* found that the school district had established the instructional validity of the test and that there was no causal link between the disproportionate failure rate of African-American students and the effects of purposeful past race discrimination.[26] As a result, the trial court upheld the use of the test. That decision was later affirmed by the Eleventh Circuit.[27]

Similarly, in *Anderson v. Banks,*[28] a federal trial court in Georgia initially struck down the use of the California Achievement Test (CAT). The CAT, used as a prerequisite to high school graduation, was challenged after a significant number of African-American students who had previously attended segregated schools were unable to pass the exam. Applying the standards identified in *Debra P.,*[29] the court found that the school was unable to provide empirical data to support a claim of instructional validity. Consequently, it prohibited the use of the CAT as violative of substantive due process.

Shortly after the initial ruling in *Anderson,* the school district was granted additional hearings based on its contention that it was unaware of the burden of proof established by *Debra P.* As a result, proceedings were held solely on the issue of whether additional evidence would have altered the earlier finding that the school district had not established the CAT to be a fair test. In light of data presented by school officials and by "recognizing the problems of justiciability inherent in judicial review of an academic standard,"[30] the court ruled in favor of the school district. It found that the district met its burden of proof in establishing the validity of the CAT, thereby upholding the future use of valid competency tests to deny diplomas to children who did not perform satisfactorily. Furthermore, it went on to reason that although "very slow learners" would not have been exposed to as many of the CAT objectives as other stu-

---

[26] Debra P. *ex rel.* Irene P. v. Turlington, 564 F. Supp. 177 (M.D. Fla. 1983).

[27] Debra P. *ex rel.* Irene P. v. Turlington, 730 F.2d 1405 (11th Cir. 1984).

[28] Anderson v. Banks, 520 F. Supp. 472 (S.D. Ga. 1981), *modified,* 540 F. Supp. 761 (S.D. Ga. 1982), *appeal dismissed sub. nom.* Johnson v. Sikes, 730 F.2d 644 (11th Cir. 1984).

[29] *Debra P.* was decided on May 4, 1981, the first ruling in *Anderson* was on June 17, 1981, and the second decision was on June 16, 1982.

[30] Anderson v. Banks, 540 F. Supp. 761, 765 (S.D. Ga. 1982).

dents, they would have had sufficient familiarity with the material to be held to the same standards.

In *Board of Education of Northport-East Northport Union Free School District v. Ambach,*[31] suit was brought on behalf of two students with disabilities who challenged the decision of the Commissioner of Education to invalidate their diplomas because they had not passed the required competency examination. Observing that the test was constructed so that the average ninth grade student could answer 80% of the questions correctly, the court rejected the students' unsupported claim that the test was invalid. The court did not require the state to prove the instructional validity of the test because, unlike *Debra P.* and *Anderson,* no prior de jure race discrimination had occurred. Accordingly, the "content validity of the basic competency tests more than adequately [resisted a] challenge on due process grounds."[32] The Court of Appeals of New York affirmed in a brief memorandum opinion.[33]

Viewed collectively, these cases indicate that MCTs are typically upheld as long as their instructional validity in relation to the material taught in the mainstream can be demonstrated. Moreover, validation does not appear to be necessary if a test is used solely for remediation or administrative purposes; however, a nonvalidated test is likely to be struck down where a property or liberty right is implicated.

Notice

The courts are not in total agreement as to whether a property or liberty interest is violated when students with disabilities are denied high school diplomas or are labeled as "certificate recipients," rather than "diploma recipients" due to their failure on an MCT. Where such interests are violated, due process comes into play. Of primary concern is the length of notice that is required prior to the use of a test to differentiate diplomas, to award diplomas, or to permit promotion.

---

[31] Board of Educ. of Northport-East Northport Union Free Sch. Dist. v. Ambach, 458 N.Y.S.2d 680 (App. Div. 1982).

[32] *Id.* at 688.

[33] Board of Educ. of Northport-East Northport Union Free Sch. Dist. v. Ambach, 469 N.Y.S.2d 669 (1983).

In *Debra P.,* a thirteen-month notice was found to be insufficient. The tests in question were used statewide in districts with a myriad of curricular innovations, emphases, methods, strengths, and weaknesses, while little time was provided for remediation between establishing the test requirement and its first administration. The court reasoned that the state had created a property right to a diploma because students were under the assumption that one would be forthcoming if they attended school and completed required courses.[34] Due to the existence of this property right, the Fifth Circuit held that the length of notice provided by the state failed to satisfy the Due Process Clause of the Fourteenth Amendment.

Standing in contrast to *Debra P.* is *Anderson,* wherein a twenty-four month notice was found to be sufficient due to the presumed general applicability of the CAT, the availability of remedial alternatives, and the ease of coordinating activities in a single district. The court did not support the students' position that more time was necessary to master material that should have been learned in earlier grades. It also rejected arguments advanced by the students that because they had been socially promoted without having acquired basic skills, it would be unfair if they were denied "a diploma on the basis of a requirement added at the eleventh hour."[35] The court reasoned that the availability and efficacy of the remedial program, the provision that the test may be retaken, and the motivational value of the diploma sanction supported the district's position.

The *Anderson* court's analysis included the observation that notice becomes constitutionally inadequate only when it renders the rule unreasonable. The court cited *Mahavongsanan v. Hall,*[36] wherein the Fifth Circuit supported a university's decision to deny a graduate student a degree because she failed a comprehensive examination which became a requirement after she had entered the program. In underscoring the fact that the student was given ample notice to prepare for the test a second time, the Fifth Circuit ruled that universities generally are not subject to the supervision or review of the courts in the uniform application of academic standards and reason-

---

[34] Debra P. *ex rel.* Irene P. v. Turlington, 644 F.2d 397, 404 (5th Cir. 1981).
[35] Anderson v. Banks, 520 F. Supp. 472, 506 (S.D. Ga. 1981).
[36] Mahavongsanan v. Hall, 529 F.2d 448 (5th Cir. 1976).

able related regulations.[37] Thus, in *Mahavongsanan,* the court found
the exit requirement to be reasonable and the student's position to be
without a constitutional basis. Similarly, in *Anderson,* the court
found the diploma requirement to be reasonable and the notice to be
adequate. It observed that "[n]o one [can] seriously contend that
academic requirements [can] never be changed during the twelve
years a child typically spends in school."[38]

In *Ambach,* discussed earlier, the Court of Appeals of New York,
noted that the students had neither a reasonable expectation of
receiving a diploma nor were they denied adequate notice since the
regulations impacting on their situation had been in effect for three
years prior to their completion of studies.[39]Furthermore, it concluded that, based on the ruling of the lower court, the students' con-
tentions did not warrant the relief they sought.

Since the Court of Appeals relied so heavily on the ruling of the
Appellate Division,[40] the earlier opinion is worthy of additional
examination. The court rejected the argument that a property or liberty right had been denied to students with disabilities, noting that a
property right exists only when there is a legitimate claim of entitlement. It reasoned that, because the district performed no acts that
would have created such an implied right, and since neither student
was capable of completing the graduation requirements, neither
should have developed an expectation of receiving a diploma. The
court also suggested that the three-year notice was of sufficient
length to permit IEP changes, where appropriate. At the same time,
in the extant case, the court did not find it necessary to alter the students' IEPs because "[n]o period of notice, regardless of the length,
would [have been] sufficient to prepare [them] for the basic competency tests now required . . . ."[41] The court did note that since future
plaintiffs with "remedial handicaps" may have the ability to pass the
examination, they may have property rights that could be compro-

---

[37] *Id.* at 449-50.
[38] Anderson v. Banks, 520 F. Supp. 472, 506 (S.D. Ga. 1981).
[39] Board of Educ. of Northport-East Northport Union Free Sch. Dist. v. Ambach,
   469 N.Y.S.2d 669 (1983).
[40] Board of Educ. of Northport-East Northport Union Free Sch. Dist. v. Ambach,
   458 N.Y.S.2d 680 (App. Div. 1982), *aff'd,* 469 N.Y.S.2d 669 (1983).
[41] *Id.* at 687.

mised. Even where such circumstances are present, however, the court noted that it would be satisfied with a three-year notice.

The *Ambach* court, relying on precedent established by the Supreme Court, also observed that liberty rights are violated only if a stigmatizing statement is false[42] and if it is made public by a governmental entity.[43] Hence, the students' rights were not violated because the district made no public statements and the students were in fact unqualified to receive a standard diploma because they had not met each of the graduation requirements.

In *Brookhart*, the Seventh Circuit provided a rationale contrary to *Ambach*. It ruled that by changing the diploma requirement and by providing only one and one-half years notice for students to prepare for an MCT, the district deprived failing students of both property and liberty rights. Although it was unwilling to define adequate notice in terms of a specific number of years, the court did stipulate that the school district must ensure that students with disabilities be exposed to most of the test material or else show that a well-informed decision was made not to pursue an MCT-based program. In closing, the court observed that due process "is not a right to a diploma . . . , but rather a right to adequate notice in order to prepare for the new requirement. Thus, the appropriate remedy for the denial of this right is an extended period for preparation."[44]

Taken in the aggregate, the above cases suggest that less than a two-year notice (possibly even three) may, under certain circumstances, be insufficient, while three years or more will suffice. Given this persuasive authority, the district court in *Williams v. Austin Independent School District* had no difficulty in determining that the seven-year notice provided in Texas was adequate. Students were periodically informed of the requirements, related information was contained in the high school guide, and teachers frequently discussed the test with their students. As a result, the court denied the plaintiff's request for a temporary restraining order and opined that it respected the principal's decision not to "allow participation [in graduation] by students who failed the [competency test] in order to send

---

[42] Codd v. Velger, 429 U.S. 624, 627 (1977).

[43] Bishop v. Wood, 426 U.S. 341, 348 (1976).

[44] Brookhart v. Illinois State Bd. of Educ., 697 F.2d 179, 188 (7th Cir. 1983).

a message to students that passing the [test] really is necessary in order to graduate and to properly recognize those students who have completed all the requirements for graduation."[45]

Conclusion

In an attempt to be "accountable" and to acquire support for public education, most states have turned to MCTs. These exams serve at least two stated purposes: they help to identify students in need of remedial help; and they assist in restoring credibility to a diploma by expecting high school students to do more than "put in their time." It is within the authority of the state to impose such a requirement, presuming adequate notice has been provided and selected tests have proven reliability and instructional validity. While all students have the right to take the tests in order to qualify for a diploma, school districts need not establish separate standards or prepare individualized tests for pupils with disabilities. Although students working within IEPs may not be exposed to as much of the test material as are students who are exclusively in regular education, assuming it is justified educationally, such a practice has not been found to violate the law.

Parents of children with disabilities are responsible for working with other members of the IEP team as they determine the components of IEPs. They should be made aware of the general content of the tests, where and how they are to be administered, and the purposes for which the results are to be used. Following the evaluation period, and prior to the placement, a decision should be made regarding the appropriateness of including MCT material within the child's IEP. If the committee determines that such content is not appropriate, the parents may always appeal the decision to an impartial hearing officer. To the extent that educators routinely follow these practices, future MCT cases will be less likely to involve children with disabilities.

---

[45] Williams v. Austin Indep. Sch. Dist., 796 F. Supp. 251, 255 (W.D. Tex. 1992).

Chapter 8

Sport Participation

Introduction

Physical education, recreation, and exercise represent essential components to the development, general health, and education of most children. However, some school-aged youngsters, because of disability, are not capable of participating in regular education related activities and, as a result, do not have them incorporated into their respective Individual Education Programs (IEPs). At the same time, most students have the ability to participate in some form of physical education and many even have the skills and endurance to compete in sports.

The IDEA maintains that in providing a free appropriate public education FAPE in the least restrictive environment LRE, appropriate physical education must be made available.[1] Furthermore, qualified students may not be denied the opportunity to participate in non-IEP athletic and recreational activities, including those that are interscholastic and intramural.[2] Yet, such laws and regulations may, at times, conflict with state athletic association regulations (e.g., those regarding age, residency, grades, health, etc.) that were intended to be applied uniformly (i.e., to all students equally).

Over the years, courts have held, with relative consistency, that if athletic association policies related to eligibility are clear and unambiguous, and then are applied uniformly and without exception, they will be upheld. Challenges were generally based on the Equal Protection and Due Process Clauses, and at times included title VI of the Civil Rights Act of 1964 when race was also a factor. In most cases, although not all, such regulations withstood judicial scrutiny. In recent years, however, the issue has appeared again, but this time the controversy centers around federal disability statutes—section 504 of the Rehabilitation Act, the Individuals with Disabilities Act (IDEA), and the Americans with Disabilities Act (ADA).

In an effort to better understand related issues, as well as the rights of student athletes, school districts, and athletic associations, this chapter has been divided into six primary areas: Constitutional Law; Federal Statutes and Regulations; American Medical Association Guidelines; State Athletic Association Bylaws; Case Law; and Policy Implications.

Constitutional Law: Fourteenth Amendment

The Fourteenth Amendment to the United States Constitution states in part that "[n]o [s]tate shall . . . deprive any person of life, liberty, or property, without due process of law; nor deny to any person within its jurisdiction the equal protection of the laws." As mentioned in Chapter 1, public schools are considered part of the "state" for

---

[1] 20 U.S.C. § 1401(a)(16), 34 C.F.R. § 300.307.

[2] 34 C.F.R. § 300.306.

Fourteenth Amendment purposes; consequently, educators are required to treat all classes of persons similarly and to provide proper due process where liberty and property interests may be denied. Where a due process violation is claimed, the courts determine whether the plaintiff had a liberty or property interest at stake; whether governmental action infringed upon such an interest; and whether adequate due process procedures were followed. Student athletes with disabilities who claim violations of the Equal Protection Clause will have rational basis scrutiny applied if the alleged discrimination is facially discriminatory and based on disability (e.g., eligibility is denied because the athlete is absent a paired organ); similarly, if the challenged act is facially neutral (e.g., eligibility is denied because the athlete failed to meet grade-point requirements), then proof of intent to discriminate will be required.

Federal Statutes and Regulations

42 U.S.C. Section 1983

Section 1983 was originally section 1 of the Ku Klux Klan Act of 1871 and is now codified as 42 U.S.C. section 1983. This section stipulates that

> "[e]very person who, under color of any statute, ordinance, regulation, custom or usage, of any [s]tate or [t]erritory, subjects, or causes to be subjected, any citizen of the United States or other person within the jurisdiction thereof to the deprivation of any rights, privileges or immunities secured by the Constitution or laws, shall be liable to the party injured in an action at law, suit in equity, or other proper proceeding for redress."

In the area of athletics, this statute is often used by plaintiffs filing Fourteenth Amendment complaints (due to the availability of attorney fees and damages) when found ineligible to participate in sports by public school districts or state athletic associations. For this law to apply, however, the contested action must be "state action," which typically requires that the actor be "public." But some courts have found private parties (e.g., state athletic associations) to have engaged in state action due to a symbiotic relationship with the state or because they were involved in activities traditionally reserved to the state.

Section 504 of the Rehabilitation Act of 1973

Section 504 states that "[n]o otherwise qualified individual with a disability in the United States . . . shall, solely by reason of her or his disability, be excluded from the participation in, be denied the benefits of, or be subjected to discrimination under any program or activity receiving [f]ederal financial assistance." Among its many regulations is one related to physical education and sport which states that:

> In providing physical education courses and athletics and similar programs and activities to any of its students, a recipient to which this subpart applies may not discriminate on the basis of handicap. A recipient that offers physical education courses or that operates or sponsors interscholastic, club, or intramural athletics shall provide to qualified handicapped students an equal opportunity for participation . . . . A recipient may offer to handicapped students physical education and athletic activities that are separate or different from those offered to nonhandicapped students only if separation or differentiation is consistent with the requirements of § 104.34 and only if no qualified handicapped student is denied the opportunity to compete for teams or to participate in courses that are not separate or different."[3]

For a student-athlete with a disability to succeed under section 504, she or he must (1) qualify as a person with a disability under the Act, (2) be otherwise qualified for the athletic activity, and (3) be excluded from the activity because of a disability. The second of these three requirements is the one most often contested.

Individuals with Disabilities Education Act (IDEA)

As discussed previously in Chapter 1, the IDEA requires recipients of IDEA funds to identify, evaluate, and appropriately place children with disabilities who are in need of special education and related services. Resulting IEPs may at times incorporate sport and thereby trigger IDEA protection for students who are later denied the opportunity to participate for whatever reason (e.g., conduct, grades, residency). Note that this law does not apply to state athletic

---

[3] 34 C.F.R. § 104.37(c)(1), (2)

associations, or to any other entity that does not receive IDEA funds. Therefore, if IEP-based sport participation is denied by a recipient school district based on state athletic association bylaws, the lawsuit typically is filed against the school, not the association.

Americans with Disabilities Act of 1990 (ADA)

Private litigants may sue under the Americans with Disabilities Act as victims of disability-based discrimination by public, private, federal fund recipient or nonrecipient institutions. The definition of disability under the ADA echoes that of section 504, and includes those who: (1) have a physical or mental impairment that substantially limits one or more major life activities; (2) have a record of such an impairment; or (3) are regarded as having such an impairment.

To date, the section of the ADA applicable to sport-related cases has been title III. Title III requires privately-operated public accommodations and services, including inns, restaurants, museums, retail establishments, and private schools, to take actions that are "readily achievable" to remove barriers to individuals with disabilities wishing accommodations.[4] This law was used for the first time in a sport-related case in 1994, where discrimination was alleged by a provider of a public accommodation (i.e., a state athletic association)—see later discussion under "Age Restrictions."

American Medical Association Guidelines

Unlike facially neutral residency or age requirements, school districts also have been charged with screening out athletes based solely on their respective disabilities. For example, an American Medical Association (AMA) publication[5] relating to the evaluation of candidates for school sports,[6] has been relied upon by school physicians

---

[4] For an update on the ADA, *see* Karen Diegmueller, A.D.A., *Sports Clash on School Playing Fields,* EDUCATION WEEK, Nov. 23, 1994.

[5] AMERICAN MEDICAL ASSOCIATION, A GUIDE FOR MEDICAL EVALUATION OF CANDIDATES FOR SCHOOL SPORTS (1972) (revised in 1976).

[6] For a thorough discussion of the AMA standards and related issues dealing with student participation, *see* Matthew J. Mitten, *Amateur Athletes with Handicaps or Physical Abnormalities: Who Makes the Participation Decision,* 71 NEB. L. REV. 987 (1992); Robert E. Shepherd, Jr., *Why Can't Johnny Read or Play? The Participation Right of Handicapped Student Athletes,* 1 SETON HALL J. SPORTS L. 163 (1991).

and administrators. Included within the AMA publication is a list of conditions that the Association considers to be disqualifying for participation in collision, contact, nonconfact, and other sports. In situations where these guidelines are rigidly adhered to, a student athlete could be qualified in spite of his or her disability, yet not be allowed to play.

State Athletic Association Bylaws

Because public education is a responsibility of individual states, each state has the authority to make and enforce rules regarding the scope of its educational programs, including physical education and sports participation. As an arm of the state, the local school board is generally authorized to develop additional rules or regulations to the extent that such provisions are not contrary to state or federal laws. Moreover, states ordinarily permit local districts to organize for sports regulation purposes and to delegate to an independent body the responsibility of making, promulgating, and enforcing rules necessary for the efficient operation of athletic programs. (See Table 8-1 at the end of this Chapter for an example of state athletic association bylaws regulating eligibility.)

State athletic associations include more than public schools, however. Private and parochial schools represent a sizeable minority in many states. Additionally, the organizations tend to be not-for-profit, are sometimes incorporated, and have some type of indirect link with the state department of education (e.g., through nonvoting membership on a state-wide board).

The associations are clearly "private," although there is disagreement as to whether they are involved in state action for Fourteenth Amendment and section 1983 purposes—see discussion under "State Action" below. This issue becomes critical when eligibility criteria are challenged under either the Equal Protection Clause or the Due Process Clause.

Case Law

Federal and state courts have been asked to address a myriad of issues related to the eligibility rights of student-athletes with disabilities. Foremost among these disputes have been those involving the presence of state action (i.e., by athletic associations), age restrictions (e.g., the athlete exceeded age limitations), academic requirements (e.g., the athlete failed to meet grade-point or credit-hour requirements), residency and transfer bylaws (e.g., the athlete moved into a district and wanted to participate in sports without meeting residency/waiver requirements), eight-semester/four season rules (e.g., the athlete failed the ninth grade and wanted to participate for a ninth semester or a fifth year), and health requirements (e.g., the athlete was absent a paired organ or limb, had impaired vision or hearing, or failed to meet other health and safety requirements). Discussion of each of these topics follows.

State Action

Prior to 1982, it appeared that private associations or corporations could be involved in "state" action by virtually having any significant relationship with state government. Examples included the receipt of funds, providing services or regulating practices. In a series of cases in the early 1980s, the Supreme Court made an effort to correct what it perceived to be the inappropriate direction taken by the lower courts.

Foremost among these cases was *Rendell-Baker v. Kohn*.[7] In this case, the Supreme Court ruled that a private school did not act under color of state law when it discharged several teachers after they had spoken out on school-related matters. The Court reasoned that although the school derived most of its funds from the government, the decision to discharge the teachers was not an act of the state; that state regulation did not require the discharge of the teachers; that the private school was not involved in state action, despite the fact that it performed a public service; and that the school's fiscal relationship with the state was not different from that of many contractors performing services for the government. No symbiotic relationship was found to exist, nor was the First Amendment or section 1983 violated.

Since 1982, federal courts have split in their determination of whether interscholastic athletic associations are involved in state

---

[7] Rendell-Baker v. Kohn, 457 U.S. 830 (1982).

action,[8] although the issue apparently has been settled with regard to collegiate sports and the NCAA. The Supreme Court, in *NCAA v. Tarkanian*,[9] held that the NCAA was not involved in state action when a public member institution disciplined one of its coaches, despite the strong relationship between the public university and the NCAA. In fact, Justice Stevens, writing for the majority, indicated that "even if we assume that a private monopolist can impose its will on a state agency by a threatened refusal to deal with it, it does not follow that such a private party is therefore acting under color of state law."[10] Given the above, the issue of state action appeared settled. But then, in note thirteen, the issue was complicated once again when Justice Stevens observed that the "situation would, of course, be different if the membership consisted entirely of institutions located within the same [s]tate, many of them public institutions created by the same sovereign."[11] This comment, although dicta, has led to additional confusion, with some courts accepting it as controlling and others ignoring it altogether.

For example, in *Burrows v. Ohio High School Athletic Association (OHSAA)*,[12] the Sixth Circuit held that the OHSAA was not involved in state action in its promulgation of eligibility requirements. The court noted that the Association was a voluntary, unincorporated, not-for-profit association made up of public, private, and parochial schools; that the NCAA was an analogous organization; and that the

---

[8] *See, e.g.*, Alerding v. Ohio High Sch. Athletic Ass'n, 591 F. Supp. 1538 (S.D. Ohio 1984), *aff'd*, 779 F.2d 315 (6th Cir. 1985) (where the OHSAA was found to be involved in state action); Griffin High Sch. v. Illinois High Sch. Ass'n, 822 F.2d 671 (7th Cir. 1987) (where the court held that the Association, although voluntary and not-for-profit with public and private members, was sufficiently public as to confer state action; Arkansas Activities Ass'n v. Meyer, 805 S.W.2d 58 (Ark. 1991) (where the court held that the Association was involved in state action for the review of constitutional claims). *But see* Burrows v. Ohio High Sch. Athletic Ass'n, 891 F.2d 122 (6th Cir. 1989) (where the OHSAA was found not to be involved in state action). For a related case, *see* Wissel v. Ohio High Sch. Athletic Ass'n, 605 N.E.2d 458 (Ohio Ct. App. 1992) (where the court held that the OHSAA was not a political subdivision within the meaning of state statutes conferring sovereign immunity and that the Association was not allowed to invoke that doctrine on the ground that it was a quasi-government body of the state).

[9] NCAA v. Tarkanian, 488 U.S. 179 (1988).

[10] *Id.* at 198.

[11] *Id.* at 193.

[12] Burrows v. Ohio High Sch. Athletic Ass'n, 891 F.2d 122 (6th Cir. 1989).

OHSAA did not perform a function traditionally reserved exclusively for the state (i.e., several organizations regulated sporting events). Additionally, the court noted that the plaintiffs failed to show that the state-supported institutions caused or procured the adoption of the contested rules. The court cited *Graham v. NCAA*[13] and *Rendell-Baker v. Kohn*,[14] but failed to note *NCAA v. Tarkanian*[15] and the infamous note thirteen.

In contrast, in *Indiana High School Athletic Association v. Schafer*,[16] the court held that the Association was involved in state action in its rule-making and enforcement, and relied in part on note thirteen in *Tarkanian*.[17] In this case, a student requested exemption from the four-fall semesters rule. Due to illness and his resulting poor grades, the student repeated the eleventh grade. However, he was enrolled long enough to have the year count toward his interscholastic sport eligibility. When the association denied his request for exemption, he filed suit under the Fourteenth Amendment and section 1983. The state court of appeals held, in pertinent part that the association was involved in state action and that the four-fall semesters rule was overbroad in its application.

Age Restrictions

Age restrictions have been, and, no doubt, will continue to be, among the more widely contested issues raised by student-athletes with disabilities. Ten related cases have been identified, with varying claims and results. Each case is presented below in chronological order.

The first case was decided in Massachusetts in 1981, *Comstock v. Teixeira*.[18] Here a twenty-one-year old Massachusetts senior was denied the opportunity to wrestle due to his age. The student had Usher's syndrome and claimed section 504 and IDEA violations. The court held that he failed to make the necessary showing for the issuance of a preliminary injunction, since he was excluded because

---

[13] Graham v. NCAA, 804 F.2d 953 (6th Cir. 1986).
[14] Rendell-Baker v. Kohn, 457 U.S. 830 (1982).
[15] NCAA v. Tarkanian, 488 U.S. 179 (1988).
[16] Indiana High Sch. Athletic Ass'n v. Schafer, 598 N.E.2d 540 (Ind. Ct. App. 1992)
[17] *Id.* at 549-550.
[18] Comstock v. Teixeira, No. 81-0355-F, *slip op.* (D. Mass. Dec. 21-22, 1981)

of age, not disability (section 504), and since sport participation was not included in his IEP (IDEA).

The next year a similar decision was handed down in Oklahoma in *Mahan v. Agee*.[19] The State Athletic Association had a rule stipulating that any student who reached his nineteenth birthday prior to September 1 was not eligible to play in interscholastic sports in any member school. The Association supported the rule by arguing that older and more mature athletes could constitute a danger to the safety of younger students, and that an age restriction would reduce the likelihood that an athlete would voluntarily repeat a grade in order to gain an advantage in competition. A nineteen-year-old senior with dyslexia was ruled ineligible. He claimed that, had school officials provided him with a FAPE in the fourth grade when he moved into the district, he would not have been required to repeat the grade and, as a result, would not have later become a nineteen-year-old senior. In rendering its decision, the court noted that school districts in Oklahoma have the authority to join athletic associations which can make and enforce eligibility requirements; that the regulation was reasonable, lawful, and in keeping with public policy; and that if the governing board interprets its regulations fairly and enforces them uniformly, there is no reason for judicial interference. Moreover, the court found that there was no violation of section 504 because the student was ruled ineligible due to his age, not his disability.

Similar decisions were reached in New York and Michigan over the next three years. In New York, in *Cavallaro ex rel. Cavallaro v. Ambach* (1983),[20] an action was brought on behalf of a student who was barred from competing in interscholastic wrestling due to age. The court averred that the student, who had a neurological impairment, was prohibited from participating because he had reached the age of nineteen and that he was not treated any differently than any other student-athlete. Thus, no Fourteenth Amendment or section 504 violation was found to have existed. Likewise, in *Nichols v. Farmington Public Schools* (1986),[21] a state court in Michigan held

---

[19] Mahan v. Agee, 652 P.2d 765 (Okla. 1982).
[20] Cavallaro *ex rel.* Cavallaro v. Ambach, 575 F. Supp. 171 (W.D.N.Y. 1983).
[21] Nichols v. Farmington Pub. Sch., 389 N.W.2d 480 (Mich. Ct. App. 1986).

that the due process rights of a nineteen-year-old student with a hearing disability, who was placed in a grade level below that to which his age cohort would ordinarily have been assigned, were not violated when he was denied the opportunity to participate in high school basketball because State Athletic Association guidelines barred his involvement based on age.

In a second Michigan case, *Cardinal Mooney High School v. Michigan High School Athletic Association* (1989), a student was initially allowed to participate in sports despite his inability to meet age requirements.[22] Involvement in sports was recommended because it would "help improve his self esteem and decrease the likelihood of the need for a more restrictive program."[23] However, the court later concluded that the Association's rules were not arbitrary and denied injunctive relief. During the interim, the student participated in several games for which the Association was going to enforce a penalty. The court held that the student participated initially through court order and that the Association could not penalize the school for permitting the athlete to play.

In 1992, the first decision on behalf of a plaintiff was handed down in Montana. The case was not resolved under section 504 or the ADA, nor did it focus on claims of discrimination. Rather, it dealt with a FAPE and the provision of services consistent with an existing IEP. In *T.H. v. Montana High School Association*,[24] a nineteen-year-old student with a learning disability was allowed to play sports during his senior year in large part due to its incorporation into his IEP as a related service.

Later during that same year, in *Thomas v. Greencastle Community School Corporation*,[25] a student-athlete with a learning disability, who had repeated the second grade, later failed to meet age requirements for interscholastic participation during his senior year. His Fourteenth Amendment claim against the school district and

---

[22] Cardinal Mooney High Sch. v. Michigan High Sch. Athletic Ass'n, 445 N.W.2d 483 (Mich. Ct. App. 1989).

[23] *Id.* at 484.

[24] T.H. v. Montana High Sch. Ass'n, No. CV-92-150-BLG-JFB (D. Mont. Sept. 24, 1992). (Cited in *J.M., Jr. v. Montana High Sch. Ass'n*, 875 P.2d 1026 (Mont. 1994).)

[25] Thomas v. Greencastle Community Sch. Corp., 603 N.E.2d 190 (Ind. Ct. App. 1992).

Association failed, given that the rule met rational basis scrutiny (i.e., it promoted safe and fair competition). It should be noted that neither the IDEA nor section 504 was involved in this case.

The first section 504 decision supporting the rights of post-nineteen-year-old student athletes was rendered in a state court in Texas in 1993, despite the claim that age, rather than disability, was the disqualifying factor and that all policies were intended to apply to all student-athletes. In *University Interscholastic League v. Buchanan*,[26] an interscholastic league had denied two athletes with learning disabilities the opportunity to participate in interscholastic sports due to the over-nineteen requirement that allowed no exemptions or special consideration. The court held that section 504 was violated and that while case-by-case considerations would constitute reasonable accommodation, this would still allow the League to limit the participation of red-shirting athletes or those who had matured to the point of representing a risk to others. Additionally, the plaintiffs were not required to exhaust administrative remedies under the IDEA, because the complaint alleged neither a violation of an IEP, nor a failure to provide a FAPE. Also, the League was not allowed to require the schools to forfeit the games in which the students had participated.

In 1994, two additional student athletes succeeded under section 504 as well as the ADA. In *Sandison v. Michigan High School Athletic Association*,[27] two twenty-one-year-old students with learning disabilities were denied the opportunity to participate in cross-country and track. In an atypical, if not curious, decision the court reasoned that, for section 504 purposes, the private association was an indirect recipient of federal financial assistance since it carried out its functions at some schools where funds were received, and since some coaches were public school district employees. Furthermore, the ADA was ruled applicable because the Association operated a place of entertainment "opened to the public," and because it was "clearly an instrumentality of the state." In light of the above, the court granted a preliminary injunction to the plaintiffs.

---

[26] University Interscholastic League v. Buchanan, 848 S.W.2d 298 (Tex. Ct. App. 1993).

[27] Sandison v. Michigan High Sch. Athletic Ass'n, No. 94-CV-73231, 1994 U.S. Dist. LEXIS 13306 (E.D. Mich. Sept. 13, 1994).

The most recent case, *Pottgen v. Missouri State High School Activities Association,*[28] also involved section 504 and the ADA. Here, an over-aged student-athlete was disqualified from playing baseball, consistent with uniformly applied age requirements. The court held that he made a sufficient showing for a preliminary injunction and reasoned that the Association should provide individual consideration, given the student's academic history and learning disability. Such a requirement would not result in undue hardship or in changes to programs or activities.

Although the majority of cases supports the uniform application of association age requirements, school officials need to confer with counsel regarding the future use of section 504 and the ADA, in light of recent case law. The uniform application of facially neutral age requirements appears to comply with both of these federal laws, while sport participation is typically not an essential component to an IEP/FAPE, thereby reducing the likelihood of an IDEA violation. The typical defense will continue to be that the student is not "otherwise qualified," while the counterclaim will be that recipients (section 504) or providers of public accommodations (ADA) are involved in discrimination and need to provide a reasonable accommodation.

Academic Requirements

Students with disabilities also have claimed a violation of their rights when they have been denied the opportunity to participate in sports due to their failure to meet grade-point or credit-hour requirements. Two cases, one from Texas and the other from Michigan, are summarized below.

In *Texas Education Agency v. Stamos ex rel. Class of All Public School Children,*[29] a "no pass, no play" statute requiring all students to meet academic standards before being eligible to participate in extracurricular activities was held not to have illegally discriminated[30] against students with disabilities. Additionally, the parents failed to

---

[28] Pottgen v. Missouri State High Sch. Activities Ass'n, 857 F. Supp. 654 (E.D. Mo. 1994).

[29] Texas Educ. Agency v. Stamos *ex rel.* Class of All Pub. Sch. Children, 817 S.W.2d 378 (Tex. Ct. App. 1991).

[30] The discrimination claim was in part based on equal protection and substantive due process guarantees in the Texas Constitution.

exhaust administrative remedies under the IDEA, limiting the court's jurisdiction to review related claims.

By contrast, in *Hoot ex rel. Hoot v. Milan Area Schools*,[31] summary judgment was denied to the State Athletic Association in a dispute over a student with a learning disability who had failed to earn sufficient credit to maintain eligibility to play football. The court determined that fact questions precluded summary judgment on claims based on the Equal Protection Clause, the Michigan Handicap-pers' Civil Rights Act, section 504, and the ADA. The student had been evaluated and found not to qualify for services under the IDEA and was later suspended for inappropriate conduct. The superintendent overruled the principal's decision not to offer a day-school schedule for the next fall term, but allowed the student's suspension from the football team to stand (i.e., he was allowed back in school, but was excluded from the team). The superintendent reasoned that the suspension from the team was required by Association regulations which required students to earn twenty credit hours for the last semester enrolled in grades nine through twelve.

Prior to the fall term, a clinical psychologist diagnosed the student as having attention deficit hyperactivity disorder. Following the receipt of this information, the superintendent advised the parents that the district would accommodate their child's disability, if it were substantiated, but that the Association's eligibility decision would be honored. The placement team later confirmed his disability. He was placed on Ritalin, then improved his social relations, and soon became an honor roll student. Given his improvement, school officials supported his athletic eligibility, but their request for a change of status was denied by the Association. Soon thereafter, the present suit was filed.

Although the Association's motion for summary judgment was denied, it cannot be assumed that student athletes with disabilities will not be required to comply with uniformly applied credit hour and grade point average requirements. In the future, related cases are unlikely to involve the IDEA, unless a FAPE is in dispute, and should comply with section 504 and ADA requirements, despite the decision in *Hoot*. Again, however, counsel should be consulted

---

[31] Hoot *ex rel.* Hoot v. Milan Area Sch., 853 F. Supp. 243 (E.D. Mich. 1994).

regarding emerging trends under these two laws (i.e., section 504 and the ADA).

Residency & Transfer Requirements

A third eligibility category is related to residency and transfer. Two cases, one from Texas and the other from Tennessee, are discussed. In Texas, the Executive Committee of the University Interscholastic League (UIL) is the rule and policy making body for most inter-scholastic public school athletic competition. Its policy stipulated that (1) student-athletes who change schools are ineligible for varsity contests if their parents live outside the district; (2) a student living with a guardian is eligible only if the guardianship has existed for one year or more; and (3) where both parents are alive, legal guardianship by others will not be recognized by the UIL. The policy was intended to help limit recruiting abuses and to reduce the competition for high school athletes but, when applied uniformly, could potentially restrict the involvement of students who transferred for reasons other than athletics. There were no exceptions to the policy and no procedures by which individual cases could be given special handling.

When UIL's policy was challenged in *Doe v. Marshall*,[32] the federal district court concluded that the student had a "compelling necessity" for living apart from his parents and a "compelling need" to participate in football, if he ever was to become a "productive happy individual."[33] The court, in ruling under section 504 in favor of the student, reasoned that the district had failed to evaluate and to provide for the student's individual needs. Additionally, the student had persuaded the court that his case had a reasonable probability of prevailing on its merits and that, on balance, the injury he would incur without an injunction would outweigh any possible injury to the district. Given the above, the court enjoined the UIL from bar-ring his participation.

In *Crocker v. Tennessee Secondary School Athletic Association*,[34] a case that was before the courts for over four years, the "individual

---

[32] Doe v. Marshall, 459 F. Supp. 1190 (S.D. Tex. 1978). This case was later vacated and remanded on other grounds, 622 F.2d 118 (5th Cir. 1980), *cert. denied*, 451 U.S. 993 (1981).

[33] *Id.* at 1192.

[34] Crocker v. Tennessee Secondary Sch. Athletic Ass'n, 980 F.2d 382 (6th Cir. 1992).

consideration" preferred in *Doe* was available, but exemption from the Association's transfer requirement was nevertheless denied. Here a student with a learning disability was denied the opportunity to participate in football because he had transferred from a private to a public school without changing residence. He argued that the transfer was made in order to gain access to remedial education programs, not to play football, and contended that it would be discriminatory to exclude him from participation. Furthermore, he proposed that without the remedial services, he would incur hardship. The Association disagreed that hardship would result and denied the requested exemption, noting that its bylaws required that he be declared ineligible for one year.

The district court initially held that the student's rights under the IDEA were violated and enjoined the Association from applying the transfer rule. Moreover, it held that the school district, rather than the Athletic Association, should determine when genuine educational motivations necessitated the transfer. However, this decision was reversed by the Sixth Circuit, due to the plaintiff's failure to exhaust administrative remedies.[35]

In addition to the above litigation, the parents obtained a due process hearing to question their son's IEP. The program prepared by school officials was satisfactory to the parents, except that it excluded football. School officials refused to include sports in the IEP and noted that it would not help the plaintiff's written language handicap. Then, despite what would appear to be appropriate procedures, the administrative judge ruled that the Association had discriminated against the student, but did not rule as to whether interscholastic sport amounted to a related service under the IDEA. However, the Association refused to comply with the decision, arguing that because it was not a party to the hearing, it was, therefore, not bound by the judgment.

As a result of the Association's position, the coach sidelined the plaintiff for fear of reprisal. At that point, the student again filed suit, this time seeking injunctive relief and compensatory and punitive damages of $1.5 million. The court held that the student failed either to state a claim for damages under section 1983 for any violation of

---

[35] Crocker v. Tennessee Secondary Sch. Athletic Ass'n, 873 F.2d 933 (6th Cir. 1989).

his rights under the IDEA or to show that the Association took retaliatory action against him after he filed his original suit.

In light of these cases, it should not be assumed that students with disabilities are exempt from meeting residency requirements. As a general rule, students with disabilities must be qualified in both ability and eligibility. Although in *Doe* the court ruled that the student had a legitimate educational and emotional need to be involved in athletics, such a conclusion generally is provided by an IEP team and not by the court, or a single therapist. However, when a responsible committee concludes that an otherwise qualified student's IEP should include interscholastic participation, it then appears that an exception to the general residency requirement would exist. Nevertheless, even this exception would become less absolute if it were to be proven that the primary factor motivating the transfer was to participate in a particular district's athletic program. Furthermore, where an IEP requires only physical education and not interscholastic participation, it is unlikely that a student's mere "desire" to play, absent a demonstrated "need" to play, would outweigh the necessity to uniformly administer residency requirements. Plus, few IEPs would teeter between appropriate and inappropriate programming, with interscholastic participation representing the decisive weight. As a general rule, such participation is not incorporated into IEPs as it is not typically an essential component to a FAPE.

Eight-semester/Four-season Rules

Of all of the eligibility criteria, the one capping semester and season participation appears least vulnerable to attack, since all students are treated equally and since its application has no relationship to a student's disability. However, one of two courts reviewing related controversies did rule on behalf of a student-athlete who proffered a unique state claim. In *Clay v. Arizona Interscholastic Association*,[36] the Interscholastic Association was found to have abused its discretion in determining that a student who was dependent on alcohol and drugs did not suffer from a "disabling illness or injury," thereby granting his petition permitting him an additional year of eligibility to play high school basketball. The court held that since the

---

[36] Clay v. Arizona Interscholastic Ass'n, 779 P.2d 349 (Ariz. 1989).

Association's act was found to be arbitrary and capricious, it was violative of state laws governing administrative agencies.

A more recent case, and one consistent with those supporting a uniform application, was *J.M., Jr. v. Montana High School Association*.[37] Here, a student who claimed to have a learning disability but who was not participating under a formal written IEP pursuant to the IDEA, unsuccessfully challenged the application of the State Athletic Association's eight semester/four season eligibility rule after he exhausted all of his allotted eligibility. The court reasoned that he had placed the "cart before the horse"[38] given that he had not been pronounced eligible for IDEA services, no IEP had been prepared based on his individual needs, and sport participation had therefore not been included in any type of specially designed program. Yet, he professed to have IDEA-based property rights. Not only did the court disagree with this reasoning, it "strongly encouraged" school districts to be prudent in including sport as a component in an IEP, as they might be "making a promise [they] simply cannot keep."[39]

Health Requirements

In circumstances where a student may be at risk of permanent and severe injury when involved in sports, district personnel routinely ask two related questions: first, will the student's participation place the student or others at risk; second, is the district at risk financially if the student participates and is injured. Students generally respond to such claims by advancing a number of related arguments. The most common positions proposed are that they are sufficiently mature to judge the advantages and disadvantages of participation, or that they have parental consent; that they are otherwise qualified to participate, as defined by section 504; that they and their parents, not the district, should be responsible for making such decisions; and that they are willing to sign appropriate forms stipulating that the district will not be held liable for injuries sustained by the student while participating in the sport. Cases involving disputes of this nature have been brought in both federal and state courts and have included a variety of disabilities and claims. With the exception of a few early

---

[37] J.M. Jr. v. Montana High Sch. Ass'n, 875 P.2d 1026 (Mont. 1994).
[38] *Id.* at 1033.
[39] *Id.* at 1032.

cases, the courts have ruled with relative consistency for the student-athlete.

Impaired Hearing. Only one case has been published regarding the sport eligibility of a student with impaired hearing, *Colombo v. Sewanhaka Central High School District No. 2*.[40] He submitted substantial testimony from a variety of witnesses in support of his athletic eligibility for high school football, lacrosse, and soccer. Included among his witnesses were an administrator at Gallaudet College, who was the president of the International Committee of Silent Sports, a former superintendent of a state school for the deaf, a parent of two children who, although hearing impaired, were currently participating in contact sports, and a noted physician who was chairman of the Committee on the Medical Aspects of Sports of the Medical Society of New York. Furthermore, although the child's doctor reported that he could participate in contact sports if he wore a specially designed helmet, the school's physician warned that, in his opinion, even a small risk was unacceptable because injury could result in a disabling disability. This latter position had additional support from recognized medical publications and AMA recommendations. The court reasoned that although there were conflicting views with respect to whether the student's participation represented a danger to himself or to others, a "determination of an administrative body, made on a rational basis, should not be judicially set aside."[41] As a result, the student was denied the opportunity to participate.

Impaired Vision. Seven cases have dealt with the rights of student athletes with impaired vision to participate in sports. Although there are two early decisions to the contrary, it appears clear that otherwise qualified individuals will be allowed to participate once certain procedures are followed: they and their parents (assuming they are minors) have been fully informed of the risks involved; they have acquired supportive statements from knowledgeable physicians; they have acquired all identified safety wear (e.g., goggles); and they have signed appropriate liability waivers. Moreover, their participation

[40] Colombo v. Sewanhaka Cent. High Sch. Dist. No. 2, 383 N.Y.S.2d 518 (Sup. Ct. 1976).
[41] *Id.* at 521.

must represent a danger to others. This procedure is now law in New York State, the origin of four related high school cases. Three higher education cases also were filed, with student-athletes succeeding in each.

High School Cases. The first related case on point, *Spitaleri v. Nyquist*,[42] was brought in 1973 prior to the enactment of section 504, and involved a New York student with a visual impairment who was medically disqualified from participating in football based totally on his disability, even though he was otherwise qualified to participate. Moreover, he and his parents were willing to sign a waiver of liability. Yet, the court upheld the Commissioner's decision, based on uncontradicted medical evidence, including an AMA recommendation and the opinion of the school's doctor.

Four years later, a similar decision was reached in *Kampmeier v. Nyquist*.[43] Pursuant to New York State statute, and under guidelines promulgated by the Commissioner of Education, two junior high school students, each with vision in only one eye, were denied the opportunity to participate in contact sports based solely on their disabilities. They were denied the chance to participate because the school's medical officer refused to give his consent, as required under state law, to qualify students for interscholastic athletics. Although blindness in one eye was among the conditions identified by the State Commissioner of Education as a disqualifying condition for participation in contact sports, the physician was also required to consider the risks of the particular contact sport in question, the athletic fitness of the candidate(s), the availability of special equipment, possible preventative measures, and supervisory control. As such, the Commissioner's guidelines were only advisory, while decisions had to be based on individual circumstances.

The Second Circuit reasoned that section 504 permits the exclusion of children with disabilities if a substantial justification is present and that public school officials, under parens patriae, have the responsibility to ensure, to the best of their ability, the well-being of students. To restrict the participation of sight-impaired students to

---

[42] Spitaleri v. Nyquist, 345 N.Y.S.2d 878 (Sup. Ct. 1973).

[43] Kampmeier v. Nyquist, 553 F.2d 296 (2d Cir. 1977). (However, the lead plaintiff ultimately triumphed in a state court action—Kampmeier v. Harris, 411 N.Y.S.2d 744 (App. Div. 1978).)

noncontact sports in order to reduce the potential for injury to each child's remaining eye appeared rational to the court, since no medical or statistical evidence was presented by the plaintiffs to support the position that such preventative measures were unnecessary. Accordingly, the Second Circuit affirmed the trial court's denial of the students' motion for a preliminary injunction, thus barring their athletic participation.

Oftentimes athletes with disabilities are capable of participating with virtually no greater (or only a slightly greater) threat to health or safety than is present for other competitors but they are, nevertheless, denied the opportunity to be involved in sports. To address this apparent injustice, in 1977 the New York State Legislature enacted a statute,[44] sometimes referred to as the Spitaleri rule (after the plaintiff in the first case), which permits a student to commence a special proceeding to enjoin a district from prohibiting athletic participation. The petition must be accompanied by affidavits from at least two licensed physicians stating that, in their opinion, the student is physically capable of participating in an athletic program and that participation is reasonably safe. Also, any special or preventive measures or devices needed to protect the student must be identified by the physicians, but the district is not responsible for providing these devices unless they are mandated by the student's IEP. In addition, the district cannot be held liable for an injury sustained by the student athlete if the injury is attributable to the physical impairment for which the court order was obtained. Both New York cases, following the passage of the Spitaleri Rule, and dealing with sight-impaired athletes, were decided in favor of the students.[45]

---

[44] NEW YORK EDUCATION LAW § 4409, recodified 1986 as § 3208-a (McKinney 1994).

[45] In *Swiderski v. Board of Educ.–City Sch. Dist. of Albany*, 408 N.Y.S.2d 744 (Sup. Ct. 1978), the court concluded that it was in the best interest of the student, who had defective vision in one eye, to participate in the athletic program and that it was reasonably safe for her to do so, provided she wore protective eye shields. The case was filed under state education law section 4409. Similarly, in *Kampmeier v. Harris*, 411 N.Y.S.2d 744 (App. Div. 1978), the parents provided affidavits of two physicians who disagreed with the school doctor and expressed the opinion that their daughter was capable of reasonably safe participation in contact sports if she wore protective glasses. The court was convinced by this and other testimony and concluded that it was in her best interest to participate in the athletic program. The case also was filed under state education law section 4409.

Additionally, cases involving vision-impaired college and university athletes were reviewed by the courts; again, consistent with the more recent K-12 cases, each court ruled in favor of the student.

Higher Education Cases. In *Wright v. Columbia University*,[46] the student had sight in only one eye but was, nevertheless, otherwise qualified to play college football and was fully informed about potential injuries and risks. In addition, he and his parents were willing to sign a waiver of liability in the event that he was injured while playing. The court agreed with the rationale proposed in *Poole* [discussed below under "Loss of Kidney"] that the football program was not outside the coverage of section 504, even though it did not directly receive federal funding. It also distinguished the case at bar from *Kampmeier* since here the student had presented evidence to rebut the University's position and was sufficiently old, mature, and informed as not to require the institution to attempt to act in loco parentis. The court concluded that the student-athlete would have incurred irreparable harm had a preliminary injunction not been issued and that he had made a prima facie case showing a reasonable probability of success on its merits. Similar results were provided in two additional cases, one from Ohio,[47] the other from Missouri.[48]

Loss of Kidney. The potential for injury to a remaining kidney has led many administrators to deny students the opportunity to participate in sport, particularly those involving collision or contact. As with other health care, they are concerned about issues related to injury or death, quality of life, and liability. To these generally well-intended educators, the gains derived from sport simply are not worth the risk, no matter how slight. However, this view often has been in conflict with the opinions of student athletes and their parents. Three published cases have dealt with this issue.

---

[46] Wright v. Columbia Univ., 520 F. Supp. 789 (E.D. Pa. 1981).

[47] In the Ohio case, the court provided a preliminary injunction to allow an Ohio University student who was sighted only in one eye to play intercollegiate basketball. *See* Borden v. Rohr, No. 75-844, oral decision (S.D. Ohio. Dec. 30, 1975). (Cited in *Wright v. Columbia Univ.*, 520 F. Supp. 789, 793 (E.D. Penn. 1981).)

[48] In Missouri two college students with sight only in one eye were denied the opportunity to play football. The court ruled that both students must be allowed to participate once they signed a waiver releasing the college from liability if they were to be injured. *See* Evans & Redding v. Looney, No. 77-6052-CV-SJ, *slip op.* (W.D. Mo. Sept. 2, 1977)

In *Poole v. South Plainfield Board of Education,*[49] the board unsuccessfully filed a motion to dismiss an action by a high school student who sought compensatory damages after he was denied the opportunity to participate in the wrestling program due to the fact that he had only one kidney. He had wrestled during the eighth, ninth, and tenth grades, but was prevented from doing so during his junior and senior years of high school. His parents supported his wrestling and were willing to sign a waiver of liability. The court, while allowing the student's suit to proceed, provided several opinions regarding section 504: a private cause of action exists; monetary as well as injunctive relief is available; and interscholastic athletic programs must be in compliance with the Act, even if no federal funds are spent specifically on athletes. In arriving at these conclusions, the court observed that medical testimony was divided regarding whether it was advisable for a student with one kidney to wrestle, but that the student should be given the benefit of all doubts. Accordingly, the court found the board's decision, although well intended, to be contrary to the informed wishes of the student and his parents and to "[stand] the doctrine of in loco parentis on its head"[50] because all of the necessary parties were present and well informed. Consequently, it reasoned that while there are times when the state may disregard parental wishes, the lack of mitigating circumstances in this case constituted a case of the school acting beyond the limits of its reasonable authority. To the court, the board's duty was to inform the student and his parents of the risks and to require them to "deal with the matter rationally," but not to prevent him from participating.

In concluding that section 504 had been violated and that the student had been otherwise qualified, the court noted that

> [h]ardly a year goes by that there is not at least one instance of the tragic death of a healthy youth as a result of competitive sports activity. Life has risks. The purpose of [s]ection 504, however, is to permit individuals with disabilities to live life as fully as they are able, without paternalistic authorities deciding that certain activities are too risky for them.[51]

---

[49] Poole v. South Plainfield Bd. of Educ., 490 F. Supp. 948 (D.N.J. 1980).
[50] *Id.* at 952 (emphasis omitted)
[51] *Id.* at 953-54.

In *Grube v. Bethlehem Area School District*,[52] a high school student with one kidney successfully obtained a preliminary injunction prohibiting the district from denying him the opportunity to play interscholastic football. The student had a history of athletic participation and, except in regard to his lack of a second kidney, was physically fit and otherwise qualified to participate. He previously had suffered a minor injury to his remaining kidney, but had purchased a specially designed "flak jacket" that would offer additional protection. Nevertheless, the school doctor, in consultation with two other physicians, recommended that he be barred from playing. The conflict was further heightened because the student had the permission of his parents and supportive testimony from the director of the Sports Medicine Clinic at Temple University. The director, a certified orthopedic surgeon, was of the opinion that the position held by the other physicians was emotional rather than medical. The trial court, although admittedly reluctant to "disturb a well-intended decision of local school authorities,"[53] asserted that the board should not have based its decision on the recommendations of medical doctors who had neither the practical experience nor the research background to evaluate the risk to the plaintiff, particularly since credible evidence from a noted authority had been presented. Accordingly, the court granted a preliminary injunction.

And finally, in *Pace v. Dryden Central School District*,[54] the district was enjoined under state law from prohibiting a seventeen year old student from taking part in high school football and basketball. The district had disallowed his participation based solely on the fact that one of his kidneys had been removed, despite the presence of affidavits from two medical doctors supporting his reasonably safe

---

[52] Grube v. Bethlehem Area Sch. Dist., 550 F. Supp. 418 (E.D. Penn. 1982).
[53] *Id.* at 423.
[54] Pace v. Dryden Cent. Sch. Dist., 574 N.Y.S.2d 142 (Sup. Ct. 1991).

participation and the fact that both he and his parents understood the health risks involved.[55]

Loss of Leg or Arm. Numerous student-athletes have been able to compete in sport, albeit at lower levels, although they were missing a leg, arm, or a hand. Some even participate in college sport and a few have become professionals (e.g., pitcher Jim Abbott with the Chicago White Sox). Where such students are otherwise qualified and their participation does not represent a risk to others, they should be allowed to play. Only one related, but unpublished,[56] case has been located. In *Suemnick v. Michigan High School Athletic Association*,[57] the court enjoined a high school from preventing a student with one leg from playing varsity football.

Loss of Testicle. In one of the more unusual cases, *Prendergast v. Sewanhaka Central High School District No. 2*,[58] the decision of the school medical director was overturned as the student, who was absent a testicle, wanted to play contact sports. He was found to be qualified to participate when the court determined that his remaining testicle could be substantially protected by wearing a proper guard and because other athletes could not conceivably be injured due to his participation. The court also distinguished between the severity of the loss of a second testicle and the loss of a second eye or kidney or hearing in a second ear.

---

[55] *See also*, Seay v. Trustees of the Cal. State Univ., No. CV-89-4791, *slip op.* (C.D. Cal. Oct. 5, 1989) (where the court denied a preliminary injunction that would have ordered Long Beach State University to permit an athlete with one kidney to play college football even though he was a two-year starter and had above average skills. Seay now plays for the San Diego Chargers in the National Football League). *See* Bob Nightengale, *Men on a Mission: San Diego is all charged up over its football team and for good reason—the Chargers have the best record in the NFL*, THE SPORTING NEWS, Oct. 17, 1994, at 12, 14.

[56] The term "unpublished" is used here to refer to cases not published by West Publishing Company in the National Reporter System. However, such opinions may be available through the respective courts or through one of the electronic services (e.g., LEXIS).

[57] Suemnick v. Michigan High Sch. Athletic Ass'n, No. 4-70592 (E.D. Mich., 1974). (Cited in *Wright v. Columbia Univ.*, 520 F. Supp. 789, 793 (E.D. Penn. 1981).)

[58] Prendergast v. Sewanhaka Cent. High Sch. Dist. No. 2, slip op. (Sup. Ct. May 14, 1975). (Cited in *Colombo v. Sewanhaka Cent. High Sch. Dist. No. 2*, 383 N.Y.S.2d 518, 522 (Sup. Ct. 1976)).

Wheelchair Confinement. In *Hollenbeck v. Board of Education of Rochelle Township*,[59] the plaintiff asked to compete with able-bodied athletes or be provided a stipend so that he might locate and compete with other wheelchair track athletes. The district refused his request and an impartial hearing, and later a suit in district court, were filed. The court held that a child's multi-disciplinary IEP team lacked the prerequisite training and knowledge to make a determination whether it was safe for him to participate in track because no one on the IEP team had any significant knowledge of athletics in general or of wheelchair track specifically. As a result, the court ruled that the student's rights under section 1983 were violated.

Policy Implications

Authorized committees of local educational units are responsible for determining the nature and extent of curricular and extracurricular activities that are made available to children with disabilities. The appropriateness of these offerings, including sport participation, can be challenged both administratively and judicially. However, where a child has been evaluated thoroughly and placed in a program designed to meet his unique educational needs, challenging such a program may prove difficult for either students or athletic associations.

It is unlikely that many IEP teams will incorporate extracurricular sport into a child's program, however, as most IEPs are not dependent on athletics to qualify as appropriate. Accordingly, as a general rule, districts are reluctant to add services or privileges that are not essential to a FAPE, because once such items are incorporated they may not be removed without proper due process (generally a second IEP meeting).

In addition to the IEP, a child with a disability has the right under section 504 to participate in extracurricular, intramural, or interscholastic activities if the child is otherwise qualified. Where school officials believe that it is not advisable for health and safety reasons for a particular student to participate in a given sport, the student

---

[59] Hollenbeck v. Board of Educ. of Rochelle Township, 699 F. Supp. 658 (N.D. Ill. 1988).

would be responsible for rebutting that position. In jurisdictions such as New York, where a state statute is controlling, challenging a board's decision would prove easier than in states without such regulations. Nevertheless, it appears that a qualified student with a disability who has acquired parental consent and supportive statements from knowledgeable physicians is likely to win judicial approval.

Table 8-1
Ohio High School Athletic Association Bylaws (1994-95)

Eligibility

Bylaw 4-1-1: Each student shall meet all requirements in this Bylaw to be eligible to participate in interscholastic athletic competition.

Bylaw 4-1-2: A student transferring from a nonmember school in Ohio to an OHSAA member school will be ineligible for interscholastic athletics in the member school for one year if the student has violated any OHSAA Bylaws or Regulations relative to eligibility or contest regulations while participating as a student for the nonmember school. The one-year period of ineligibility shall begin on the day after the last violation occurred.

Age Limitation

Bylaw 4-2-1: If a student enrolled in high school attains the age of nineteen before August 1, the student shall be ineligible to participate in high school interscholastic athletics for the school year commencing in that calendar year.

Bylaw 4-2-2: If a student enrolled in grades 7 or 8 attains the age of fifteen before August 1, the student shall be ineligible to participate in 7-8th grade interscholastic athletics for the school year commencing in that calendar year.

Bylaw 4-2-3: A student shall become eligible for high school athletics when the student attains the fifteenth birthday before August 1, or when the student attains 9th grade standing. The student is eligible at the school where the student is expected to enroll at the 9th grade level.

Bylaw 4-2-4: In determining the age of a student, the date of birth as recorded in the school records shall be considered as final, except that when birth records, filed within six years after date of birth, are available in the State

Bureau of Vital Statistics or a comparable governmental agency, it shall be used. If this information is not available and if the school records do not agree, the earliest date of birth shall be considered the valid date of birth.

Bylaw 4-2-5: Family Bibles, physician's statements, parents' affidavits, baptismal certificates etc., will not be accepted in lieu of birth certificates. Amendments to birth certificates filed after six years from date of birth will not be considered.

Enrollment & Attendance

Bylaw 4-3-1: All students on a high school athletic squad shall be enrolled in the high school sponsoring the squad and living in the high school attendance area.

Exception #1: Students enrolled in the 9th grade separate from the high school (grades 10-12) are eligible to participate with the school squad of the high school they will be assigned to attend provided the superintendent of the high school and the 9th grade is the same person.

Exception #2: Students enrolled in a joint vocational school are eligible at the high school where they would normally attend if not enrolled in at the joint vocational school. All students on a 7-8th grade school athletic squad shall be enrolled in the 7-8th grade school sponsoring the squad and living in the 7-8th grade school attendance area.

Bylaw 4-3-2: To be eligible for participation in interscholastic contests a student shall be enrolled in a school by the fifteenth calendar day of the credit grading period (quarter, trimester, semester). Enrollment shall be continuous after a student has officially enrolled in a school until the student is officially withdrawn.

Bylaw 4-3-3: The student shall attend school according to the officially adopted attendance plan of that school unless the principal of the school authorizes an excused absence. Unless excused, a student not attending the first day of a credit grading period shall be ineligible to participate in interscholastic contests until the fifteenth calendar day after that student's first day of attendance. Transfers from other states as well as Ohio schools must comply with this Bylaw.

Bylaw 4-3-4: After a student completes the 8th grade, the student shall be eligible for a period not to exceed eight semesters taken in order of attendance, whether the student participates or not. A student in grades 7 or 8 who attains the age of fifteen before August 1, shall be eligible only at the high school level for a period not to exceed eight semesters taken in order of attendance, whether the student participates or not. The Board of Control may permit a student who completes the eighth semester of eligibility during the season of a sport to complete the sports season of the sport in which the student is participating provided the student is enrolled in school. If such extension is granted, the student is ineligible for further interscholastic participation when the sports season, regular and tournament, has ended.

Bylaw 4-3-5: A student who is enrolled fourteen or more school days after the first day of attendance in any semester, or who participates in an interscholastic contest prior to or in a semester, shall have that semester count as one semester of eligibility.

Bylaw 4-3-6: When a student is enrolled in high school courses with a value of more than two credits, the student shall be counted as a high school student insofar as the Semester Bylaw is concerned.

Bylaw 4-3-7: A student is considered a graduate when the student has completed the work required for graduation and is declared a graduate by the Board of Education. Such student is no longer eligible for interscholastic sports except for participation in the remaining contests of that semester.

Bylaw 4-3-8: Member schools containing grades 7 and 8 may combine students from two or more schools within the school district to form an interscholastic team in a sport. Requests for permission to combine students from two or more schools in the same private, parochial, or public school system must be submitted annually to the OHSAA in writing by the superintendent of the nonpublic or public school system. The written request must contain the following: (1) names of schools involved; (2) total number of students from each school involved in the sport; (3) total number of boys or girls in each grade of each school in the combination; and (4) the name of the principal, name of the school, and the complete address of the administrator responsible for the conduct and operation of the combined team or teams.

Scholarship

Bylaw 4-4-1: In order to be eligible in grades 9-12, a student must be currently enrolled and must have been enrolled in school the immediately preceding grading period. During the preceding grading period, the student must have received passing grades in a minimum of four one-credit courses or the equivalent which count toward graduation.

Bylaw 4-4-2: The eligibility or ineligibility of a student continues until the start of the fifth school day of the next grading period, at which time the grades from the immediately preceding grading period become effective. Exception: Eligibility or ineligibility for the first grading period commences with the start of the fall sports season.

Bylaw 4-4-3: A student enrolled in the first grading period after advancement from the 8th grade must have passed 75% of those subjects carried the preceding grading period in which the student was enrolled.

Bylaw 4-4-4: A student enrolling in the 7th grade for the first time will be eligible for the first grading period regardless of previous academic achievement. Thereafter, in order to be eligible, a student in grades 7 or 8 must be currently enrolled and must have been enrolled in school the immediately preceding grading period and received passing grades during that grading period in 75% of those subjects carried the preceding grading period in which the student was enrolled.

Bylaw 4-4-5: The eligibility of a transfer student must be established by school records or verification from the sending school. The responsibility for establishing eligibility rests with the receiving school.

Bylaw 4-4-6: Summer school grades earned may not be used to substitute for failing grades from the last grading period of the regular school year.

Bylaw 4-4-7: Tutoring or examinations to complete the preceding grading period requirements is permissible provided the inability to complete the required work on time is due to illness or accident verified by a physician and the procedure applies to all students in the school.

Bylaw 4-4-8: The Commissioner may waive the requirement of preceding grading period enrollment if a student has been withdrawn or removed from school because of circumstances due to personal accident, illness, or family hardship. The principal or the official designee of the school shall appeal in writing to the Commissioner. The appeal shall contain documentation with school and medical supporting evidence. The decision of the Commissioner may be appealed to the Board of Control.

Conduct, Character, Discipline

Bylaw 4-5-1: In matters pertaining to personal conduct in which athletics are not involved, the school itself is to be the sole judge as to whether the student may participate in athletics.

Bylaw 4-5-2: In matters pertaining to personal conduct in which athletics are involved, the principal or the official designee of the involved schools or game officials may file a report and the Association shall have jurisdiction to determine the penalties involved and whether or not the student may participate in athletics.

Bylaw 4-5-3: Physical attacks on any official shall be reported to the Association office immediately by the officials involved. The Commissioner shall conduct an investigation and determine the penalties involved.

Bylaw 4-5-4: Any students who are ejected from an athletic contest in any sport for unsportsmanlike conduct shall be immediately placed under direct supervision of a school official.

Residence

Bylaw 4-6-1: A student is eligible at the school located in the district where the parent resides. If, however, the student is a ward of a court appointed guardian, the student is eligible at the school located in the district where the guardian resides provided the student lives with the guardian. A student may be eligible at only one school.

"Parent" refers to the natural and/or adoptive parents of the student. If the parents are divorced, or their marriage has been dissolved or annulled, "parent" means the "residential parent" and "legal custodian" (pursuant to O.R.C. Chapter 3109) of the student. If the student has been temporarily or permanently removed from the home, "parent" shall mean the person or government agency with legal or permanent custody.

When a change of "residential parent" and "legal custodian" results in a change of school districts, the student is not eligible until ruled eligible by the Commissioner.

Bylaw 4-6-2: A student who does not live in the same school district as parents or legal guardian and who is financially self-supporting may be ruled eligible upon approval of the Commissioner at a school in the district where the student resides. The Commissioner is empowered to establish the requirements for a student to be determined to be self-supporting. These requirements shall be established for each school year by May 15th of the preceding year. Self-support documentation must be submitted for approval. The student is not eligible until ruled eligible by the Commissioner.

Bylaw 4-6-3: Parents of students attending a nonpublic school shall be school residents of the nonpublic school district.

Bylaw 4-6-4: If the residence in which a student and a student's parents reside is annexed to a school district, the student must attend the school in the student's district subject to modification by formal action by the Boards of Education concerned. A copy of such action by Boards of Education must be on file in the Association office before the Commissioner can rule such students eligible.

Bylaw 4-6-5: Students attending a vocational school are eligible at the high school in the district of residence of parents.

Bylaw 4-6-6: A student whose parents move from the district during the school year may finish the school year and be eligible but is ineligible for one year from date of enrollment if the student returns the following school year. A student whose parents move during the summer is not eligible for one year from date of enrollment should the student return to the former school.

Bylaw 4-6-7: A student enrolled in a special education program at a school outside of the district of residence of parents is eligible at the school where the student attends classes or the school located in the district of residence of the parents. Definition of Special Education Program: (1) special education curricula as described in P.L. 94-142 as amended; (2) gifted and talented programs; and (3) alternative education programs as conducted by member schools of the OHSAA.

Bylaw 4-6-8: A student entering a high school from an elementary or middle school may choose either the nonpublic or the public high school in the district of residence of parents.

Bylaw 4-6-9: A student whose parents live in another state will be ineligible for athletics in an Ohio member school.

Exception #1—A student who has attended a minimum of fifteen days in the 11th grade and whose parents move outside the State of Ohio may be declared eligible for the 12th grade provided the student maintains continuous enrollment in the Ohio school.

Exception #2—A student who enrolls at 1st grade level in a school consisting of grades 1-12 and who maintains continuous enrollment shall be eligible for interscholastic athletics in grades 7-12 in that school regardless of place or state of residence of parents.

Exception #3—A student who resides within the boundaries of a parochial school system consisting of grades 1-12 that has multiple sites organized into elementary schools (1-8) and secondary schools (9-12), and who has enrolled at 1st grade level of an elementary school in that system and has maintained continuous enrollment in that school system through grade 8, shall be eligible for interscholastic athletics in grades 9-12 providing the secondary school attended by the student is the school designated by the school system for the continuance of the student's educational program.

Exception #4—A student who resides within the boundaries of a public school district in a neighboring state; and who attends an Ohio public school system under an arrangement through which the entire grade of the out-of-state student attends the Ohio public school system; and for who the tuition or cost of education for said out-of-state student is paid by the neighboring state's school district of residence; and who will be eligible to receive a high school diploma from an Ohio public school system shall be eligible for interscholastic athletics in grades 7-12 at the schools designated by the Ohio school system for attendance by the students from the neighboring state.

Transfers

Bylaw 4-7-1: The Transfer Bylaw applies to all students enrolled in grades 7-12. It applies to all member schools, both public and nonpublic.

Bylaw 4-7-2: If a student transfers to a school from the district in which the parents reside without a corresponding change in the residence, the student shall not be eligible until one year from date of enrollment except as provided in this Section.

Bylaw 4-7-3: A student is considered to be establishing eligibility in a school and may not transfer that eligibility except as provided in this Section if the student: (1) participates in an interscholastic contest prior to or in a semester; or, (2) is enrolled fourteen or more days after the first day of attendance. A transfer student who has not participated in an interscholastic contest and has not been enrolled fourteen or more days after the first day of attendance in a new school is not considered to have established eligibility in the new school.

Bylaw 4-7-4: If the parents of a student move during the school year from the district of the school which the student attends, the student may transfer to the new school at the time of the moving or any time thereafter during the school year and be eligible so far as transfer is concerned.

Bylaw 4-7-5: The districts for all member schools, both public and nonpublic, are defined for athletic purposes. Such districts shall be fixed by the Board of Control after consultation with the involved school districts. If a student changes from a nonpublic to a public school or a public to nonpublic school, or from a nonpublic to a nonpublic school, or from a public to a public school, the student will not be eligible for one year from date of enrollment.

Exception #1—If the parents or legal custodian change residence from one public school tax district to another public school tax district, the student may enroll in either the public or nonpublic school, whose district includes the residence of the parents or legal custodian, and be immediately eligible.

Exception #2—A student who has completed the 8th grade may enroll in a four-year high school whose district includes the residence of the parents or legal custodian and be eligible at the 9th grade.

Exception #3—If the student completes the work of the school from which the student transfers, the student may be eligible upon enrollment in a school whose district includes the residence of the parents or legal custodian. Examples of completing the work of the school include: (1) completes the 8th grade in an elementary or middle school; (2) completes the 9th grade in junior high school (7-9, 8-9, 9); and (3) the school closes.

Bylaw 4-7-6: If a student transfers from a school within the student's districts (nonpublic and public) to another school within the student's districts, the student shall be ineligible until one year from date of enrollment has elapsed unless change of residence of parents within the districts is recognized by the Commissioner as necessitating the change except as provided in this Section.

Bylaw 4-7-7: The superintendent or person delegated by the superintendent of either a nonpublic or public school system may transfer students within the system without jeopardizing their eligibility. Such transfers are eligible only after approval by the Commissioner.

Bylaw 4-7-8: The Commissioner may rule a student eligible if released to a designated school by formal action of the Board of Education or similar governing body of the public or nonpublic school from which the student transfers. Such students will not be declared eligible until a copy of the formal action is on file in the Association office and the Association declares the student eligible. If a student returns to the school in the district of residence the student shall be ineligible for one year from date of enrollment. No more than one such release may be granted to an athlete. The Commissioner or the Board of Control may approve a second release if the student never participates in an interscholastic contest under the first release. Note: the OHSAA release form must be used.

Bylaw 4-7-9: A student may transfer to a school (nonresident school) outside the district of residence of the parent and be eligible insofar as the Transfer Bylaw is concerned provided the student is enrolled and in attendance at the nonresident school not later than fifteen days following the beginning of the school year in the nonresident school. A student who transfers at any other time in the school year shall be ineligible insofar as the Transfer Bylaw is concerned but subject to other provisions of Bylaw 4-7. At the beginning of the next school year, such student may return to the school in the district of residence of the parent (resident school) or may enroll in another school (nonresident school) and be eligible if enrolled within fifteen days following the beginning of the school year in the nonresident school.

Bylaw 4-7-10: Whenever a new high school has been established in a school district in which the student's parents reside, all students whose parents reside in that new school district, and who enroll in the new high school, are eligible for interscholastic athletics insofar as the Transfer Bylaw is concerned. This applies to students from both public and nonpublic schools whose parents reside in the new school district defined by the local board of education. This rule applies only at the beginning of the school year when the new school first opens. After the first year of operation, the eligibility of any future transfers from one school to another will be determined in accordance with applicable paragraphs of this Section.

Bylaw 4-7-11: In order for a transfer student to be eligible for OHSAA tournament competition at a school, the student's name must be listed on the eligibility certificate submitted at the first tournament level in the sport.

Bylaw 4-7-12: The Commissioner shall have discretionary power to waive the transfer requirements in the case of orphans; students from broken homes; students from foreign countries, or any exchange program contained in the Advisory List of International Educational Travel and Exchange Programs published by the Council on Standards for International Educational Travel, students legally and entirely self-supporting; students whose parents live outside the school district at the start of the school year whose contracted domicile within the district is not available for their habitation; those who are wards of the court or of the state.

Bylaw 4-7-13: Students transferred to the State School for the Blind or State School for the Deaf become eligible upon enrollment insofar as the Transfer Section is concerned.

Students From Foreign Countries and Exchange Students

Bylaw 4-8-1: A student from a foreign country participating in an exchange program set forth in Bylaw 4-7-12 may be eligible to participate in interscholastic athletics for a maximum of one school year provided the student complies with all provisions of Bylaw 4—Student Eligibility (except that the Commissioner may waive the requirements of Section 6—Residence and Section 7—Transfer). Such a student is not eligible until ruled eligible by the Commissioner.

Bylaw 4-8-2: An Ohio student returning from a domestic or foreign exchange program may resume interscholastic competition in an Ohio member school at the point of interruption provided the student did not receive credits toward graduation while participating in the exchange program and provided the student meets all requirements relative to age, semesters of eligibility as well as preceding grading period scholastic requirements in the grading period immediately preceding enrollment in the exchange program. Such a student is not eligible until ruled eligible by the Commissioner or the Board of Control.

Recruiting

Bylaw 4-9-1: A student is considered a prospective athlete upon enrolling in the 7th grade, or the grade corresponding to the 7th grade for a student from a foreign country.

Bylaw 4-9-2: The use of influence by any person connected or not connected with the school to secure or to retain a prospective athlete is not permitted and shall cause the student to be ineligible upon transfer and shall jeopardize the standing of the school in the Association.

Bylaw 4-9-3: Prior to enrollment a prospective athlete may visit a nonpublic or public school within the district of residence of parents, provided the arrangements for the visit are cleared through the principal of the school to be visited.

Bylaw 4-9-4: No employee of the school system shall initiate any communication with a prospective athlete, parents of an athlete, guardian or family member, in person or through a third party prior to enrollment.

Bylaw 4-9-5: A prospective athlete shall not be offered or accept any inducement, such as free tuition, employment, books, complimentary tickets, uniforms and supplies, other than that which is provided to all students.

Amateur

Bylaw 4-10-1: A student who represents a school in an interscholastic sport shall be an amateur in that sport. An amateur athlete is one who engages in athletic competition solely for the physical, mental, social, and pleasure benefits derived therefrom. An athlete forfeits amateur status in a sport by:

(1) competing for money or other monetary compensation (allowable travel, meals, and lodging expense may be accepted);

(2) receiving any award, playing equipment or prize of monetary value which exceeds the amount provided by the Association;

(3) capitalizing on athletic fame by receiving money or gifts of monetary value (scholarships to institutions of higher learning are specifically exempted);

(4) signing a professional playing contract in that sport;

(5) failing to return player equipment and uniforms issued by a nonschool or school team or organization when the season for the sport is concluded.

Bylaw 4-10-2: Accepting a fee for instructing, supervising, or officiating in an organized youth sports program or recreation, playground, or camp activities shall not jeopardize amateur status.

Bylaw 4-10-3: Only awards approved by the Association may be accepted by a high school student-athlete as a result of participation in school or nonschool competition in a sport recognized by the Association.

Bylaw 4-10-4: The purchase of memberships for specific school students participating in interscholastic athletics, in youth serving agencies, athletic clubs, recreation centers, etc., would be a violation of this rule. This does not infringe on the right of such organizations to provide anonymously sponsored memberships for individuals in the community proven financially in need.

Bylaw 4-10-5: A high school student who loses amateur status may apply to the Association for reinstatement in the interscholastic program after a waiting period of one year.

Bylaw 4-10-6: Professional, amateur, and college tryouts or auditions which may interfere with a high school student's school work or which involve a contest in violation of Association rules shall result immediately in that student's ineligibility for further interscholastic athletic competition in that sport.

Source: OHIO HIGH SCHOOL ATHLETIC ASSOCIATION, 1994-1995 Handbook (1995).

Chapter 9
Child Abuse

Introduction

Child abuse and neglect are, most unfortunately, a tragic fact in American life. However, while cases of abuse and neglect of children are filed more often today than at any time in American history, it is not entirely certain whether child abuse actually has increased or is simply being reported more regularly. An illustration of these harsh realities may be found in the congressional hearings preceding the passage of the Child Abuse, Domestic Violence, Adoption, and Family Services Act of 1992, codified as the reauthorized version of the Child Abuse Prevention and Treatment Act.[1] Testimony introduced at the Senate hearings on this Act estimated that in 1990 some 2,508,000 children were reported as victims of child abuse or neglect, an increase of 31% since 1985.[2] The data from the Senate hearings are even more stark when considered in light of the fact that in 1984 the number of reported cases of child abuse rose to over 1,727,000, an increase of 158.1% since 1976.[3] Furthermore, a 1991

---

[1] 24 U.S.C. § 5101 *et seq.* (1994).

[2] SEN. REP. NO. 102-164, 102d Cong., 2d Sess. at 135 (1992). Deaths attributed to the maltreatment of children rose by 38% over that same period, with an estimated 1,211 children found dead in 1990 alone.

[3] Clearinghouse on Child Abuse and Neglect, *Child Abuse and Neglect: An Informed Approach to a Shared Concern* (1986), at 3.

study conducted on behalf of the National Center on Child Abuse and Neglect estimated that while 21.3 per 1,000 children without disabilities are subjected to varying forms of maltreatment, this figure leaps to 35.5 per 1,000 when dealing with children with disabilities, a 67% higher rate.[4]

What is clear is that the abuse of children is neither unique to the United States nor to the twentieth century. In fact, child abuse dates back over 4,000 years. The mistreatment of children has been motivated by a variety of reasons including the need to discipline, to please certain deities, or to expel evil spirits, particularly when children with mental disabilities have been involved. At other times, abuse was based on tradition or custom, or was the result of frustration, jealousy, or anger.[5]

When children were beaten, whipped, mutilated, castrated, enslaved, prostituted, starved, burned, abandoned, or murdered it often occurred without government intervention and, at times, happened with the knowledge, encouragement, or even at the command of officials. Among the myriad of examples of sanctioned abuse were the flattening of the heads of children by some Native Americans, the shaping of youngster's heads into elongated cones by the Melanesians, the binding of feet of young girls in China, the selling of offspring by the Romans, and the killing or ostracizing of illegitimate

---

[4] *A Report on the Maltreatment of Children with Disabilities,* National Center on Child Abuse and Neglect, United States Dep't of Health and Human Serv. at 2-4, Table 2-2 (Incidence of child maltreatment: Overall and by whether or not children have disabilities (1992).) The weighted percents of the most common forms of maltreatment suffered by children with disabilities are physical abuse, 34.6%; inadequate supervision, 22.0%; sexual abuse, 21.6%; physical neglect, 20.6%; medical neglect, 18.8%; and emotional abuse, 12.0%. *Id.* at 3-11, Table 3-3 (Maltreated children with and without disabilities by type of maltreatment). These data are further broken down into weighted percents of types of disabilities that were suspected to have led to maltreatment of children: any disability, 47.2%; physical health problem, 76.1%; serious emotional disturbance, 66.6%; hyperactivity, 59.2%; mental retardation, 43.4%; learning disability, 32.8%. *Id.* at 3-13, Table 3-4 (Percent of maltreated children for whom disabilities were suspected by caseworker to have led to maltreatment, by type of disability) (totals are greater than 100% since children often incur multiple forms of abuse or have more than one disability).

[5] For a good background discussion on the history and epidemiology of child abuse, *see* CYNTHIA CROSSON TOWER, UNDERSTANDING CHILD ABUSE AND NEGLIGENCE (2d 1993).

children in many societies. Moreover, in the United States there has been a long history of abuse of children who were placed in institutions as well as the many who were required to serve apprenticeships during colonial times, enslaved prior to the Civil War, or made to work in factories during the latter nineteenth and early twentieth centuries.[6]

Despite these unpleasant realities, child abuse, far from being reduced, remains present in much of the world (including the United States), as many cultures continue to bind children's bodies to produce fashionable configurations; to pierce their ears, lips, and noses; or to put to death or brutalize unwanted children. Youngsters who are housed in institutions as well as those in foster homes and natural homes are known to suffer all forms of abuse, often at the hands of those they love and trust the most. Child abusers come from all economic, social, racial, and cultural groups, although some factors (e.g., household poverty, family conflict, and alcohol abuse) may exacerbate incidences of abuse.

Over the years, efforts to reduce, if not eliminate, child abuse have met with mixed success. The Constitution was amended in 1865 prohibiting slavery[7] and numerous laws were passed regarding child labor and factory safety conditions. Additionally, societies for the prevention of cruelty to children, beginning in New York City in 1871, were organized in many communities; a variety of children's aid societies were formed during the 1890s; the White House Conference on Children was held in 1909; the National Children's Bureau was formed in 1912; and tremendous growth in the number of humane societies occurred during the first half of the twentieth century. During the 1960s each state passed a child abuse law and in 1974 Congress enacted The Child Abuse Prevention and Treatment

---

[6] *See* SAMUEL RADBILL, A HISTORY OF Child ABUSE AND INFANTICIDE IN THE BATTERED CHILD (Helfer & Kempe, eds. 2d ed. 1974), at 3-21; SHIRLEY O'BRIEN, CHILD ABUSE: A CRYING SHAME (1980), at 5-8; PAMELA MAYHALL & KATHERINE NORGARD, CHILD ABUSE AND NEGLECT: SHARING RESPONSIBILITY (1983), at 3-21.

[7] Section 1 of the Thirteenth Amendment states that "[n]either slavery nor involuntary servitude, except as a punishment for crime whereof the party shall have been duly convicted, shall exist within the United States, or any place subject to their jurisdiction."

Act which created the National Center on Child Abuse and Neglect.[8]
Today, numerous governmental and private organizations have as
their primary focus the prevention of child abuse and neglect. See
Table 9-1 for a partial listing of such organizations.

Table 9-1
Selected Organizations
Opposing Child Abuse & Neglect

Name	Address	Phone
American Humane Association— Children's Division	63 Inverness Dr. Englewood, Colorado 80112	303-792-9900
National Resource Center on Child Abuse and Neglect	Same as American Humane Association	800-227-5242 303-695-0811
C. Henry Kempe National Center for the Prevention and Treatment of Child Abuse and Neglect	1205 Oneida St. Denver, Colorado 80220	303-321-3963
International Society for the Prevention of Child Abuse and Neglect	Same as C. Henry Kempe National Center	303-321-3963
National Association of Counsel for Children	Same as C. Henry Kempe National Center	303-321-3963
National Child Abuse and Neglect Clinical Resource Center—University of Colorado Health Sciences Center	Same as C. Henry Kempe National Center	303-321-3963
National Center on Child Abuse and Neglect—Administration for Children, Youth, and Families	U.S. Department of Health and Human Services, P.O. Box 1182 Washington, D.C. 20013	202-205-8586

---

[8] SEN. REP. NO. 102-164, 102d Cong., 2d Sess. at 134 (1992).

Name (cont.)	Address	Phone
National Clearing House on Child Abuse and Neglect	Same as National Center on Child Abuse and Neglect	703-385-7565 800-FYI-3366
National Child Abuse Hotline	None	800-422-4453
National Anti-Child Abuse Movement	None	703-550-4123
National Resource Center on Child Sexual Abuse	2204 Whitesburg Huntsville, Alabama 35801	301-949-5000 (Maryland) 205-534-6868 (Alabama) 800-KIDS-006
National Committee to Prevent Child Abuse	332 S. Michigan Suite 1600 Chicago, Illinois 60604	312-663-3520

In light of the epidemic of abuse and neglect, especially as it relates to children with disabilities, the remaining sections of this Chapter examine legislative definitions and related legal requirements affecting educators, including mandates for reporting child abuse, immunity from civil liability based on good faith reporting, and civil and criminal liability for failure to report. The Chapter concludes with policy recommendations for educators to help ensure compliance with statutes aimed at obviating child abuse.

Definitions

The Child Abuse Prevention and Treatment Act defines child abuse and neglect as: "the physical or mental injury, sexual abuse or exploitation, negligent treatment or maltreatment of a child by a person who is responsible for the child's welfare."[9] In most states similar provisions have been interpreted to mean parent, guardian, or caretaker abuse, but are seldom sufficiently broad to also include educa-

---

[9] 42 U.S.C. § 5106g(4). The statute defines a child as a person who has not reached the lesser of age 18 or when dealing with sexual abuse, the age specified by state law where the child resides. *Id.* at (3).

tor abuse of children[10] or the abuse of one child by another,[11] although those issues are of importance and have often been the subject of litigation.

---

[10] For cases involving the schools generally, *see, e.g.,* Zmijewski v. B'Nai Torah Congregation of Boca Raton, 639 So. 2d 1022 (Fla. Dist. Ct. App. 1994) (where the court held that the trial court erred in failing to provide a hearing regarding hearsay statements of a child who was alleged to have been abused by a school janitor); United States v. Booth, 996 F.2d 1395 (2d Cir. 1993) (where a teacher's status was held to be sufficiently related to facilitating the crime to permit sentence enhancement where he was convicted of interstate transportation of minors for unlawful sexual activity); State v. Moses, 615 So. 2d 1030 (La. Ct. App. 1993) (where a band director who was convicted of sexually molesting students could be given a more severe penalty for persons in a position of control or supervision over a juvenile); Jones v. Board of Educ. of Sch. Dist. 50, 854 P.2d 1386 (Colo. Ct. App. 1993) (where a student who was sexually molested by a teacher was not deprived of her right to due process under § 1983 since the board and superintendent did not know or have reason to know of the charges until after the teacher was suspended); Franklin v. Gwinnett County Pub. Sch., 112 S. Ct. 1028 (1992) (where a district was held liable under title IX when a male teacher engaged a female high school student in nonconsensual sexual relations); Doe v. Taylor Indep. Sch. Dist., 975 F.2d 137 (5th Cir. 1992) (where a fourteen-year-old female student who was sexually molested by a teacher had a right to be free from sexual molestation); Helena-West Helena Sch. Dist. v. Doris, 843 S.W.2d 873 (Ark. Ct. App. 1992) (where a school board's dismissal of a nonprobationary teacher accused of sexually molesting a student was upheld); Williams v. Columbus Bd. of Educ., 610 N.E.2d 1175 (Ohio Ct. App. 1992) (where a district was not held liable for injuries sustained by a female student who stayed after school to work on a science project and was raped by three male students who were released from detention); People v. Peters, 590 N.Y.S.2d 916 (App. Div. 1992) (where the admission of testimony about a male teacher's prior sexual relations with a seventeen-year-old female student on school grounds was reversible error when he was convicted of the sexual abuse of a thirteen-year old female pupil); Thelma D. *ex rel.* Delores A. v. Board of Educ., 934 F.2d 929 (8th Cir. 1991) (where the school board could not be held liable unless the plaintiff showed that it either had knowledge of the teacher's abuse of the child or that its procedures were inadequate); Daly v. Derrick, 281 Cal. Rptr. 709 (Ct. App. 1991) (where the statute of limitations did not begin to run until the victims of sexual molestation by a teacher discovered or should have found all of the facts essential to their action); Tinkham v. Groveport-Madison Local Sch. Dist., 602 N.E.2d 256 (Ohio Ct. App. 1991) (where a child with a developmental disability was sexually assaulted by a cab driver hired by the district to take her to and from school, the district was not liable since contracting for transportation was an exercise of its discretion).

[11] For cases involving students with disabilities and other students, *see, e.g.,* L.K. v. Reed, 631 So. 2d 604 (La. Ct. App. 1994) (where a school district was not liable when an eighteen-year-old male student had sex on school grounds with a thirteen-year-old female special education student); Dorothy J. v. Little Rock Sch. Dist., 7 F.3d 729 (8th Cir. 1993) (where the mother of a high school student who was mentally retarded failed to state a § 1983 claim when her daughter suffered a sexual attack at the hands of another pupil at school as the district and its employ-

The Act continues on to define sexual abuse as including:

(A) the employment, use, persuasion, inducement, entice-
ment or coercion of any child to engage in, or assist any
other person to engage in, any sexually explicit conduct or
simulation of such conduct for the purpose of producing
any visual depiction of such conduct; or

(B) the rape, molestation, prostitution, or other form of sexual exploitation of children or incest with children.[12]

State statutory definitions typically are similar to the federal standard, but may vary slightly.[13]

Responsibility to Report

All fifty states and the District of Columbia have mandatory
reporting statutes, although they include a degree of latitude regarding who must report,[14] to whom a report must be submitted,[15] what a

---

ees had no constitutional duty to protect her from assault by another student);
Doe v. Escambia County Sch. Bd., 599 So. 2d 226 (Fla. Dist. Ct. App. 1992)
(where summary judgment was precluded when there was a genuine issue of
material fact as to whether a school board breached its duty to supervise adequately the pupils under its control where two students with disabilities were
taken from the school grounds and raped by other students).

12 For a discussion of issues related to the sexual abuse of children, *see* Richard
Fossey, *Law, Trauma, and Sexual Abuse in the Schools: Why Can't Children
Protect Themselves?*, 91 EDUC. L. RPTR. 443 (1994); Gail P. Sorenson, *Sexual
Abuse in Schools: Reported Cases from 1987-1990*, 27 EDUC. ADMIN. Q. 460
(1991).

13 For example, a review of the reporting statutes of the 50 states and the District of
Columbia reveals 240 distinct terms. The two most commonly defined terms are
abuse and child, both of which are present in the laws of 32 states. KAREN L.
MICHAELIS, REPORTING CHILD ABUSE: A GUIDE TO MANDATORY REQUIREMENTS
FOR SCHOOL PERSONNEL at 33 Appendix 6-A: Definitions (1986). *See also* Danny
R. Veilleux, *Annotation, Validity, Construction, and Application of State Statutes
Requiring Doctors or Other Persons to Report Child Abuse*, 73 A.L.R. 782 (1993).

14 A total of 131 professional positions are named in the statutes of the 50 states and
the District of Columbia. The most commonly identified educators are teachers
(31 states and the District of Columbia); school officials (12 states and the District
of Columbia); school administrators (eight states); and school personnel (eight
states). Michaelis, *Id.* at 2 (Appendix 1-A: Mandatory Reporters).

15 Reports made in school must be submitted to the chief administrator or a designated substitute in 20 states and the District of Columbia. Other commonly identified recipients are law enforcement agencies (10 states) and departments of
social services (eight states). *Id.* at 31 (Appendix 5-D: Recipient of Report).

report is required to include,[16] the method of reporting[17] and when a report must be filed.[18] In developing their respective laws, four models were made available to the states. The models were offered by the United States Children's Bureau,[19] the American Humane Association (AHA),[20] the Council of State Governments (CSG),[21] and the American Medical Association (AMA).[22] The Children's Bureau placed a primary duty on medical professions including physicians and osteopaths;[23] the AHA suggested that the reporting requirement extend to all hospital personnel coming into contact with children;[24] the CSG recommended that registered nurses be

---

[16] The most common elements of a report are the child's name (33 states and the District of Columbia), address (31 states and the District of Columbia); and age (29 states and the District of Columbia); the name (31 states and the District of Columbia) and address (29 states and the District of Columbia) of the child's parents, guardians, or caretakers; the identity of the abuser (26 states and the District of Columbia); information about the nature or character and extent of injuries (32 states and the District of Columbia); other pertinent information to establish the cause of injuries (32 states and the Districts of Columbia); and evidence of previous injuries (26 states and the District of Columbia). *Id.* at 29-31 (Appendix 5-B: Content of Report).

[17] Statutes in 36 states and the District of Columbia have provisions for oral reports while 23 states include provisions for written reports. *Id.* at 28-29 (Appendix 5-A: Type of Report).

[18] All of the statutes require reports to be filed immediately. *Id.* at 7. However, the time for making an oral report is specified as within 48 hours in three states and 24 hours in two states; written reports must be filed within 48 hours in six states, 72 hours in three states, and five days in two states. *Id.* at 28-29 (Appendix 5-A: Type of Report).

[19] United States Department of Health, Education, and Welfare, Welfare Administration, Children's Bureau, The Abused Child—Principles and Suggested Language for Legislation on Reporting of the Physically Abused Child (1963).

[20] Council of State Governments, Program of Suggested State Legislation (1965).

[21] The American Humane Association, Children's Division, Guidelines for Legislation to Protect the Battered Child (1963).

[22] American Medical Association, Physical Abuse of Children—Suggested Legislation (1965).

[23] Medical professionals continue to be identified as reporters at about the same rate as educators. For example, statutes require a doctor/surgeon (32 states and the District of Columbia), medical examiner/coroner (28 states and the District of Columbia), osteopath (21 states), and dentist (27 states and the District of Columbia) to report suspected cases of child abuse. Michaelis, *supra* note 13 at 2 (Appendix 1-A: Mandatory Reporters).

[24] An additional 14 states and the District of Columbia require medical personnel engaged in the admission, examination, care, or treatment of children to report suspected cases of abuse. *Id.*

responsible for reporting;[25] and the AMA argued that registered or visiting nurses, school teachers, and social workers be encouraged to report.[26]

The requirement to report suspected child abuse notwithstanding, educators have been reluctant to act.[27]   Among the justifications offered to support educators' unresponsiveness to statutory obligations are a lack of diagnostic capabilities; a tendency to report only severe injury; a feeling that reporting abuse may only result in more excessive abuse and impair the student-teacher relationship; limited knowledge of policy and procedure; a possible conflict with the federal right to confidentiality;[28] fear of suit based on invasion of privacy or defamation; and a preference not to interfere with parental rights.[29]

The level of suspicion necessary to file a report of suspected child abuse is substantially less than probable cause.   In fact, statutes employ a variety of terms including reasonable cause or grounds to believe,[30] reasonable cause to suspect,[31] reason to believe,[32] and knows or has reasonable cause to suspect.[33] Accordingly, laws do not require an educator to know, as a matter of fact, that a child was

---

[25] Registered nurses are identified as reporters in 33 states and the District of Columbia while licensed practical nurses are addressed in the statues of 14 states and the District of Columbia. *Id.*

[26] Social workers are identified as reporters in 32 states, social services workers in eight states, and clinical social workers in one state. *Id.*

[27] *See, e.g.,* Daly v. Derrick, 281 Cal. Rptr. 709 (Ct. App. 1991) (where teachers who knew of the sexual molestation of students by another teacher were not excused from the reporting requirement where they believed that it had ceased); People v. Bernstein, 243 Cal. Rptr. 363 (App. Dep't Super. Ct. 1987) (where a school official was held to have appropriately reported child abuse when he reported an incident to the school district police).

[28] Pesce v. J. Sterling Morton High Sch. Dist. 201, 830 F.2d 789 (7th Cir. 1987) (where a teacher/school psychologist was disciplined for failure to disclose suspected child abuse, notwithstanding her belief that to do so would violate the student's confidentiality).

[29] *See* Robert J. Shoop & Lynn M. Firestone, *Mandatory Reporting of Suspected Child Abuse: Do Teachers Obey The Law?*, 46 Educ. L. Rep. 1115 (1988); Patricia Levin, Teachers' Perceptions, Attitudes, and Reporting of Child Abuse/Neglect, 62 Child Welfare 14, 14-20 (Jan./Feb. 1983).

[30] This standard is present in 17 states. Michaelis, *supra* note 13, at 11 (Appendix 2-A: Standard [for Reporting]).

[31] This is the standard in 13 states. *Id.*

[32] This is the standard in nine states. *Id.*

[33] This is the standard in eight states and the District of Columbia. *Id.*

abused or that a particular person was responsible for the abuse. Rather, state laws typically require individuals to report immediately[34] if they form the opinion that there are reasonable grounds to suspect that a child's injury was not due to an unavoidable accident. Who is responsible, when the abuse occurred, and the degree or severity of the abuse are areas to be investigated, are not typically prerequisites to reporting.

Once the stipulated level of suspicion is present, the person must report the suspected abuse either to a superior or directly to a designated authority, depending on state law. Reports may be directed to an investigator of a children's services board of the county department of welfare, municipal or county peace officer, juvenile court, or other authorized official or body. Furthermore, state law determines whether the report must be oral, written, or both. Most states mandate that the report first be oral, so that any investigation not be delayed, and require a written statement to follow soon thereafter.

Immunity

After a report of suspected child abuse has been filed, it is investigated to determine whether any action is necessary. By this time, an adversarial relationship between the investigator and the child's parent(s) is possible and the threat of legal action is common. In order to encourage educators to report suspected child abuse and to offer a measure of protection based on the potential for an explosive encounter with a parent charged with abuse, most statutes provide qualified immunity for good faith reporting,[35] while a handful of states offer absolute immunity from suit.[36] Moreover, the Child Abuse Prevention and Treatment Act predicates eligibility for federal

---

[34] For a case involving a teacher's duty to report suspected child abuse immediately, *see* Aigner v. Cass Sch. Township of Laporte County, 577 N.E.2d 983 (Ind. Ct. App. 1991) (where the cancellation of a permanent teacher's contract was upheld in part due to her failure to follow state law by immediately reporting a suspected case of child abuse).

[35] The statutes of 43 states and the District of Columbia explicitly contain provisions for immunity based on good faith reporting; of these, 32 states and the District of Columbia require that the reporter act in good faith while 14 states and the District of Columbia also include language presuming good faith. Michaelis, *supra*, note 13 at 18-19 (Appendix 3-B: Immunity).

[36] Only four states offer absolute immunity. *Id.*

financial assistance on a state's inclusion of immunity provisions in its statute.[37]

Immunity for reporting was examined in an Oregon case, *McDonald v. State*.[38] Here parents brought an action against public officials to recover damages that they claimed were caused by a teacher's report of suspected abuse to the Children's Services Division. When the teacher spoke with the child about the marks on his neck, he first claimed that a cat had scratched him, but later stated that he had been choked by his mother and that she had done so on numerous occasions. Based on these conflicting statements, the teacher suspected abuse and, as required by state law, reported the incident. Consequently, the child was removed from school and placed in a foster home. At trial, the defendant's suspicions of abuse were not substantiated either by a medical examination or by the child's testimony. However, since the parents were unable to prove that the report of child abuse was motivated by bad faith, the court ruled that the defendants were immune from liability.

In a second case, *Roman v. Appleby*,[39] a federal district court in Pennsylvania was asked primarily to determine whether the federal rights of a high school student and his parents had been violated under the First and Fourteenth Amendments and section 1983.[40] The complaint was premised upon a high school counselor's recommendation to the parents of a student, who may have been emotionally disturbed and mentally unstable, to contact a mental health counseling service in order to provide the young man with the opportunity to undergo treatment. Yet, his parents did not seek help even

---

[37] 42 U.S.C. § 5106a(b)(1)(B).

[38] McDonald v. State *ex rel.* Children's Serv. Div., 694 P.2d 569 (Or. Ct. App. 1985).

[39] Roman v. Appleby, 558 F. Supp. 449 (E.D. Pa. 1983).

[40] For two other cases in which § 1983 liability was raised *see* C.M. v. Southeast Delco Sch. Dist., 828 F. Supp. 1179 (E.D. Pa. 1993) (where school officials were not entitled to qualified immunity in a § 1983 action by a special education student for sexual, physical, and verbal abuse by a teacher when the action or inaction of school officials amounted to custom, practice, or policy of indifference for the purposes of a § 1983 action); K.L. v. Southeast Delco Sch. Dist., 828 F. Supp. 1192 (E.D. Pa. 1993) (where a district and school administrators were not liable under § 1983 for a teacher's sexual abuse of a middle school student for injuries that occurred after the student graduated from the middle school; however, the defendants were not entitled to qualified immunity under § 1983 for sexual, physical, and verbal abuse that occurred during the school year).

though the counselor had told them that their son's problems were potentially serious. When the parents failed to cooperate in seeking treatment, the counselor made an oral referral to Children's Services to have the child evaluated and tested; also, the counselor charged that the parents had refused to provide sufficient psychiatric care. Following appropriate hearings, the parents unsuccessfully filed suit claiming violations of their federal statutory rights as well as for emotional distress and humiliation.

The trial court ruled in favor of the counselor, holding that the parents were unable to overcome the presumption of good faith reporting on her part. In developing its rationale on qualified immunity, the court followed the position adopted by the Supreme Court in *Harlow v. Fitzgerald*.[41] The Court, in *Harlow*, noted that traditionally defendants who asserted a defense of qualified immunity had to meet both an "objective" and a "subjective" standard. Under these measures, qualified immunity could be defeated if a person knew or reasonably should have known that his or her official action would violate the rights of the plaintiff (objective standard), or if there was a malicious intent to deprive such rights (subjective standard).[42] However, in *Harlow* the Court dispensed with the subjective element of malicious intent and ruled that good faith immunity will defeat claims if the official conduct does not violate clearly established statutory or constitutional rights of which a reasonable person should have known.

Applying *Harlow* to *Roman*, the trial court ruled in favor of the counselor. It reasoned that since she had not violated clearly established law in conducting interviews with the student, referring the matter to Children's Services, or providing an affidavit for use in a petition to have the student adjudicated dependent, she was entitled to statutory immunity.

In addition to immunity for constitutional, civil rights, and tort claims, the counselor asserted good faith immunity pursuant to the State Child Protective Services Law which, under threat of criminal sanction, required her to report to the county welfare agency whenever she suspected that a child had been physically or mentally

---

[41] Harlow v. Fitzgerald, 457 U.S. 800 (1982).
[42] Wood v. Strickland, 420 U.S. 308 (1975).

injured. The court again ruled in favor of the counselor, observing that probable cause, was not required prior to making a report, but rather a lesser quantum, such as reason to believe, was sufficient.[43]

A final case on immunity, *Krikorian v. Barry*,[44] involved the owner and operator of a preschool and a licensed clinical psychologist. The owner had sued the psychologist for professional negligence and intentional infliction of emotional distress because the psychologist had provided psychotherapeutic services to a preschool child, collected data, and made observations that culminated in her filing a report that the child had been abused. The court noted that the psychologist was required by statute to report suspected child abuse and that she was therefore entitled to absolute immunity from liability.[45]

Failure to Report

Although reporting statutes often do not allow for a private right of action by the child,[46] an educator's failure to report a suspected case of child abuse still may result in the imposition of a civil or criminal penalty. Related civil suits have been brought based either on state tort law[47] or section 1983,[48] while state criminal codes may impose a fine, generally between $100 and $1,000, or require imprisonment of

---

[43] Roman v. Appleby, 558 F. Supp. 449, 459 (E.D. Pa. 1983).

[44] Krikorian v. Barry, 242 Cal. Rptr. 312 (Ct. App. 1987).

[45] *See also* Landstrom v. Illinois Dep't of Children and Family Serv., 699 F. Supp. 1270 (N.D. Ill. 1988) (where a child was subjected to a physical examination to determine whether she had been abused); E.Z. v. Coler, 603 F. Supp. 1546 (N.D. Ill. 1985) (where parents brought action to enjoin an agency from conducting searches of their children who had been suspected of being abused).

[46] *See, e.g.*, Letlow *ex rel.* Bacon v. Evans, 857 F. Supp. 676 (W.D. Mo. 1994) (where the state child abuse law did not create a private right of action).

[47] Although not a case of caretaker abuse, *see* Phyllis P. v. Superior Court, 228 Cal. Rptr. 776 (Ct. App. 1986) (where a special relationship existed between a school and a mother such that educators had a duty to notify her upon learning that her child had been sexually assaulted numerous times by a fellow student).

[48] For a related case, *see* Stoneking v. Bradford Area Sch. Dist., 882 F.2d 688 (2d Cir. 1989), *cert. denied*, 493 U.S. 1044 (1990) (where a principal and assistant principal could be sued under § 1983 for failing to respond to repeated complaints of sexual misconduct by a teacher against a student).

one year or less.[49] Although the criminal liability issues are fairly straightforward (i.e., if a mandatory reporter is proven to have failed to report suspected abuse, such person could be fined and/or imprisoned), the issues related to negligence and section 1983 liability merit further discussion.

Negligence

Where an individual claims negligence for failure to report child abuse, a court typically examines how the four elements of negligence apply. More specifically, it must determine first, whether the person had a legal duty to report suspected abuse; second, whether the duty was breached; third, whether the child suffered actual injury; and, fourth whether the breach was the proximate cause of the injury. The first three elements often are proven easily in this type of case. The final element, proximate cause, represents a more difficult problem, because the actual injury is inflicted by a third party. However, most courts have held that foreseeable intervening acts of third parties do not amount to a superseding cause relieving the negligent defendant of liability.[50] Moreover, at least as applied to the battered child syndrome,[51] when it is clear that assaults on a child are not isolated, but rather are "part of an environmental mosaic of repeated beatings and abuse that will not only continue but will become more severe unless there is appropriate medicolegal intervention,"[52] then liability is more likely to attach.

An early case examining the battered child syndrome is *Landeros v. Flood*,[53] a 1976 decision of the Supreme Court of California, involving a child who had been beaten regularly and abused by her

---

[49] *See* Morris v. State, 833 S.W.2d 624 (Tex. Ct. App. 1992) (where the criminal conviction of a teacher's aide and the imposition of a $1,000 fine for failing to report child abuse when aides placed the hands of a child who was mentally retarded under hot water, causing them to blister, was upheld as the statute was not unconstitutionally vague); State v. Grover, 437 N.W.2d 60 (Minn. 1989) (where the statute charging a principal with a misdemeanor offense of failing to report child abuse was not unconstitutionally vague or overbroad).

[50] *See, e.g.*, Landeros v. Flood, 551 P.2d 389, 395 (Cal. 1976).

[51] For an earlier case involving battered child syndrome, *see* State v. Loss, 204 N.W.2d 404 (Minn. 1973). *See also* C. Henry Kempe, *The Battered-Child Syndrome*, 181 J.A.M.A. 17 (1962).

[52] Landeros v. Flood, 551 P.2d 389, 395 (Cal. 1976).

[53] *Id.*

mother and her mother's common law husband. Once taken to a hospital, the child was diagnosed as suffering from a comminuted spiral fracture of the tibia and fibula, but was not diagnosed for multiple bruises, superficial abrasions, and a nondepressed linear fracture of the skull. No explanation was sought from the mother, nor was one tendered. The physician treated the child and released her to her mother, but did not file a report with the juvenile probation department or law enforcement officials even though an injury of this type generally would result in a further examination, including X-rays.

The complaint asserted that had the examination been conducted properly, the child would have been diagnosed as suffering from the battered child syndrome, thus requiring a report to the proper authorities and the child's withdrawal from her present household. Yet, the child was released to her mother who continued to abuse her. When the child later was examined by a second physician at a different hospital, she was diagnosed as a victim of battered child syndrome; this second diagnosis was reported immediately. The child was then taken into custody and placed with foster parents. In applying the elements of negligence, the court ruled that the first physician and hospital could be held liable for injuries sustained by the child if it could be shown that the doctor negligently failed both to diagnose battered child syndrome and to make the required report, resulting in her being returned to her home where it was foreseeable that she could be further injured.

Section 1983 Liability

Along with state tort claims involving the failure to report suspected child abuse, suits have been filed claiming a section 1983 violation.[54] The term person is not defined in 42 U.S.C. section 1983, but since the Supreme Court has concluded that local governments

---

[54] 42 U.S.C. § 1983, originally part of the Civil Rights Act of 1871, stipulates that: "[e]very person who, under color of any statute, ordinance, regulation, custom, or usage, of any [s]tate or [t]erritory, subjects or causes to be subjected, any citizen of the United States or other person within the jurisdiction thereof to the deprivation of any rights, privileges, or immunities secured by the Constitution or laws, shall be liable to the party injured in an action at law, suit in equity, or other proper proceeding for redress."

(including public school boards,[55] cities, and counties) are persons, they may be sued under section 1983. Furthermore, individuals acting under color of state law may not claim Eleventh Amendment immunity,[56] although those performing their responsibilities in good faith, even if later proven to be in error, may claim good faith immunity. However, such immunity does not extend to public institutions, or to individuals who act in bad faith.

No substantive rights are provided in and of themselves under section 1983. Accordingly, any liability must be attached to a constitutional or civil rights violation. Related cases have averred that a child has a liberty right under the Fourteenth Amendment to be free from harm;[57] that the family has a liberty right to remain together and not be separated;[58] that an affirmative obligation to protect or intervene on behalf of a known or suspected child abuse victim may arise from a special custodial or other relationship, such as a mandatory requirement to report abuse;[59] that it is not necessary for the perpetrator of the actual harm to be in control, custody, or supervision of the state or local government entity to impose an affirmative obligation to protect or to impose liability for the failure to protect a child abuse victim;[60] and/or that liability may result from omissions if officials acted intentionally or if they exhibited deliberate indifference to a known injury or risk and failed to carry out the duty to ameliorate that injury or risk resulting in the proximate cause of the deprivation of the child abuse victim's rights under the Federal Constitution.[61]

---

[55] Private schools do not operate under color of state law and therefore may not generally be sued under § 1983. *See* Rendell-Baker v. Kohn, 457 U.S. 830 (1982).

[56] The Eleventh Amendment to the United States Constitution states that: "[t]he Judicial power of the United States shall not be construed to extend to any suit in law or equity, commenced or prosecuted against one of the United States by Citizens of another State, or by Citizens or Subjects of any Foreign State."

[57] DeShaney v. Winnebago County Dep't of Social Serv., 489 U.S. 189 (1989) (where a boy and his mother unsuccessfully brought suit alleging a violation of a liberty right when the department of social services failed to intervene to protect the child from continued abuse by his natural father).

[58] LaBelle v. County of St. Lawrence, 445 N.Y.S.2d 275 (App. Div. 1981) (where two children were "home alone" and were removed from their home and held overnight until their parents returned from vacation).

[59] Jensen v. Conrad, 747 F.2d 185 (4th Cir. 1984).

[60] Doe v. New York City Dep't of Social Serv., 649 F.2d 134 (2d Cir. 1981).

[61] *Id.*

In any of these settings, plaintiffs will have difficulty substantiating a section 1983 claim because an error in judgment or an unforeseeable tragic event, a good faith but misinformed professional decision, or mere negligence will not suffice to impose liability. If anything, plaintiffs will have to prove gross negligence establishing that the practices were so far below minimum accepted and generally prevailing professional standards as to infer deliberate or reckless indifference or callous disregard for the safety of children.[62]

Policy Recommendations

To protect the health and safety of all children it is imperative that related school policies be developed and implemented.[63] Although most districts have child abuse reporting policies in effect, some are not comprehensive, while many more are neither promulgated nor understood by faculty, staff, or other mandatory reporters. Thus, the following guidelines are recommended.

The policy should include a brief statement that the administration will support the good faith reporting of suspected child abuse. Moreover, it should explicitly incorporate a provision indicating that interference with reporting will not be tolerated and that individuals who file reports in good faith do so with the full support and protection of the school district.

The policy should be written in lay terms, explaining all relevant sections of state statute, including specific references to who must report; when to report; to whom to report; how to report; what kinds of information to include in the report; and, if forms are used, where they may be acquired. It should also summarize the law regarding confidentiality, immunity for good faith reporting, and the potential for criminal and civil liability for failure to report. Finally, the district should provide in-service training for all mandatory reporters regard-

---

[62] Estate of Bailey *ex rel.* Oare v. County of York, 768 F.2d 503, 508 (3d Cir. 1985).
[63] *See also* Richard Fossey, *Child Abuse Investigations in the Public Schools: A Practical Guide for School Administrators*, 69 EDUC. L. REP. 991 (1991).

ing the legal requirements for reporting as well as how to recognize a child abuse victim.[64] (See Table 9-2 for indicators of child abuse.)

Table 9-2
Indicators of Child Abuse

Type of Abuse	Physical Indicators	Behavioral Indicators
Physical	**Unexplained bruises and welts:** °on face, lips, or mouth °on torso, back, buttocks, or thighs °in various stages of healing °clustered or forming patterns °shaped like recognizable object (e.g., belt buckle) °appearing regularly after absences, weekends, or vacation periods **Unexplained burns:** °by cigars or cigarettes, especially on soles, palms, back, or buttocks °by immersion in hot liquid, especially on hands, feet, buttocks, or genitalia °shaped in a recognizable form (e.g., electric range coils, electric iron) °by rope on arms, legs, neck, or torso	°wary of adult contact °apprehensive when other children cry °extreme aggressiveness or extreme withdrawal °fear of parents °fear of going home °reporting of injury by parents of others

---

[64] A report by the National Teacher Survey sponsored by the National Committee to Prevent Child Abuse revealed that only 49% of teachers reported that their schools provided workshops on topics related to child abuse and neglect. Furthermore, of this total, 62% responded that while training was mandatory, it was ordinarily offered only once a year. Mary Nowensnick, *Shattered Lives: Why Schools Must Face Up to the Harsh Realities of Child Sexual Abuse*, AM. SCH. BD. J. 14, 17 (Oct. 1993).

Type of Abuse	Physical Indicators	Behavioral Indicators
Physical (cont.)	**Unexplained fractures:** °of skull, nose, or facial bones °in various stages of healing °in multiple locations **Unexplained lacerations or abrasions:** °on mouth, lips, gums, or eyes °on external genitalia	
Sexual	°difficulty in walking or sitting °torn, stained, or bloody underclothes °pain or itching in genital area °bruises or bleeding in external genitalia, vaginal, or anal areas °venereal disease symptoms, especially in pre-teens °pregnancy	°unwillingness to change clothing or to participate in physical education classes °withdrawal, fantasy, or infantile behavior °bizarre, sophisticated, or unusual sexual behavior or knowledge °poor peer relationships °chronic delinquency °reporting of sexual assaults
Emotional	°speech disorders °lag in physical development °severe allergies, asthma, or ulcers °alcohol or drug abuse	°habit disorders (e.g., thumb sucking, lip biting, rocking) °antisocial or destructive conduct °psychoneurotic traits (e.g., hysteria, obsessions, compulsions, phobias, hypochodria) °behavior extremes of compliance or aggression °inappropriate adult or infantile behavior °mental and emotional developmental lags °suicide threats or attempts
Neglect	°consistent hunger °poor hygiene °inappropriate dress	°begging or stealing food °early arrivals and late departures

Type of Abuse	Physical Indicators	Behavioral Indicators
Neglect (cont.)	°unattended physical problems or medical needs °alcohol or drug abuse	°constant fatigue or listlessness °chronic delinquency, especially theft °reporting of no caretaker at home

Source: Myra Herbert, *What Principals Should Know About Child Abuse*, PRINCIPAL (November 1985), at 12.

Appendix 1
Federal Circuit Courts (1995)

Circuit Court	State or Territory	Circuit Court	State or Territory
Federal Circut	none	Sixth Circuit	Kentucky Michigan Ohio Tennessee
District of Columbia	none	Seventh Circuit	Illinois Indiana Wisconsin
First Circuit	Maine Massachusetts New Hampshire Rhode Island Puerto Rico	Eighth Circuit	Arkansas Iowa Minnesota Missouri Nebraska North Dakota South Dakota
Second Circuit	Connecticut New York Vermont	Ninth Circuit	Alaska Arizona California Hawaii Idaho Montana Nevada Oregon Washington Guam North Mariana Is.
Third Circuit	Delaware New Jersey Pennsylvania Virgin Islands	Tenth Circuit	Colorado Kansas New Mexico Oklahoma Utah Wyoming
Fourth Circuit	Maryland North Carolina South Carolina Virginia West Virginia	Eleventh Circuit	Alabama Florida Georgia
Fifth Circuit	Louisiana Texas Mississippi		

Appendix 2: Supreme Court Appointments (1965-95)

1965	1970	1975	1980	1985	1990	1995

Earl Warren 1953-69 Eisenhower Appt.

Warren Burger, 1969-86, Nixon Appt.

William Rehnquist, 1986-, Reagan Promo.

Byron White, 1962-93, Kennedy Appt.

Ruth Ginsburg, 1993-, Clinton Appt.

Abe Fortas 1965-69 Johnson Appt.

Harry Blackmun, 1970-94, Nixon Appt.

Stephen Breyer, 1994-, Clinton Appt.

William Douglas, 1939-75 Roosevelt Appt.

John Paul Stevens, 1975-, Ford Appt.

Potter Stewart, 1958-81, Eisenhower Appt.

Sandra Day O'Connor, 1981-, Reagan Appt.

John Harlan 1955-71 Eisenhower Appt.

William Rehnquist, 1972-86, Nixon Appt.

Antonin Scalia, 1986-, Reagan Appt.

Hugo Black 1937-71 Roosevelt Appt.

Lewis Powell, 1972-87, Nixon Appt.

Anthony Kennedy, 1988-, Reagan Appt.

William Brennan, 1956-90, Eisenhower Appt.

David Souter, 1990-, Bush Appt.

Thurgood Marshall, 1967-91, Johnson Appt.

Clarence Thomas, 1991-, Bush Appt.

Table of Cases

Index

Please remember that this is a library book,
and that it belongs only temporarily to each
person who uses it. Be considerate. Do
not write in this, or any, library book.